WAVES
OF
CHANGE

WAVES
OF
CHANGE

Business Evolution through Information Technology

JAMES L. McKENNEY
Harvard Business School

with

Duncan C. Copeland
University of Western Ontario

Richard O. Mason
Southern Methodist University

Harvard Business School Press
Boston, Massachusetts

Library of Congress Cataloging-in-Publication Data

McKenney, James L.
  Waves of change : business evolution through information
technology / James L. McKenney with Duncan C. Copeland, Richard O.
Mason.
    p. cm.
  Includes index.
  ISBN 0-87584-564-9
  1. Information technology—United States—Management—History.
2. Business enterprises—United States—Automation—History.
3. Organizational change—United States—History. I. Copeland,
Duncan C., 1956–   . II. Mason, Richard O. III. Title.
HD30.2.M4   1994
658.4′038—dc20   94-3471
                                                                          CIP

The paper used in this publication meets the requirements
of the American National Standard for Permanence of Paper
for Printed Library Materials Z39.49-1984.

Dedicated to the
Maestros
for
Their Unique Information Technology
Leadership Role

Contents

Preface

Waves of Change focuses on the development by innovative managers of an evolving strategy to exploit the potential of information technology (IT). The CEOs of these organizations were typical Joseph A. Schumpeter entrepreneurial managers who creatively destroyed established means of competition, thereby gaining market share and improving profits. They had no grand plan but persistently pursued the technology in a learning-by-using effort that eventually established a unique information-processing design for their markets. Although competitors were quick to copy the designs, most of them lacked the necessary perspective to exploit the potential of the technology.

The historical paradigm allows readers to understand these executives' mistakes as well as their clever moves but equally important were their investment of requisite time and effort to truly invent and adapt new information-processing systems. The core of such a difficult task lies in the nature of the necessary change—shifting the information-processing habits of a working group. IT often induces profound transitions that demand faith on the part of the recipients that the invisible new process has integrity. This situation requires a leader who is both the catalyst and executor of a strategy that leads the organization to a new plane of operation. As the narratives that follow show, these leaders never had a complete picture of their destinations; they just took the next few steps toward a strong goal to solve a limiting processing situation. Successful in achieving their objectives, they demonstrate following a common set of procedures to achieve their ends. The stories therefore focus on the roles, decisions, and shifts in their responsibilities as they forged new IT-based information-processing systems.

Our objective is to influence management practice by providing historical evidence of how successful managerial teams created and implemented innovative information technology systems. The companies are American Airlines, Bank of America, American Hospital Supply/Baxter Travenol, Frito-Lay, and USAA Insurance. All are IT leaders in their industries as well as effective competitors. The advantage of a historical perspective is to document the elapsed time and complexity of not only managerial actions and results but the cumulative effect of actions and their consequences on an organization. All our companies were early IT innovators in their industries and learned by using. A few had relapses and bounced back; others started late and caught up. All created an IT design that became a competitive necessity in their industries.

The patterns of managerial behavior described center on the actions and decisions the managers made as they fashioned an IT strategy. All learned by using IT and from their competitors, suppliers, and consultants. Their early moves were to gain competence to develop an IT system to resolve a processing bottleneck that was inhibiting their growth. They grew beyond that challenge to perceive a broader set of opportunities and established an evolving IT strategy. The emphasis of the stories is on managerial actions, organizational changes, and mutations in the use of IT, all woven into a set of patterns that reflects shifts in competencies of the organizations.

Our effort started as a history project to document the managerial maneuvers and activities of two pioneering firms, American Airlines and the Bank of America, which created competitive IT systems in the 1960s. In analyzing the managerial moves, we were struck by a common pattern and set of roles in both companies. This led us to expand the project to test whether the same pattern existed in other firms that had successfully created innovative IT designs. We found that they did.

The model that emerged from our analysis is termed a "cascade," because the technology continues to expand in processing power, thus enabling new designs. Firms that do not keep abreast of the technology become stuck in an application that is approaching obsolescence, and their competence begins to erode. Firms that copy an original design and gain IT competence can create a better design, passing the innovator and taking market share from the earlier innovator. The five companies vary in their traverse of the cascade owing to the nature of their processing requirements, the capabilities of available IT, and their culture. Among the pioneers, American Airlines lost the lead for a few years but regained it quickly. The Bank of America got so far ahead of its competition that when it stopped investing in information technology, it required eight years to notice the economic impact, then four more years to start to regain momentum. The recent histories depict the ease of matching existing designs; and the alternative means of gaining IT competence that allowed them to move ahead of their competitors.

The ultimate test of a design is whether it stimulates instant emulation by all competitors. Within a year, most leading banks were moving to adopt the magnetic ink computer recording (MICR) check-processing system of the Bank of America. With American Airlines' SABRE reservations system, all competitors quickly initiated a reservations development program; within four years most airlines relied on SABRE-like systems. We borrow the phrase "dominant design" from William J. Abernathy and James M. Utterback's analysis of the automobile industry; when the all-metal body, rear wheel drive, internal combustion engine, and wheel brakes design emerged, all manufacturers quickly developed their own versions. Thereafter the design was the norm; firms moved into an extended era of improving productivity and competing with styling and features. As IT continues to change, competitors have to experiment just to keep up. There have been at least two shifts in banking and airlines since the original designs. In both it was an extension to remote inputs, be they terminals in travel agents' or treasurers' offices or ATMs. As they became competitive airlines focused marketing on yield management and banks on electronic transactions, allowing treasurers to handle their own services. The highly heralded home banking still seems to lurk on the edges while the debit card is growing. The conclusion is that a dominant design in IT is typically a temporal one that will be cannibalized when IT enables a better mousetrap.

In modern jargon, one could suggest that these firms reengineered their systems to transform their organizations into a lean, competitive force. The salient differences between them are the CEOs and their teams, who framed the issue as one of solving a processing problem that was threatening their growth. They sought technology within the confines of organizational procedures by creating new IT systems and adapting their organizations to the opportunities as they arose. They adjusted their management processes to exploit the available information and learned to anticipate the potential IT would bring to their activities. They gained competence in managing the deployment of IT-based systems as competitive means.

Our analysis covers the years 1950 to 1993, when the basic driver of computer and communication switching went from electro-mechanical devices and vacuum tubes with millisecond speed and memory capacity in thousands to today's nanosecond speeds and, for practical purposes, infinite memory capacity for normal online response. The functionality and power of IT systems, which include computing power, accessible storage, input/output devices, and communication links, has grown exponentially. IT systems are at the stage where they can support active visual and audio interaction through TV-like links complemented by shared reference to electronic files of text and graphic displays. Soon they will be voice activated rather than manually activated. The recent stories relate how organizations are exploiting recent information-processing innovations by providing tailored interactive systems that aid both managerial activities and analytic work. Their implementation processes have broader sources of technical competencies as well as a variety of means of developing services either in-house or through an outside source. However, the managerial process is similar to that of the pioneers' establishing an ongoing dialogue among key managers, covering recent developments both as to their economic impact and organizational impact as means to shape future IT investments. Although the implementation of technology can be accomplished quickly, changing an organization still takes years.

Acknowledgments

This book draws its general managerial perspectives from Alfred Chandler and Joseph Schumpeter. The theme is an extension of how technology changes organizations described in Chandler's "The Visible Hand," namely, how persistent managers changed their companies by creating divisions on the basis of markets and production functions. Schumpeter's analyses of the forces of growth in a capitalistic economy ascribe the basic cause to entrepreneurial managers who fearlessly destroy existing systems to exploit the potential of new technology, thereby reducing costs and expanding markets. These perspectives were sharpened in two Harvard Business School seminars—Tom McCraw's Business History seminar and Dick Rosenbloom's Technology and Competition Colloquium. Our concepts lean heavily on authors who have captured the management perspective on organizational change, technological innovation, and IT manageral issues. Organizational constructs were drawn from Paul Lawrence, Schein, Richard Walton, and Shoshana

Zuboff; technology, William Abernathy, Robert Burgleman, Kim Clark, Paul David, Richard Nelson, Nathan Rosenberg, Sidney Winters, and Joanne Yates; IT systems from Linda Applegate, James Cash, Peter Keen, John King, Kenneth Kramer, F. Warren McFarlan, Richard Nolan, Jack Rockart, Michael Scott-Morton, and James Short.

The result is a product of the efforts of a broad range of colleagues and vital support from the Division of Research at the Harvard Business School. I have had steadfast support from my colleague and long-time associate Warren McFarlan, who encouraged me to pursue the project and provided constructive feedback, made me aware of deadlines, and provided innovative support by sponsoring an ad hoc history group.

The history group is comprised of persons with an impressive collective background in information technology with whom I had worked and who I knew had wide-ranging contacts from the early years of IT to the present. They provided valuable assistance as I set about documenting the activities of managers in the 1950s and 1970s. Dick Canning, an early author on the use of information technology, is founder and editor of the popular "Data Analyzer." Walter Carlson, former IT manager at DuPont, marketing manager at IBM, and president of the Association of Computer Machinery, is now an author. Duncan Copeland, assistant professor at the University of Western Ontario, as a doctoral student piqued my interest in history by tracing the evolution of American Airlines' use of IT for his dissertation. The late Phil Dorn was an early innovator at Systems Development Corporation, designer of General Motors' computer-based design system, and consultant and author. George Glaser, employed early by McKinsey & Co. on the use of information technology, consults independently. Richard Mason, a Burroughs salesman in the 1950s, is a professor at Southern Methodist University and a management science scholar, strategy consultant, and distinguished author. Ted Withington, Arthur D. Little's computer maven since the 1950s until recently, has become an independent computer consultant. These individuals made time to meet as a group each fall and spring to discuss working papers, formulate issues, and identify relevant individuals. Between meetings they edited drafts and made suggestions for contacts. I am deeply indebted to them for their help, critical analysis, and continuing interest and support.

During the development of the book I came to rely increasingly on Duncan Copeland and Dick Mason, not only for editorial support but also for creative development of the rationale for salient organizing concepts to interpret the information we were gathering. Duncan is the principal author of Chapter 4, and Dick is the key conceptualizer of the cascade metaphor and the role of the maestro.

The project has involved a host of helpful colleagues, in particular Linda Applegate, Al Chandler, Tom McCraw, Richard Vietor, Richard Rosenbloom, Dick Walton, Jim Emery, John King, Michael Scott-Morton, and Joanne Yates. I am also indebted to the many company representatives who were patient not only through interviews but during follow-up phone calls and the editing of drafts for accuracy. This effort could have not been created without the help of Amy Weaver Fisher, my research assistant for three years while we organized the bank story and refined the airline story as well as shaped the themes in the book. She was an effective note taker, editor, organizer, and metronome of the project, which has developed three articles in addition to this volume. John Simon, a patient and thorough editor, helped develop a story from the historical descriptions. Espen Andersen, a graduate student, created the excellent exhibits. A special word of appreciation is due my secretary, Mary Kennedy, for her good humor, patience, and meticulous attention to detail to ensure a well-organized manuscript. I have published with four other publishers and found Carol Franco and her staff to be the most effective and supportive in the process of both bringing closure and providing superb editorial services. They did an outstanding job in bringing the book to fruition.

I owe a special debt to Al Zipf, an AMP student of mine in 1967, who was the catalyst of this effort. I started the project by writing to Tom Clausen, because I was aware of the untold bank story, and he suggested that I visit Al. The chemistry worked, and I began to document the bank story. A brilliant critic and source of perspective on the challenges facing managers in the early days, he was the exemplar of an IT entrepreneur.

Finally, a note of thanks to my wife, Mary, who provided early morning breakfasts and supportive ambiance to the effort. She was the first reader, critic, and enthusiast who maintained the momentum.

WAVES
OF
CHANGE

Chapter 1

Creating Competitive Information-Processing Designs

Surprisingly few firms have broken the mold of history and transformed their industries with a new dominant design for information processing.[1] We present an in-depth study of perhaps the most notorious and influential — American Airlines and Bank of America — and examine others that are prominent — United Services Automobile Association in insurance, Baxter Travenol/American Hospital Supply in medical supplies, and Frito-Lay in retail foods. The difficulty of truly innovating with information technology (IT) accounts for the small number of vivid successes. Most firms simply automate, eliminating clerical tasks but requiring only modest process adjustments. To innovate with IT involves changing an organization's information-processing infrastructure.

Arriving at a Dominant IT Design

Changing an information-processing infrastructure is akin to engaging in guerrilla warfare, in which the competent, effectively led group wins. It requires extensive financial resources, a long-term view, and a capacity to learn by using.[2] Harvard Business School case studies document more than a thousand interesting disasters — interesting from the perspective of what not to do and how not to proceed. This book, in contrast, offers accounts of successful innovation accomplished by managers who marshaled their resources to change organizational habits and enable their firms to function in radically new ways. Over four- to seven-year periods, these managers effectively reengineered their organizations to implement an IT-driven strategy.

As these stories show, each successful implementation of an IT innovation creates a new infrastructure with latent potential for new functionality. Successful leaders perceive this functionality and its utility; they see, for example, the potential to substitute for an order book a hand-held calculator and systems designed to receive order-entry input directly, effectively shifting the entire order-entry infrastructure to an IT base. These descriptions of managerial actions document their growth in competence to forge the technology and to shift the organization to gain competitive advantage.

The successful leaders epitomize Joseph Schumpeter's[3] creative destructive managers, who fashioned innovative IT designs that destroyed the effectiveness of existing processes, thereby winning distinct competitive advantages. As Schumpeter predicted, the managers changed their organizations to exploit the potential and became adept at using the technology that supported market growth and penetration. This growth fueled competitive responses, shifting the nature of their industries and expanding their markets. We document the unique aspects of IT in the destructive process: not only does IT demand new structures, but it also enables market-oriented managerial processes and radical infrastructures. Redesigning the way an organization functions is critical to leading the industry in the exploitation of newly available information.

Major corporations today are increasingly deploying IT as a key element of their strategies. Specifically, they are using IT to radically alter production functions and to shift cost structures, evolving in the process a new bureaucratic form: the "information-based organization."[4] Each of the organizations we describe has established a new IT infrastructure, and two have continued to evolve their IT use, requiring no transformation today. In all cases, innovating with IT engendered a realignment of the entire competitive structure of the organization's industries.

These developments, and others, raise a host of questions: What has occasioned the need and opportunity for businesses to change what they were doing and how they were doing it? What level of understanding did business leaders possess at the time? Why did change come when it did and take the form that it did? What role did information technology play in the process?

Creating Dominant IT Designs

Consistent patterns in the leadership of and progress made by the companies we studied suggested a framework for understanding how companies arrive at a dominant design for information processing. The basis of this framework, extended longitudinal analyses of American Airlines and Bank of America, was subsequently tested and expanded through in-depth studies of American Hospital Supply/Baxter Travenol, Frito-Lay, and United Services Automobile Association (USAA).

The histories of these businesses reveal persistent patterns of managers' engaging in learning-by-using ventures that evolved gradually, and of technical teams' following unique paths to tailor specific technologies to the needs of their businesses. As they gained experience, the managers of these firms expanded and enriched their portfolios of system projects and continuously adjusted organizational structures to better exploit the potential of each new system. Understanding why their predecessors succeeded can help contemporary managers cope with a rapidly accelerating pace of technological change.

Each story begins with a management crisis, a business circumstance that simultaneously poses a threat and presents an opportunity. In banking during the early 1950s, the crisis stemmed from growth in check writing and the use of other banking services. Expanding volume was rapidly escalating check processing processing time and labor costs, precipitating excessive employee turnover and significantly lengthening float. For the airlines, the problem was matching passenger lists with seat inventory and obtaining timely flight information. The debut of commercial passenger jets and the attendant reduction in the duration of flights, coupled with growth in demand for flights, frequently resulted in passengers' arriving before manifests. American Hospital Supply was beset by an inventory-management problem elevated to crisis proportions by large numbers of low-cost items, long lead times, unreliable delivery, partial shipments, and criticality of availability; Frito-Lay management had to cope with a dramatic shift from stable national brands to quarterly new product introductions and fierce regional competition; and USAA, faced with 80,000 pieces of mail and 120,000 phone calls per day and a reference file of 2.6 million pages, anticipated gross deterioration in customer service with future growth.

CEO, Maestro, and Technical Team

Each history centers around a few key protagonists who perceived information technology as a solution to an organizational crisis, innovated, and managed the resulting change. All were insiders looking out, not outsiders, such as vendors, rushing in with a solution. For the most part, our prime movers were experienced managers aware of their industries' impending crises and actively looking for solutions.

We have discerned three essential roles in management's response to crisis. Two are at management level, one filled by a high-level executive, the other by a manager of technological innovation. The third is filled by an implementation team. These roles, as will be seen, are highly interdependent. Only when all three are effectively filled is success likely.

The CEO

First, a firm's top-level executives must include a technology champion with sufficient power and prestige to drive technological innovation. Typically, though not always, this is the CEO. Over a period of years the CEOs in the companies we surveyed nurtured electronic solutions to problems that were constraining growth, in the process searching for technology, manufacturers, and insightful people with ideas about how to change business processes dramatically. They built on their successes and learned from their failures. They had the latitude to allocate funds to specific projects without formal review, but they demanded payback on these investments, requiring managers to realize identifiable savings and holding them accountable by auditing results. These executives were an interesting combination of visionary and bookkeeper.

The Technology Maestro

To harness the technology to the needs of the firm, the CEOs recruited able technology managers, individuals with a remarkable combination of business acumen and technological competence. It was up to them to recruit first-class teams of competent technologists and, working with planning teams of business managers, to establish the direction of automation.

A manager of technological innovation is vital to maintaining momentum in IT-based systems development. The person in this role must understand technology as it affects both the organization and the industry and must plan and implement a new technology infrastructure and effect concomitant shifts in organizational processes. Arthur Squires, who calls such managers "maestros of technology," observes that many successful technology projects (e.g., the Manhattan Project) have been led by these maestros, while many failed projects (e.g., the Army's development of the M16 rifle) have lacked players in this crucial role.[5]

Effective maestros are akin to start-up managers as the founts of strong financial and moral support that project teams need to deliver systems that achieve economies of scale. They understand how the technology's capabilities address the needs of their businesses and can recruit and lead bright, energetic technologists. They are confident in their ability to deliver working systems on time and within budget. It is the maestros who establish the close alliances between high-level executives and other key business managers needed to ensure an organization's ongoing adaptation to new procedures. Maestros who achieve exceptional results are trusted and their business and technological judgment respected by executives and team members alike.

Maestros constantly survey the technology landscape for relevant IT, and they pace organizational learning to its use in the context of a shared vision of a technology's potential payoffs and risks, costs and impact. Maestros trusted to make a technology work are able to make that technology understandable to the CEO and management team.

Successful maestros recognize the talents of their teams and value the ideas and innovations their teams originate. They enable the development of these ideas, weaving them into a fabric that supports the overall vision of the senior executive and grounds it in a sound technical design. And they motivate their teams by cultivating a supportive environment and minimizing bureaucracy.

The Technical Team

The technical team recruited and assembled by the maestro is responsible for the managerial, technological, and systems analyses needed to realize the leader's vision. A well-functioning team unfreezes old thinking and develops new procedures and functions to take advantage of the speed, reliability, and other attributes of emerging technology. Frequently, team members are unsung players who make many important contributions to a technology, develop new concepts and ideas and subsidiary innovations, and solve the many problems that invariably arise. They engage in detailed systems planning and help to adapt existing policies to accommodate new skills and career paths.

Effective technical groups persist not only in developing solutions, but also in improving the operation of their solutions. They possess a genuine interest in changing business processes for the better.

These three roles — a strong CEO convinced of the utility of IT, an empowered entrepreneurial manager of IT who understands the business, and an innovative group of IT technologists — are essential to the effective deployment of IT. Each story in these pages vividly illustrates how the people in these roles functioned and interacted to change their firms and, ultimately, their industries.

The Cascade Phenomenon: Experiential Growth of IT Design

An analysis of the managerial activities of American Airlines and Bank of America shows that the managers exhibited a consistent set of actions as they gained experience in using the technology. As the technology's processing capabilities grew to allow more functions, the managers' learning process was both cumulative and expanding. Disciplined analysis, cost evaluation, training, and organizational change remained constant throughout. Planning procedures, management control, and new products or services continued to emerge with each shift in the power of IT. It became clear that if the managers failed to exploit new opportunities or adapt to timely information from the stream of innovations, their companies would fall behind their competitors and stagnate. Thus, these successful managers came to master the five phases of a cascade in the stream of ever-changing technologies.

The five phases of the cascade represent the learning path managers traverse as they explore the potential of technology and experiment with organizational structures designed to exploit that potential. The energy generated by these activities leads to organizational understanding relative to how to proceed. We ascribe this genesis to decisions of the principal actors — the CEO, the maestro, and

EXHIBIT 1-1   Phases to an Evolving IT Strategy

	CEO	Maestro	Technical Team
Phase 1 Information-processing crisis and search for an IT solution	Identifies processing crisis and seeks electronic solution; grooms or recruits maestro; with maestro, designs an IT project	Analyzes problems and evaluates available technologies and vendors; identifies skill needs and assembles team of technologists	Becomes organized and trained; becomes involved with users in system planning
Phase 2 Building IT competence	Approves/funds requisite R&D; tracks progress; maintains close liaison with vendors	Plans implementation; sets ROI goals; establishes user organization	Revises work flow and design system in collaboration with users; tests system and trains users
Phase 3 Expanding the scope of IT	Supports expansion of applications portfolio; reviews relationships with vendors and consultants; champions new projects	Implements and evaluates system; identifies and prioritizes additional applications; plans subsequent implementations	Undergoes expansion of staff and functions; creates new, leading-edge system
Phase 4 Using IT to enable structure and drive strategy	Fashions IT management system and establishes direction for IT strategy	Manages project portfolio and participates on senior management committee	Organizes to support 24-hour data-processing shop; expands training and systematizes processes
Phase 5 Evolving IT strategy; competitors emulate	Promotes/supports exploitation of emergent dominant design; anticipates/monitors adoption of dominant design; competitors adopt design	Pushes IT organization to maintain momentum; stays abreast of IT developments; monitors/assesses IT activities of competitors	Hones skills; fortifies liaisons with users and vendors

the technical team. Exhibit 1-1 shows the individual and interactive tasks of these players in each phase of the cascade.

Phase 1: Information-Processing Crisis and Search for an IT Solution

Operating conditions, new technology, or market shifts that seriously threaten a business's trajectory give rise to a management crisis, spurring some managers to become Schumpeterian, innovative entrepreneurs who seek solutions in the enhanced processing capability and capacity of information technology. Rejecting standard automation procedures, they search for new means to capture and process information electronically. While searching, they frequently recruit a technical partner to build prototypes and help test the feasibility of various IT solutions.

 ## Phase 2: Building IT Competence

Phase 2 begins when users are involved with project teams in analyzing detailed procedures and conceptualizing an automated system, and with the maestro in redesigning work flows and developing new procedures. Ultimately, implementation of a system, typically a prototype or limited application, exerts an impact on the structure of an organization, often by eliminating or redefining some staff positions and occasionally introducing new ones. Organizational changes necessitated by the implementation lead to deeper CEO involvement and greater collaboration between the information systems people and users. If the system works and yields projected savings, the CEO is encouraged to expand the IT effort and continue the search for applications.

Phase 3: Expanding the Scope of IT

Expansion of the domain of IT prompted by growing understanding of its potential marks the start of Phase 3. The CEO and the maestro explore radical new IT designs that reduce requisite activities and make information accessible electronically. One of these designs becomes a vision and a basis of the firm's strategy. The CEO becomes the product champion and, with the maestro, searches for and selects a supplier with the competence and resources to build the design. They strive assiduously to realize the most robust design possible, given the state of the technology. The project grows to encompass and exert influence over a broad spectrum of the organization. IT becomes a normal topic in senior management discussion, and the maestro becomes a member of the senior management group.

 ## Phase 4: Using IT to Enable Structure and Drive Strategy

The operational design that emerges as the system is tested and resolves the processing crisis provides a competitive edge in service improvement and cost reduction. More timely and accurate information becomes accessible throughout the organization, linking formerly disparate groups. A significant effort is made to exploit the system's productivity and provide a dynamic basis for managing and augmenting the firm's marketing programs. If the system improves profit and market share, the CEO further expands IT's domain of influence to encompass all segments of the value chain, and the maestro looks to IT to improve the firm's management procedures. IT becomes both an integrative and a strategic force in the organization.

Phase 5: Evolving IT Strategy; Competitors Emulate

Continuing the evolution of the organization's IT strategy and competitors' emulation of the new system design constitute Phase 5 of the cascade. Few organizations, however, can fully exploit the potential of a new information-processing design, and lack of experience results in costly failure for some. The leader typically enjoys a comfortable two-year lead and begins to introduce new products and services and more effective marketing programs. Occasionally, competitors that have been experimenting on their own expand on the original design and improve the system's capability, which levels the playing field and initiates another round of IT innovation. The competence a leader gains in traversing the phases of the cascade usually enables it to prevail over competitors' advances. But if a discontinuity in leadership causes disinterest and emphasis on cost minimization, the leader may lose organizational adaptability and technical competence and end up watching helplessly as a competitor creates the next dominant design for information processing.

Evaluating the Robustness of the Framework

Our analysis both documents the pattern of evolution and captures the Darwinian contingency forces that engender the development of revolutionary IT systems and the new organizational structures they occasion. The principal forces are the nature of a business, its CEO's style and organizational competence, and IT functionality relative to processing needs. Each organization arrived at a dominant design for information processing via a unique set of experiences and a maturation process that rendered it a different organization with a newfound competence in the use of IT. Organizational competence is a salient force, being a composite of shared and individual knowledge. Competitors' responses, contingent on their own experience and competence, give rise to a new set of circumstances for exploiting the emerging potential of an IT design for competitive ends.

The following chapters flesh out the framework provided in this chapter, describing in detail the situation, rationale, and managerial moves the principals made for each company. The parallels are readily apparent, as are certain differences arising from firm or industry circumstances, management and organizational culture, and the growing sophistication of technology.

Each company provides an example of a different route to attaining a dominant IT design in its industry. Bank of America's CEO was an IT product champion and the architect of a new organization. American Airlines' CEO, with a small management team, ran a tight ship and managed the deployment of IT, allowing his key managers to adapt the organization. At American Hospital Supply, the CEO exploited an innovation by encouraging a decentralized culture and nurturing an IT champion. United Services Automobile Association's CEO acquired three maestros to achieve his dream of a paperless office. At Frito-Lay, the CEO who initiated the IT program became corporate CEO and nurtured his maestro through four successive CEOs. Each of these companies sustained the momentum of its evolving IT strategy.

Different routes notwithstanding, firms that create dominant designs for information processing in the modern context follow much the same path as did the pioneering firms, which first saw in information technology potential solutions to constraints on growth imposed by manual, labor-intensive, paper-based systems. The constraints have changed, but the need remains for technical competence assembled and guided by a business-savvy maestro with the confidence and support of an involved CEO-level executive throughout the lengthy process of learning by using that is the basis of technological leadership.

Notes

1. W. J. Abernathy and J. M. Utterback, "Patterns of Innovation in Technology," *Technology Review* 80, no. 7 (1978): 40–47.

2. N. Rosenberg, "Learning by Using," *Inside the Black Box: Technology and Economies* (New York: Cambridge University Press), 120–140.

3. J. A. Schumpeter, *Capitalism, Socialism and Democracy* (New York: Harper Torchbooks, 1976), 81–86.

4. P. F. Drucker, "Coming of the New Organization," *Harvard Business Review,* 1989. Reprint 88105.

5. Arthur Squires, *The Tender Ship: Government Management of Technology Change* (Boston: Birkhauser, 1986).

Chapter 2

Information Technology and the Revolution of Information-Processing Designs

Among the most forceful drivers of social and economic change in the twentieth century is the revolution in communications and information processing wrought by information technology (IT) developments. IT is more than a set of machines and procedures; used increasingly to afford knowledge workers direct access to vast amounts of information, it has spawned a set of social innovations that has altered the way organizations create and finance the introduction of products and penetrate new markets. For example, as Walter Wriston noted in 1988, nations no longer control their money supplies; on-line money traders do.[1]

IT is the latest and arguably most influential in a long chain of potent forces that have had an impact on the restructuring of business and the political economy as a whole. It follows the technologies that led to the rise of the railroads, concentration of urban markets, emergence of mass-production technology, electrification, introduction of the internal combustion engine. In addition, the necessary scale of operations led to adoption of a systematic management approach based on formal procedures and specified information.[2] New procedures in turn exploited new communication and office technologies. The bureaucratic form that evolved to support these innovations — the vertically integrated, multidivisional corporation — was attended by a new concentration of economic power guided, as Al Chandler aptly put it, by a "visible hand."[3]

Chandler's longitudinal analyses of a number of successful firms revealed that they had adapted structurally to support changes in strategy which, generally, reflected a shift from strong, central, functional control to decentralized control molded by the needs of particular geographic or product markets. DuPont and General Motors were characteristic of the divisionalized companies of the 1920s, in which product and marketing decisions were made within divisions and financial decisions centrally, all being subject to headquarters review. Punched-card systems that automated accounting and material control were the processing innovation of the day. Most organizational changes begun in the 1920s were completed, and information processing was largely systematized (though still dependent on human interaction through meetings and telephone), by World War II. The strategies of firms that adapted their organizational structures generally succeeded; those which did not frequently failed.

Transferring power over basic business decisions to divisions enabled companies to focus on markets and orient production toward achieving economies of scale. The result was to transform the design of information-processing systems. Staff analysts became common in divisions, and finance and systems analysts were employed to design paperwork flows.

Finance being the primary link with headquarters, financial systems were designed centrally by the headquarters group, strongly influenced by financial accountants. Production control systems, on the other hand, were usually designed on-site in a decentralized fashion to meet local production and, often, distribution needs. Because production depended on economies of scale and the nature of the driving technology, its information-processing designs tended to be strongly influenced by the notions of scientific management, particularly emphasis on detailed analysis of local conditions.

The design of marketing support depended on firm strategy, which was strongly influenced by the nature of markets and technology. Large retailers like Procter & Gamble and Sears evolved centralized marketing information systems along with the execution of national-brand strategies associated with coordinated brand identities. Firms that chose a regional approach (e.g., National Dairy) or product-line structure (e.g., General Electric) tended to decentralize the design and evolution of their marketing systems to regional or product divisions. These approaches reflected differences in the nature of competition in different industries.

Conceptual Foundations

As industrial growth exploded following World War II, a new set of managerial concepts emerged. Robert Anthony articulated a framework comprising three levels of control systems: operational control, focused on assuring that task execution is effective and efficient; management control, aimed at ensuring the efficient procurement and effective use of resources; and strategic planning, undertaken to establish the nature of — and prescribe the means and policies for achieving — company objectives.[4] This framework spawned a new, highly specific philosophy of operational control that in many industries became computer based. Managerial control came to rely increasingly on budgeting and marketing programs and a strategic process that fit market and management objectives. Anthony's notion of control together with Kenneth Andrews's articulation of the range of and means of implementing strategic processes capable of creating and sustaining market growth changed management process. CEOs extended planning beyond the accounting equation and framed management situations in a way that was ideally supported by computer-based information, which was timely, accurate, and accessible within the context of the operation or forecast.[5]

Computer use in the late 1950s and early 1960s stimulated a range of speculation and thoughtful analysis. Herbert Simon of Carnegie-Mellon University developed a pivotal set of concepts pertaining to the nature of man-machine potential.[6] He proposed and substantiated a series of iconoclastic notions, for example, that managers who devise a workable solution which meets their goals do not optimize but "satisfice," and that such solutions are products of managers' domains. He demonstrated that for some problems search was much more efficient with computers, which he labeled heuristic systems, implying that they possessed an ability to "learn" through repeated trials to improve their solutions. He thus proposed the unthinkable — that computers could "think" — giving rise, as was his intention, to a wonderful tempest in a teapot.

Research at Case Western Reserve University was directed at applying computers to new forms of systematic analysis. C. West

Churchman, Russell L. Ackoff, and E. L. Arnoff, working with industrial users, popularized the use of mathematical programming
to optimize product flow through production and logistic systems,
which literally transformed planning and control methods in most
process industries.[7] The Massachusetts Institute of Technology's Jay
Forrester developed dynamic simulation models that could replicate
the time dynamics of complex industrial systems and, together with
others, devised analytical procedures that could be tailored to particular markets and production systems to improve overall system
performance.[8] These innovations provided companies with an analytical base for sophisticated long-range planning that constituted a
new competitive weapon with a potential for significant market impact. Oil companies that appropriated these innovations significantly improved yield and inventory control, and large distributors
were able to locate warehouses to reduce overall logistics costs.
Such modeling became one of the fastest growing uses of computers
in the late 1960s.

The Evolution of Information Technology

Today's information technologies link organizations in real time
without regard to geography, effectively globalizing society. The
evolution of these technologies, characterized by decreasing cost
and increasing capacity, has shaped the functionality of information-processing designs and, ultimately, industry competition (see
Figures 2-1 and 2-2; Table 2-1). Over the course of forty years, we
have seen the computer's role shift from central processor for
groups in many different functions — the mainframe era — to personal aide to individuals (albeit frequently linked to extant mainframes) — the distributed era. The emerging ubiquitous era frequently linked diffuse use of the technology by building upon
existing habits that a few innovators transformed. The ubiquitous
era will allow employees and citizens access to multimedia terminals, most of which will be linked to one another, and to increasingly capable computers. The figures depict the growth of power
of electronic circuitry and the resulting economies of scale in the
basic circuits as increasing from 1,000 circuits per chip to 2 million.
Figure 2-1 documents the relative growth of the three genres of
computers in the mainframe, the minicomputer/client server, and
the personal computer (PC); Figure 2-2 shows the price performance in computer power per genre; and, Table 2-1 provides exam-

FIGURE 2-1 **Worldwide Computer Sales**

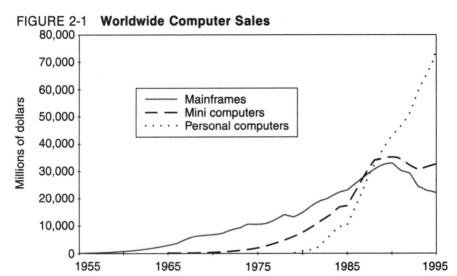

Sources: For 1955–1978, Montgomery Phister, Jr., *Data Processing Technology and Economics,* 2d ed. (Burlington, Mass.: Digital Press, 1979); for 1979–1985 and 1988–1995, Gartner Group (Stanford, Conn.), fax to author; for 1986–1987, author's interpolations.

FIGURE 2-2 **Price per MIPS (million instructions per second)**

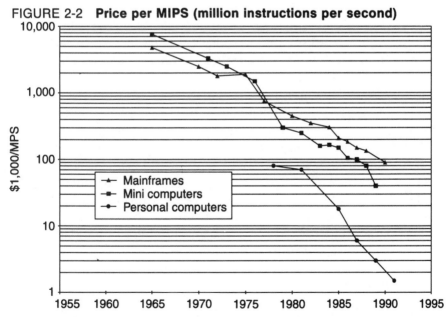

Source: N. Weizer et al., *The Arthur D. Little Forecast on Technology and Productivity: Making the Integrated Enterprise Work* (New York: John Wiley & Sons, 1991): 34. Reprinted with permission.

TABLE 2-1 **Actual Cost and Processing Power for Popular IBM Computer Models**

IBM Model	First Installed	Price $000	Memory (typically)	Add Time (microseconds)	CPU MIPS
704	December 1955	1,390	192Kb	24	
7090	November 1959	1,658	196,600 bytes	4.36	
7070	March 1960	372	25,000 bytes	72	
7074	November 1961	735	50,000 bytes	10	
360/65	November 1965	2,560	1,152 Kb	1.40	.241
370/165	June 1971	3,050	2 Mb	.16	
3033	March 1978	3,685	8 Mb	.08e	1.963
Intel 486DX2-66 PC	1992	6	16 Mb		45

Sources: Data from Montgomery Phister, Jr., *Data Processing Technology and Economics*, 2d ed. (Burlington, Mass.: Digital Press, 1979) and Bay Arinze, *Microcomputers for Managers* (Belmont, Calif.: Wadsworth, 1994).

ples of the actual power and cost of the most popular computers in the different periods. The 1994 PC is more powerful than a 1988 mainframe.

The mainframe era provided an impetus to change that stimulated a broad range of innovations formed largely by the nature of its technology. The distributed IT era added new functionality to the base established by mainframe systems and led to the creation of a new set of procedures, assimilation and modification of old procedures, and maintenance of a core of older, but still useful, systems. A Hartford insurance company is emulating a 1967 computer system within a 1991 computer to process customer activities for a product introduced in the latter year.[9] Present systems are products of leadership's exploitation of the available technology, drawing on past leadership's insights into the implementation process and best practice for information-processing design. But policies and premises that emerged to deal with management issues raised by the earlier design are often irrelevant to, and even impose unnecessary constraints on, subsequent IT innovation; blind subscription to dated procedures and beliefs can be dysfunctional rather than useful or even neutral. The intent is to review the policies of earlier eras as perspective for today's managers to better understand their heritage and basis for future adoption.

The Mainframe Era

Few people are familiar with the drudgery associated with the detail-oriented nature of manual, paper-based systems. Not so long ago, bank middle management was preoccupied with organizing and checking the work of young clerks who had to read signatures to identify accounts and enter draft amounts on ledger cards; the typical department store devoted so much supervisory and clerical time to processing bills and credit purchases that merchandise buyers had to walk the aisles to determine what was selling. Middle managers of necessity focused on operations and training to ensure that flow procedures were being followed and that information was accurate. Sending bills on time was a significant objective. In manufacturing environments, e.g., aircraft and automobiles, the bulk of engineering time was spent proving slide rule computations with punched cards, calculators, or comptometers. Typically, firms pursued and refined a single product design, there being too little time to consider alternatives.

Business managers who attempted to apply early information technologies were pioneers who, in retrospect, might be viewed as having managed research and development projects. They used mainframe computers to automate a broad range of clerical and computational activities and provide middle managers with timely and accurate, if sometimes voluminous, information; at the same time they were creating new jobs in data collection and processing. Buyers could suddenly determine gross sales by product and department; branch bankers could obtain exception reports on overdue loans; design engineers could create alternative designs to better trade off costs and marketability. But gathering transaction details and transforming them into electronic format was a cumbersome, time-consuming task. Success was measured by their ability to close the books by midmonth. Detailed product information was lacking, the principal source of profitability information being income statements by organizational unit.

Firms that engaged in technological innovation in the 1960s had to learn the nature of their investments quickly. For insurance companies accustomed to buying $1,200 calculators, purchasing computer represented an awesome capital decision that demanded months of study and detailed analysis. Although IT innovation was a more normal domain for large manufacturing organizations, they, too, had to learn quickly that IT was not a typical capital investment, that the human accouterment was often more daunting than the requisite capital. Moreover, IT introduced a litany of problems. It was soon discovered, for example, that approximately every four years the technology transformed into something less expensive and more powerful, that usage was inclined to outgrow system capacity far more quickly than anticipated, that new opportunities (e.g., emergency power and backup systems) emerged continuously, and that new systems de-skilled some jobs and expanded responsibilities in others.

Transistor computers, with their intriguing blinking lights, became a status symbol of modern management. Many organizations housed their new computers in glass cages on the first floor or in the lobby for all to see. Access was not an issue, as few needed or wanted to approach a computer. This changed during the Vietnam era, when a series of physical assaults on computers led many firms to find secure, inconspicuous sites for their mainframes. At about the same time, suspicions of data snooping and even deliberate falsification of information in computers became news. These developments were attended by restricted access to computer rooms and greater attention to data security and control of the overall computer resource. Challenged to provide security and assure data integrity as they gained experience and perspective, companies instituted comprehensive central controls that proved a hindrance in subsequent eras.

Mainframe era policies and practices were developed around the ability to centralize processing to exploit economies of scale. General Electric, for example, taking advantage of the new economy of scale in computing to develop an efficient logistics system and automate clerical support, consolidated its entire appliance division in Louisville, Kentucky. The company's first computer, a UNIVAC 1, supported sophisticated production control, logistics planning, and comprehensive payroll systems that enabled a massive organizational shift.

For most firms, the primary criterion for computers was cost reduction through automation of clerical activities or computational tasks. In more progressive firms, such as those whose stories appear in subsequent chapters, IT was directed at solving information-processing crises. As they gained experience, managers turned their IT innovations to competitive advantage.

Companies that focused on automating clerical activities and routine calculation tended to organize the IT function under finance, focusing first on accounting, then on budgeting and overall planning systems. They emphasized capturing and analyzing historical information and making it available to relevant managers. To this end, many companies created active operations control systems to provide timely information on planned versus actual and eventually exception reporting. Many of these firms established a strong tradition of cost reduction, central control, and minimal user involvement in system development. Robert Kling's review of this era documents how successful finance groups quickly understood that the computer, as an effective power base, worked to maintain control over the form and content of its systems.[10] In a number of finance-dominated companies, for example, computer systems became the basis of complex centralized planning and control methods.

Centralized efforts often stimulated local-product champions to create their own IT systems. McKenney's 1964 system audit for the chief operating officer of a large oil company discovered three large mainframes with greater capacity than the headquarter's computer. Finance, which believed that it managed all major computers, knew nothing of these "geological data," "production analysis," and "oil field" systems.

Production systems generally tended to grow in a decentralized manner under the control of the production manager, research groups, or marketing research teams without much coordination with finance. In the 1960s Procter & Gamble developed an on-line marketing system that allowed product managers to analyze effects of alternative marketing programs by city. But except in companies with a strong analytical marketing tradition, marketing tended to be ignored, partly because of the control exerted by finance, but also because the large databases required for marketing applications were difficult to justify on a cost-reduction basis.

Beyond finance, the computer encouraged a broader application of mathematical concepts to problem resolution, resulting in systems that yielded significant economic benefits. Old concepts such as control became the basis of automated production-planning systems capable of responding quickly to fluctuations in demand by way of improved forecasting techniques to establish economic order quantity. New analytical tools, such as mathematical programming, became the foundation for systems that, for example, optimized shipping schedules for oil and minimized cost for grain mixes.

Effective use of these new tools relied on the nurturing of a cadre of professionals who practiced management science. Firms typically hired such individuals into an independent group that was subsequently aligned with either the management information systems group or a functional department. New concepts (e.g., global logistics planning and design support) emerged to enable individuals and functions to take advantage of timely, accurate information and to broaden and deepen the scope of management. IT and management science were practically synonymous in major oil companies, most of which developed sophisticated, mathematically based planning systems.

Firms that recognized the potential of the new analytic base initiated continuous organizational change to integrate it into their normal management procedures. In 1967, Michael Scott Morton, a doctoral student at the Harvard Business School, conducted a pioneering study of the benefits of a Westinghouse decision support system designed to make accessible to washing machine division management up-to-date inventory status and information on planned production and sales.[11] Previously, division managers had met quarterly with marketing and production managers to establish a production plan and anticipated inventory levels and to set warehouse distribution for the next period. Because the managers' inventory and sales data were usually a month old, a three-day negotiation meeting was required to define the plan. The new system's timely information on production schedules, inventories, recent sales, and likely forecasts eliminated the need for both the long meeting and the sales manager, whose role was subsumed by the division manager, as decisions then tended to relate to when to cannibalize products, expand capacity, or inaugurate a new product line. Scott Morton confirmed that timely information can change an organization.

Another lesson many firms learned during the mainframe era, often the hard way, was that system development is best shared by an IT group and the affected organization. Effective system design builds on understanding the functions and information needs of knowledgeable users. Moreover, managers in user organizations are best held accountable for the costs and benefits of a new system. The requisite analysis includes a detailed definition of the proposed application and its postinstallation functioning. Design should be a give-and-take process aimed at evaluating future services and benefits, as well as development and operational costs and implementation the responsibility of the line manager supported by the IT group.

Early system development efforts most commonly failed as a consequence of a firm's delegating full responsibility for design and implementation to the head of MIS. Without senior management leverage and strong line involvement, it is virtually impossible for a complex system implementation to work, never mind achieve projected benefits and productivity gains. Too often, benefits are identified as objectives by the MIS team plus involved users with no delegation of control to the responsible line manager. We have documented system development efforts three years overdue and were continuing to slip as a consequence of, among other things, successive changes in design to accommodate emerging needs and lack of involvement by responsible managers. Such projects are frequently accompanied by at least one turnover in senior MIS management. A typical response, one that persists to this day, is to fire the MIS manager and start over. Taking charge of and managing change to control costs and realize productivity improvements demands constant line-management involvement. This is even more true as information technology begins to penetrate the professional and managerial levels.

By the end of the mainframe era, there were a few acknowledged leaders in the most intensive information-processing industries, a large number of excellent functionally oriented systems, and a group of financially oriented automators or pure data-processing shops. Strong line involvement was in evidence in the leaders' experimentation and in many of the functional systems. Most had more than one data center and their system efforts were characterized by decentralized control and central coordination. Fairly strong, centrally controlled, technologist-dominated MIS groups focused on reducing costs by taking advantage of the economies of scale of the centralized mainframe. With too few competent people to meet demand, consulting grew, and university and vocational school curricula expanded to accommodate the intellectual needs of the emerging technology.

The standard design of information processing at the end of the mainframe era was a large central computer. Usual inputs were punched cards and magnetic tape and, somewhat less commonly, remote typewriter-like terminals. Mainframe computers were generally located apart from operations and attended by specialists who made their careers in IT. Keypunchers, programmers, and systems analysts predominated. Management was generally supplied by individuals with business backgrounds and ties to the company. Most middle managers, trained in the technology and information systems staffs, tended to be young vis-à-vis the rest of the organization.

Another fact of life about computer systems which became evident during this period was that programs had to be changed to accommodate changing requirements. When the need to migrate to more powerful computers every three or four years and increasing growth in salaries for computer personnel were factored in, computer costs overall became an insatiable economic sump. For firms focused on cost reduction, this was a paradox and a source of considerable discussion and study. Firms that imposed arbitrary limits on budget growth effectively limited programming to essential maintenance. Leading-edge firms, recognizing the bottom-line impact of computer investments, viewed them as a strategic necessity.

The number of organizations that had become knowledgeable buyers of information services and were actively utilizing information technology had grown considerably by the end of the mainframe era. Innovative systems had been developed in financial services, aerospace, large manufacturing, oil, and chemicals, among other industries. A number of these had strong professional groups and had evolved career paths and profitable system portfolios. A few companies were led by executive product-champion innovators who appreciated the potential of the computer and created effective IT-based information-processing designs. Such organizations understood the value of software and enforced standards for applications, data storage, and programming.

But many more organizations were still learning the complexities of computers, or had learned the wrong lessons. In companies that viewed them as an expensive investment best utilized to improve productivity in finance and planning, computers had only modest visibility. A handful of firms which had tried and failed to implement computer systems concluded that they were irrelevant except for accounting, an attitude that still has subscribers. We suggest that a computer is what a company makes of it; well managed within its technological bounds, a computer is completely pliable to the needs of an organization.

To be sure, employing the technology of the day was not a productive use of capital for a large segment of the economy. A boon to the engineering and accounting professions, it had only a modest impact on law and medicine, for example. In industries such as retailing and construction, the technology simply was not capable of supporting dramatic new system designs. The portfolios of small- and medium-size businesses that used time-sharing or finance and payroll services were limited by cost and competence requirements. The benefits of mainframe computers accrued primarily to large organizations that had to control massive product volumes and satisfy large numbers of customers. IT proved to be strategically important to them and to large government agencies.

Capable firms learned that organizational impacts were as significant as technological impacts. Hal Leavitt and Thomas Whisler suggested in an elegant and insightful 1958 *Harvard Business Review* article that computers would replace middle managers, a prediction intended to focus managers on organizational as well as technological issues.[12] This is even more important today. Automation influences the flow of work and individual tasks and tends to integrate activities across, and thereby blur, normal functional or product boundaries. This, in turn, has the effect of altering managers' responsibilities. Who, for example, is in charge of customer delivery, the mill manager or the logistics manager? Exception operating-control reporting was common by the mid-1960s and the first steps were taken toward developing comprehensive management control systems to appraise markets and technology.

The Distributed Era

The distributed computing era was built on a reliable, relatively inexpensive, and predictably changing technology — the large-scale integrated circuit, or chip. The building block of all computing and communications, the chip provided the basis for undreamed-of functionality at an ever-increasing pace. Advances in communication technology facilitated, for example, the electronic transfer of large amounts of information between centralized computers and geographically remote sites.

The emergence of the computer on a chip quadrupled the total hardware power in organizations from 1982 to 1986 and provided thousands of people with hands-on computing experience. The distribution of computing diffused awareness of the technology throughout organizations and began to erode the dominance of the central mainframe. Applications grew beyond finance, production control, and analysis as managers began to see opportunities and become more involved in the deployment of information technology. Point-of-sale and automatic credit card scanners that accumulate accurate, detailed information about item sales to customers eliminated an entire chain of data input and processing, and CAD/CAM (computer-aided design and manufacturing) systems sped turnaround for trial parts and supported testing of multiple designs. More timely and useful information became available to all functions in a geographically independent fashion.

Distributing functional computer support, which began as an extension of mainframe computing in most organizations, became rampant with the second generation of personal computers and IBM's entry into the market. By the 1980s, computing had become commonplace and there existed a broad base of persons who possessed some computing experience. Most U.S. organizations employed some form of IT, and there was a general awareness of the dramatic changes electronics had wrought, as evidenced by the prominence of the personal computer.

The ability to manage an orderly transition to distributed processing depended on an organization's experience, attitudes, and policies toward the use and value of IT, that is, on its mainframe experience. For firms with time-sharing experience and a tradition of strong user involvement in system design and development, the personal computer was a natural extension of past practice. Firms previously uninvolved with IT tended to focus on cost savings and ignore the evolution of distributed systems. Such organizations invited the development of an uncoordinated set of innovations by individual product champions' targeting specific needs. The control firms exerted through budgets was unable to contain personal computer use.

In the distributed as in the mainframe era, the driving force for investigating the IT option was typically a business problem for which the computer, in this case a personal computer, seemed to provide an answer. Often a local hacker would fashion a trial solution and local managers, encouraged by the trial, would sponsor the effort, intentionally not informing the information systems function for fear it would be quashed. Some of these efforts proved quite successful and their fruits were transferred to other groups within the company, occasionally emerging as a standard. Support ranged from active involvement by local management teams and their managers to benign neglect, much as in the pioneering days of the mainframe.

Champion/hacker teams produced many useful systems, a number of which became indispensable but grew beyond their base technology and required costly efforts to maintain. And a few were debacles. These efforts tended to create islands of technology constrained by their original design and limited by the particular computer systems on which the applications were created. The saving grace was that subsequent generations of personal computers were typically faster and accompanied by more useful software, so reprogramming was not overly complex. The real cost lay in converting complementary data and rolling out a new system. Most firms quickly learned to shift to systems they knew would evolve with the chip. Thus were lessons in system development requirements learned by the pioneers relearned by a broader, more diverse set of managers and users. System standards assumed added importance, and purchasing software, not developing programs, became the formative step.

Low entry cost and, in most companies, the absence of strong or obvious technical constraints resulted in much more rapid progress in the distributed than in the mainframe era. There existed a broad and relatively knowledgeable consumer group of managers and professionals, and little technical input was required to get a personal computer up and running. Furthermore, the distributed era accompanied many firms' rapid expansion into global markets and need for international communications. The distributed era represented ideal technology transfer, with IT both leading and being driven by user needs. Unbeknownst to the information systems group and even senior management, many departments purchased personal computers with spreadsheets and other software. Responses to the discovery of such efforts ranged from "Great idea, how can we help?" by enlightened, progressive managements to confiscation of equipment and systems by strong, control-oriented MIS managers.

IT groups that did not appreciate the personal computer's potential banned its distribution; experimenters and product champions who understood its potential moved quickly to get in front. Passive observers that had consciously turned to outside suppliers or intentionally lagged behind seemed to tolerate innovation as long as it involved a department manager. A nationwide corrugated box company with a modest IT investment which permitted its plants to experiment soon had a grassroots marketing program on linked personal computers that leapfrogged the systems of competitors relatively advanced in mainframe use.

Superficially, distribution and market penetration were much faster and deeper than in the early part of the mainframe era as a result of the user appeal and initial surge of personal computer implementations. Much of this growth seems to have resulted from pent-up demand for service among users who had had little access to helpful IT support. Frustrated practitioners who could visualize solutions that employed personal computers found ways to acquire them. Moreover, the expanded base of computer terminals in educational settings increased the number of people who felt more comfortable with a personal computer than without one. A new role emerged that had always existed in the professional IT group, but rarely had been seen in public — that of the creative hacker who loved solving complex problems with a computer. Such individuals became indispensable.

The flash of new systems development by departments produced both successes, such as the corrugated box company's marketing system, and visible failures, such as the one that left 1,500 personal computer table sculptures in the headquarters of a large company. In large part, the basis of success was similar to that of the mainframe era: the vision and competence of the innovator. The box company's plant manager, for example, knowing that he wanted to organize all the market data he could find on major competitors and potential customers, had recruited a bright hacker and a market research consultant to design and test a system. His sales force, which he had involved in the project from the start, soon came to rely on the new data to expand market share.

The visible failure, by no means an isolated example, resulted when an IT manager and an enthusiastic cohort senior production manager became fascinated with the personal computer's potential. They developed a modest system to link to the regional plant managers in order to provide timely information on production versus plan. The system worked and the production manager began to exchange electronic mail with his managers. Together they developed an ad hoc adaptive planning and control system. Seeing the personal computer as the wave of the future and encouraged by the IT manager, the production manager convinced the executive committee to put personal computers on the desks of most headquarters staff and relevant field managers.

Given little rationale, all managers were required to attend a three-day introduction to personal computers; the executive committee received a one-day tutorial. Subsequently, only the original product champion and the system manager used their computers; the other senior executives persisted in their old habits of communicating through secretaries. Six months after the system was introduced, most of the personal computers had migrated from the office so that managers could "work at home." A follow-up survey found that the most of the "workers" were managers' children, who used the systems for games. That company is still gun-shy of personal computers.

The intellectual intimacy of working with a personal computer presents a formidable challenge to obtaining active involvement programmatically. Our field studies suggest that personal computer implementation comes down to the need for senior managers to lead by example and provide individual training to all who are interested. Patience and the passage of time seem to be key to involvement, particularly for those at the senior level, for whom the value of the personal computer is truly ambiguous. Jack Rockart's study of senior management use of terminals emphasizes the importance of a CEO leader effect.[13] At the organizational level, carefully planned experiential training and encouragement to experiment and rethink procedures are important. In large organizations, coaching one group with representatives of the next groups in line helps the latter adapt to the training and become insiders with respect to what it means. Training has proved important for a much broader spectrum of the organization in the distributed than in the mainframe era.

Firms that moved from tight control to managing a distributed support system found that it took time to build trust and skills, create new policies, and shift responsibilities. Organizations typically required about three years to fashion a serviceable user-MIS relationship, including jointly setting standards and arranging for support and training. Activities such as data backup, installation and maintenance of networks, and enforcement of security were frequently returned to the information systems group. User-assimilated training, new systems deployment, and architectural issues became shared responsibilities. A number of companies developed strong joint-planning committees to set standards, explore new application software and hardware, and encourage technology transfer among user groups. Whether training and software support migrated to users or the IT group depended on competence and attitude. Organizations that could not make the shift often found outsourcing for mainframe services and distributed support a useful gambit.

Communication as an Integral Function

New chips supported reliable, high-speed transfer of unlimited amounts of information but required tailored software to control and store the data flow. The expanded capacity of channels and storage in available computers and communications devices enabled these devices to assimilate automatically, and exchange with other computers, large flows of data. This released pent-up demand for wide-band communication channels, and markets such as linking CAD systems with CAM grew quickly.

Communications became a leading competitive opportunity as

firms learned the advantages of linking to customers, suppliers, and various groups within their own organizations. As electronic data interchange among companies grew, an entire new set of opportunities appeared or reappeared. The need for technology standards to govern the transmission of information within an industry or between cooperative groups intensified. Some companies built proprietary networks — Citibank, for example, to support its early entry into the automated teller machine (ATM) market — while others formed cooperatives in order to go nationwide.

The experiential growth of organizations was more heterogeneous in the distributed era, as more individuals and organizations were influenced by IT. Growing use of ATMs, point-of-sale (POS) checkout devices, and credit cards, as well as greater educational involvement at all ages, lent computers and their presumed potential a period of notoriety. Many industry leaders held their positions, a number of firms caught up and became innovators in their industries, and quite a few bailed out and today outsource IT support. The results reflect industry and managerial perspectives and firm competencies. Strengths in the distributed era evolved — from managing technological issues and large organizational shifts to exploit the potential of mainframe innovations to managing organizational change as a continuous process supported by planned technological advances.

In industries whose leaders were competent to deliver and knew that the expanding capacity of IT would support their innovations, the focus was on new services and processes. In industries without clear leaders and a relatively stable dominant IT design, the early shifts were modest, limited to moving to new distributed systems that provided better information. Retailing, for example, viewing the technology as relatively expensive and not up to handling massive volumes of data, focused on using POS data to automate ordering and reduce stock-outs.

Wal-Mart was an exception. Having decided that IT made a significant difference in economy of scale, the firm undertook to develop a system that enabled it to operate decentralized stores in a centralized mode via tight electronic links to headquarters. The firm's early growth was attributed to its small-town locations and upbeat style of business, but it soon learned to use POS data to improve its stores' merchandising efforts and refine its logistics system as a way to bargain with suppliers for reduced prices.

The key to developing a logistics control system from shelf to factory was to organize the mass of distributed data into large, efficient databases. Wal-Mart's system captured data at the POS checkout, organized it at the store level, and transmitted it to Arkansas for sophisticated, detailed analyses of trends and likely sales rates. Today, the company knows hourly the status of its plans versus actions and sends POS data to the suppliers that keep its shelves stocked. The company no longer "buys"; it establishes year-long contracts for filling shelf space.

Ultimately, the distributed era afforded the ability to link any form of digital computer to any other, one consequence of which has been a growing market in specialty services. Most companies contract with specialists for some outside services. An intriguing example is the outsourcing of payroll, typically one of the primary justifications for early IT investments, to service companies. Tax code changes in 1990 caused payroll service providers' business to surge, as companies considered the cost of reprogramming their own payroll systems to accommodate the innumerable federal, state, and foreign government permutations of these changes.

The core competence here remains specialists who can make systems function as a seamless operation. Skilled development staff and an alert technology-purchasing group that insists on strong user involvement have become the basis of this technical know-how.

The Ubiquitous Era

Megabyte chips and optical fiber communication systems are generating a fundamental integration of communication and computers. Intelligence is the watchword of this ubiquitous era, information distributed instantaneously in graphic form its medium. Managing this latest structural shift effectively requires persistence and experimentation to create new forms of storage and retrieval, and to develop new schema by which individuals might relate to new forms of organizational information.

The ubiquitous era will see both the business transaction data that began to be captured in the mainframe era and the access to multiple files and data services that became the hallmark of the distributed era become a foundation for more human-friendly means of use. Combined with "consumer and entertainment services" they will provide increasingly rich menus of support and communications for businesspeople and private citizens across a range of activities. The era will evolve slowly because of the requisite huge capital investments and data integration efforts involved, but its effect will be profound. Indeed, in time the computer may take entirely unfamiliar forms.

The innovative process is driven by the increasing capacity of the chip to deliver user-friendly, sophisticated processing capability. The trend toward systems that can accommodate human needs without cumbersome input devices and complex means of extracting information seems promising. Intel's chief scientist expects the chip of the future, circa 1998, to have the capacity of a large Cray computer, weigh less than a pound, and be about the size of the present laptop.[14] Concurrent developments in batteries will make possible smaller portable computers that can communicate wirelessly with home systems. The next growth business is likely to be individualized pocket- or purse-size computers that have the ability to interpret their owners' handwriting and voices. Given the requisite infrastructure, these devices will make it possible to communicate with other devices and the telephone system.

Adaptive support systems that can absorb and respond to large flows of information will render unbounded potential to these new computer systems. Organizing and making these large data flows accessible may, in the short run, be the gating factor — the elapsed time required to train individuals and adapt roles to exploit the potential. We do not have effective systems to store and retrieve voice-annotated dynamic electronic visuals. That is, we are soon to have useful portable machines that have decent human ergonomics, but their productivity will be similar to that of personal computers used as individual intellectual aides because the infrastructure to support organizational use is not in place. Given that most companies understand its value and have a greater range of communication suppliers to choose from, developing the needed infrastructure should be economical and relatively timely. The eight-year period to evolve an infrastructure to support organizational use of the personal computer, as documented below, will likely be considerably foreshortened.

Development challenges will be similar to those of the past, but the process will involve a greater degree of search and select. Unfortunately, most organizations do not have a track record in managing the growth of intellectual systems that have many designers and users. It is probable that the links between systems and structure will become seamless, and possible that managers who assume new roles will build upon the previous incumbent's personal computer system.

The Emergence of Competitive Systems

Information technology is the modern equivalent of steam power and electricity, which in their time transformed industries and competition by shifting the nature of production power and the focus and locus of control. Many authors have emphasized IT's uniqueness in terms of competitive impact, potential for organizational transformation, high rate of change, and the time and resources required to build expertise for effective use.

Annual investment in IT today exceeds 20 percent of capital investment in many firms and is growing in most. Peter Keen has reported that IT investment grew from $55 to $190 billion per year in the 1980s, a rate of 15 percent at a time when capital investment was declining. In light of this level of investment, IT has become an integral part of many firms' strategic plans. According to Keen, between 25 and 80 percent of major businesses's cash flows depend on electronic processes.[15]

With the maturing of IT systems in the 1980s has come a need for increasing sophistication and depth. Whereas the mainframe era generated explosive growth in the number of books that described how to build systems and extolled the potentialities of IT, the distributed era stimulated a succession of thoughtful commentaries that serve as the basis for managing an evolving IT strategy.

Michael Porter has substantiated that IT provides vital support in some, if not all, stages of the value chain in all industries.[16] His analysis suggests that IT reduces overhead and increases the pace of activities by integrating functions and providing more links between organizational units, essentially tying disjointed activities into coherent systems that can better anticipate market moves. Such systems enable management to quickly formulate, test, and implement revisions to strategy, accommodate changing relationships with customers and suppliers, which can yield tremendous economies of scale and drastically reduce reaction times, and spawn new businesses that depend entirely on competence in innovating with IT.

McKenney, with James I. Cash, Jr., and F. Warren McFarlan, analyzed a number of industries' dependence on IT for logistics, production, distribution, and marketing. We found only a few industries in which IT progress was not essential to competitiveness (see Figure 2-3), and even these had strong IT dependencies in operations and finance.[17] Because there was little opportunity for significant improvement, these systems required little attention. The lumber industry, for example, employs optical laser-driven

FIGURE 2-3 **IT Impact: Current Position of Industry Leaders**

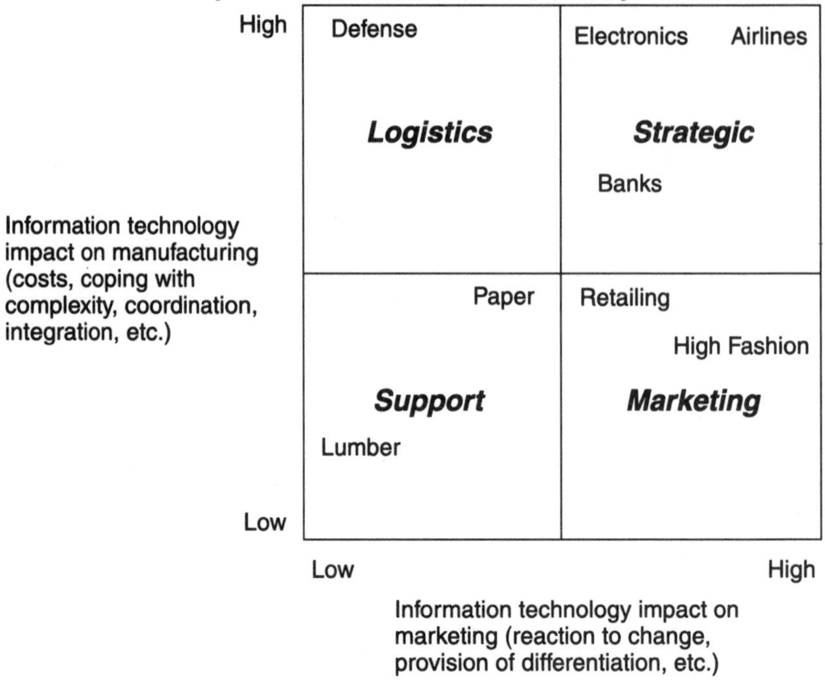

Information technology impact on manufacturing (costs, coping with complexity, coordination, integration, etc.)

High

Defense

Logistics

Electronics   Airlines

Strategic

Banks

Paper   Retailing

High Fashion

Support

Lumber

Marketing

Low

Low   High

Information technology impact on marketing (reaction to change, provision of differentiation, etc.)

Source: J. I. Cash, F. W. McFarlan, and J. L. McKenney, *Corporate Information Systems Management: The Issues Facing Senior Executives* (Homewood, Ill.: Richard D. Irwin, Inc., 1992), 24.

sawing and sophisticated logistics systems, as well as complex support systems that track market prices throughout the nation, but the driving cost factors are raw materials and logistics costs, which are based on overall demand and location. Technology has rendered the lumber industry — a group of survivor companies with similar computer-process control and order-entry systems for which competition is dependent on execution — an organizational game. Their need to invest in innovative systems is modest — they merely have to stay current.

Even more vital is the human side of the organization, which is coming more and more to rely on IT for information sharing, control of activities, and maintenance of customer and supplier links. Shoshana Zuboff has advanced the notion that one of IT's fundamental capacities is the ability to "informate" an organization.[18] Tracking the production of goods and services for control purposes, for example, not only improves control of the process, but also accumulates a precise history of what has happened, often supplemented with contextual information that enables managers to determine why it happened. This information can be used to continuously improve the human operational system, thus expanding the organization's knowledge base and increasing its competence. Alternatively, it can be used to discern causality and refine control, fix responsibility, and, over time, concentrate knowledge in a few specialists, thereby reducing human participation and commitment. The former application reflects the "informating" power of IT. The latter, which reflects the persistent control mentality, is attended by a potential long-term loss of competence. Whether IT is to be used as an effective controller based on understood conditions and human noninvolvement or an adaptive knowledge development base that relies on competent individuals must be decided by top management.

Richard Walton has proposed a phased process that builds commitment to organizational goals by aligning the use of IT with the organization and its strategy. This process emphasizes the importance of interaction among strategy, structure, and systems to effective competition.[19] Because strong ownership is essential to the effective deployment of IT-based systems, organizational members must be stakeholders in their design and development. Key to all the successes Walton relates in this regard is top management involvement.

The increasing capacity of IT to informate and link its component units independent of space and time has created an opportunity to transform an organization, to organize, as Harold Leavitt and Thomas Whisler suggested in the 1950s, with empowered decision makers situated where the action is. Lynda Applegate et al., in a series of interviews with Leavitt and Whisler, confirmed that what is at issue is transforming the firm by empowering managers.[20] Frito-Lay's decentralization of product-line decision making from the top to the field to compete more effectively with regional brands, a move that decentralizes product strategy to specific territories, is an example. The impact of the IT transformation process on structure is to foster simultaneously highly adaptable focused groups and large economies of scale while preserving and extending expertise and encouraging better training and greater autonomy for workers.

The end of the distributed era is fuzzier than the end of the mainframe era. There is no wave of dramatically new technology such as the personal computer and the explosion in connectivity that followed. All the basic technological components of the ubiquitous era have been proffered at intervals since 1939, when the picture phone was shown at the New York City World's Fair. At the 1963

Fall Joint Computer Conference, Doug Englebart demonstrated a terminal system with mouse, windows, and the capacity to see and talk with a geographically distant person, all supported by a powerful database.[21] The slow accretion of concepts and rapid improvement in the power of the chip ultimately yielded the coordinated realization of a number of innovations that had previously languished for want of adequate channel capacity and logic speed. Exception reporting on the basis of color is an example. Highlighted numbers in a report on a screen need no explanation to provide a vivid message. A viewer is able to place the exceptions in context and click on particular entries for further analysis or explanation.

Competitive Advantage and Dominant Designs

Tactically, competitive advantage accrues to the system which first provides a unique processing capability that delivers better service at lower cost. Such a design supports the extension of the electronic base throughout the value chain and its application to informating the process. Human competence is needed to develop and implement innovative systems that capture necessary information electronically and process it in a way that supports an organization's objectives; management guidance is required to structure organizations in a way that enables them to exploit the novel functionality of such systems. A company's long-term advantage thus lies in the knowledge and experience of its management and IT organization.

The histories we relate document companies that invented the dominant information-processing design of their industries — American Airlines and the Bank of America. In the formative stage of computers, the airline and bank developed dramatically new computer-processing systems that transformed the competitive basis in their industries. Both industries moved from paper-based systems to computers within three years. The notion of dominant design was first defined by William Abernathy and James Utterback's analysis of the automobile industry in its formative stage and the impact of the all-metal body, rear-wheel drive and the dramatic changes in the car.[22] These changes standardized design and competition, which shifted to execution, styling, and marketing, and IT firms developed efficient technology and complementary assets to produce it. In our studies, all firms moved quickly to adopt the innovative design as it enabled competitive advantage through better service or new products. The design changes the character of innovation and competition in a firm and an industry.

Once defined, the dominant design of information processing in an industry becomes obvious, and most firms move quickly either to adopt it or to shift to an atypical strategy that reduces their reliance on IT. The rate of adoption depends on the ability of competitors to manage the change to a new mode of information processing. The overwhelming evidence from Harvard Business School case studies is that firms without much experience find making the change a painful and costly effort, requiring several attempts over a number of years.

There is also strong evidence for the alternatives of leading or adopting a fast second policy with respect to IT. Both require sustained competence and the continuous scanning of alternatives to discern probable future designs. Firms that do not invest in IT probably lack management ability to understand the nature of potential changes and their impact on the industry competitive situation and the need for organizational adaptation. Such skill is not readily available from consulting firms; when it can be found, it is expensive and often too late.

Because the evolution of an emergent design depends on the needs and history of the industry and the innovativeness of the firms that exploit it, constant surveillance and occasional testing are needed. Future designs are not well understood at the beginning of the development cycle; rather, they evolve with experience into reasonably well-understood visions that continue to shift with experience and changing technological opportunities. Early point-of-sale efforts aimed at capturing information at a store and making it available to store managers proved interesting, but not very useful. Store managers could obtain the same information less expensively by walking the aisles with a clipboard. Not until links to central systems became efficient did reordering information become valuable, at which point companies that had experimented with electronic data interchange (EDI) links to their suppliers for replenishment had a solid base for moving forward.

The real challenge for most organizations is not technology per se, but the ability to adapt to take advantage of its emerging functionality, which requires both an understanding of how it might function and a readiness to change. In retailing, the role of buyer is shifting dramatically from bargainer to long-term planner-negotiator because IT systems provide real-time information to the supplier of customer purchases. The buyer and supplier work together on promotion to expand on sales within the context of targeted sales levels. Changing solely for the purpose of introducing a new technology is akin to automating and often proves difficult. A technology introduced in a believable form in the context of improving a firm's ability to compete realizes its potential. A modest investment in experimentation with systems enables an organization to learn how to test and use new technologies to evaluate their limitations and potential.

Competent managers and technicians shape an information-processing design as their understanding of a technology's true potential emerges, then alter the organization to make IT investments and adaptations to take advantage of incremental changes that yield better information. This approach has led American Airlines and Frito-Lay to the development of communities of experimenters distributed broadly throughout their organizations. Such breadth tends to produce more capable and robust systems as well as prepare an organization for change. Growth in the rate and breadth of change was clearly in evidence at Bank of America as it gained momentum. Once a system is up to speed, the issue becomes managing the rate of innovation, not initiating change.

Progress toward new industry designs is driven not by the technology, which is an enabling force, but by market need. IT innovation normally requires dramatic changes in entire processes. The requisite understanding of these processes and the market needs which dictate that they be changed can be supplied only by knowledgeable IT users.

The evolution of IT will continue to be an exciting and interesting adventure, more and more dependent on the ability of managers and technologists to design and implement solid system designs. These must exploit the expanding capacity of IT to support effective market moves by organizations whose boundaries are expanding to encompass suppliers, customers, and global markets. The challenge to management is to formulate an effective IT strategy that builds a competence to invent and exploit systems which improve a firm's ability to compete. The secret is management involvement and leadership. The following stories articulate what that means.

Notes

1. Walter B. Wriston, "Technology and Sovereignty," *Foreign Affairs*, February 1988, 71.

2. Joann Yates, *Control through Communication: The Rise of System in American Management* (Baltimore, Md.: Johns Hopkins University Press, 1989).

3. Alfred D. Chandler, Jr., *The Visible Hand: The Managerial Revolution in American Business* (Cambridge, Mass.: Harvard University Press, 1977).

4. Robert N. Anthony, *Planning and Control Systems: A Framework for Analysis* (Boston: Harvard Business School, 1966).

5. Kenneth R. Andrews, *The Concept of Corporate Strategy* (Homewood, Ill.: Dow Jones, Irwin, 1980).

6. H. A. Simon, *Models of Man: Social and Rational, Mathematic Essays on Rational Human Behavior in Social Setting* (New York: Wiley, 1957).

7. C. W. Churchman, R. L. Ackoff, and E. L. Arnoff, *Introduction to Operations Research* (New York: Wiley, 1957).

8. Jay W. Forrester, *Industrial Dynamics* (Cambridge, Mass.: MIT Press, 1961).

9. Interview with Irwin Sitkin, retired CFO, February 17, 1992.

10. Robert Kling, "Computing and Urban Services," in James N. Danziger, William Dutton, Robert Kling, and Kenneth Kramer, *Computer and Politics — High Technology in American Local Governments* (New York: Columbia University Press, 1986), 211–217.

11. Michael S. Morton, *Management Decision Systems* (Boston: Harvard Business School, 1971).

12. Hal J. Leavitt and Thomas L. Whisler, "Management in the 1980's," *Harvard Business Review* 36, no. 6 (November–December 1958), Reprint 58605.

13. John F. Rockart and Adam D. Crenscenzi, "Engaging Top Management in Information Technology," *Sloan Management Review* 25, no. 4: 3–16.

14. D. Gelsinger, D. Gargin, G. Parker, and A. Yu, "2001: A Microprocessor Odyssey," in *Technology 2001: The Future of Computing and Communication*, ed. D. Leebart (Cambridge, Mass.: MIT Press, 1992), 84.

15. Peter G. W. Keen, *Shaping the Future: Business Design Through Information Technology* (Boston: Harvard Business School Press, 1991).

16. Michael E. Porter and V. E. Millar, "How Information Gives You Competitive Advantage," *Harvard Business Review* 63, no. 4 (July–August 1985), Reprint 85415.

17. James I. Cash, Jr., F. Warren McFarlan, James L. McKenney, and Lynda M. Applegate, *Corporate Information Systems Management Text and Cases* (Homewood, Ill.: Irwin, 1992), 628–634.

18. Shoshana Zuboff, *In the Age of the Smart Machine* (New York: Basic Books, 1988).

19. Richard E. Walton, *Up and Running: Integrating Information Technology and the Organization* (Boston: Harvard Business School Press, 1989).

20. Lynda M. Applegate, James I. Cash, Jr., and D. Quincy Mills, "Information Technology and Tomorrow's Manager," *Harvard Business Review* 66, no. 6 (November–December 1988), Reprint 88601.

21. Doug Englebart, excerpt from Conference on Personal Computer Proceedings, San Francisco, 1993 (Boston: Harvard Business School Film Archive), TV clip.

22. William J. Abernathy and James M. Utterback, "Patterns of Industrial Innovation," *Technology Review* (June–July 1978): 41–47.

Chapter 3

Bank of America: Breaking with 500 Years of Tradition

The early 1950s found the banking industry on the brink of a crisis. Check use in the United States had doubled between 1943 and 1952, from four billion to eight billion checks per year, and bankers were projecting continuing increases of one billion checks per year by 1955. Banks were at a standstill, unable to expand, or, in some cases, even to keep pace with the increasing flow of paper.

The immediate culprit was the check clearing process. Each of the 28 million checks written every business day passed through approximately $2\frac{1}{3}$ banks, taking more than two days to be processed. The result was a staggering 69 million checks in process throughout the United States on an average day. Unless deposited at the bank where both accounts were located, a check had to be sorted by hand and individually tallied on an adding machine at least six times during the clearing process.

In a 40-person branch, seven or more people were kept busy sorting, adding, and bundling checks. Most were young female bookkeepers between the ages of 18 and 24. Given the drudgery of the work and the age of the women, who traditionally left the banks upon marrying, turnover was exceedingly high, in some instances 100 percent per year.[1]

Bank of America (called Bank of Italy until 1930) was founded in 1904 as a small San Francisco savings and loan. A single branch, opened in 1909, grew to 24 by the end of 1918 and to 292 by the bank's twenty-fifth anniversary in 1929, at which point Bank of

America employed more than 7,000 people and had more than $1 billion in assets. L. M. Giannini, some of founder A. P. Giannini, took the bank to 495 branches and $2.1 billion in assets by the end of 1941. With World War II, California's population and economy mushroomed, boosting the bank's resources to more than $5 billion. Following the war, Bank of America opened nine overseas offices; by 1946, it was the largest bank in the world.

Former national bank examiner S. Clark Beise, who had come to Bank of America under A. P. Giannini and risen to senior vice president by 1950 (and to president in 1954 to 1964), was acutely aware of the serious problems that faced the nation's banks in general and Bank of America in particular. The bank was managing more than 4.6 million checking, savings, and Timeplan loan accounts, with checking accounts growing at a rate of 23,000 per month. Realizing that growth would be limited not by new business, but by inability to service new accounts adequately, Beise became the first of the bank's senior managers to seek a solution in the automation of check handling. Exhibit 3-1 lists key events in Bank of America's use of IT.

EXHIBIT 3-1 Development of the Bank of America Dominant Design

Year	Event	Significance
1920s	Establishes systems analysis department	Competence in systems analysis
1950	SRI hired to analyze potential of IT for check processing	Beise learns of potential of IT; forms joint study team
1951	Beise hires Zipf as IT manager	Forms IT function
1952	SRI to build ERM	Prototype check-processing system
1953	Zipf orders IBM 702	Credit automation initiated
1954	Eldredge invents MICR	Human- and machine-readable type
1955	SRI's ERMA works; Zipf installs 702 and it works	Proves electronic check processing; begins automating credit applications

EXHIBIT 3-1 Continued

Year	Event	Significance
1956	GE to build ERMA; initiate loan exceptions	Joint development project; automates credit management
1958–1959	Links branches to headquarters; proofing in ERMA; introduce credit card	Develops electronic infrastructure; enables electronic processing; expands electronic product base
1960–1961	Finishes installing ERMA; installs 7070s; expands credit card to U.S.	Expands branches to small towns; new capacity for new services; national market
1963–1964	Credit card restricted to California; Beise retires; Peterson CEO; Zipf orders new computer	Bank banned from interstate acts; given charge to expand overseas; new generation must reprogram
1966–1968	System failures plague IT; Zipf head of retail bank	Loses confidence of management; S&ER leaderless; loses momentum
1969–1978	Cost-minimization IT era; Zipf retires; IT skills depart	Full generation behind in use of IT; loses momentum; ATMs vetoed
1978–1981	Clausen recognizes problem; works to bring in ATMs	Hires competent IT manager; rebuilding IT infrastructure
1981–1992	Armacost and then Clausen CEO; Clausen empowers a maestro; management becomes involved; establishes evolving IT strategy	Hopper designs new architecture; Simmons builds on Hooper's effort; creates ongoing planning process; strengthens IT competence
1993–present	Rosenberg CEO picks Maestro; continuing IT strategy	Swartz experienced IT manager; expanding in new products

The Searching Phase: 1950–1953

When a promotional meeting at the Emporium department store near Bank of America headquarters ended earlier than expected, Dr. W. B. Gibson of the Menlo Park, California, Stanford Research Institute (SRI), an independent technology research institution at the leading edge of electronics, decided to call on Beise. "I told Beise that this was just a 'shot in the dark,' but that I thought Bank of America should be thinking about electronic applications," Gibson later recalled.[2]

Beise had previously approached several business equipment manufacturers about creating an automated bookkeeping system. Although willing to improve their basic proof machines, none of the manufacturers was interested in investing time or capital to create an entirely new system. Beise acted quickly on Gibson's advice; vice president of operations Frank M. Dana, asked by Beise to follow up and develop a proposal, contacted SRI's director of engineering research, Thomas H. Morrin, and immediately commenced a series of meetings to explore the automation of check processing, account numbering, and paper handling. SRI seemed to Beise to be the perfect solution. As a prominent research and development organization with a strong track record in electronics research, it could establish the possibilities in automated check handling and design a model to test or sell to a manufacturer. Beise formed a close relationship with Morrin, vice president of SRI Engineering and R&D. Working under a charter from L. M. Giannini to solve the banking crisis, he signed a contract, with the understanding that no publicity would be given to the effort. Morrin became his R&D manager. Subsequently, a highly secret feasibility study was initiated. Beise assigned Charles Conroy as systems analyst to work with the SRI team.

Automating Check Processing

When a check was deposited at a bank, two steps had to be accomplished quickly: proofing and bookkeeping. Each afternoon, "on us" checks, meaning checks drawn on the bank that held the account, were sorted by signature and taken to a conventional ledger-card accounting machine whose operator entered the dollar amount on a ledger card and subtracted it from the balance, thereby creating a permanent record for month-end reporting. Daily deposits and withdrawals were subsequently posted to customers' account balances. All other checks were batched into proofed totals and forwarded to other branches and banks. To finish proofing early enough to catch stop payments or overdrafts, most banks were forced to shut their doors to business by 2:00 P.M.[3]

The check was central to SRI's feasibility study. Bank of America, regarding it as an important emotional link to customers, wanted few, if any, changes to the check. One of the first critical choices was between customers' usage habits and system needs with respect to the account filing system. Standard banking practice was to organize customer files alphabetically, which resulted in changing the order of sorting with the addition of each new account, and to identify and verify checks against customers' signatures, which were maintained on index cards at branch offices. SRI engineers suggested that a numerical accounting system would make check processing easier to automate and provide a more reliable means of identifying checks. Conroy worked with them to develop a revised paperwork flow to articulate the potential savings. The proposed change would entail distributing new checkbooks with customer name and account numbers printed on checks and warning customers against loaning bank checks to friends, a common pre-automation practice.

The feasibility study provided an opportunity for engineers and bankers to learn the complexities of each other's businesses. Bank of America vice president Ranaulf Beames stressed to SRI engineers the service-industry/customer-focus character of banking, emphasizing that prompt, reliable banking services engendered customer loyalty. He also underscored the bank's desire that customers be inconvenienced as little as possible and that usage habits be changed only as necessary. Beames discussed with Beise the alternative work flows resulting from printing identification numbers on the checks, and Beise quickly agreed the change was essential. They encouraged SRI to explore the means of electronically identifying the account number, thereby changing a banking tradition established in Venice in 1431.[4]

In late September 1950, Morrin informed Beames that SRI's feasibility study "indicated it was technically possible to build an automatic bookkeeping system for ledger posting and processing of commercial checking accounts" and suggested a three-phase project approach entailing (1) a study of banking procedures external to the machine, (2) logical design, and (3) development, construction, and testing.[5] Because manufacturing ran counter to SRI's mission statement, the last phase was to be carried out by an equipment manufacturer. Beise approved the project under CEO funds and made the fixed investment toward electronic banking. The $15,000 contract (later augmented by $5,000) for SRI's part in the project referred to the system as an electronic recording machine (ERM).

Although the Bank of America was interested in using the proofing process as an input to bookkeeping activities, an April 30, 1951, interim report described the machine as fundamentally a bookkeeping device. Completion of the first two phases of the project found the bank and SRI in agreement that the system would have to perform five basic bookkeeping functions: credit and debit all accounts; maintain a record of all transactions; retain a record of current customer balances to be printed as needed; respond to stop-payment and hold orders on checks; and notify operators of checks that caused accounts to be overdrawn.

SRI subsequently began what was supposed to be its final project for the bank, estimation of optimal account capacity for and cost of constructing the ERM. An initial rough estimate of $750,000, with an additional $15,000 for development of a check reader, was arrived at by comparing it with estimated construction costs incurred by other companies for such large-scale computer projects as the Mark III, UNIVAC, EDVAC, and Whirlwind I. When ERM development was broken down into specifics, the final estimate was $949,000, a figure deemed high by Morrin, who suggested estimating minimum and complete systems. The readjusted figures were $530,000 and $830,000, respectively.

Only Burroughs expressed an interest in building an ERM for the bank, and its proposal to modify an existing system that would deliver less functionality at twice SRI's cost estimate was rejected. Consequently, Beise asked SRI to construct an engineering prototype of the ERM, a decision motivated to some extent by his belief that confidentiality was less at risk with the research firm. Although it had no interest in manufacturing and was ill equipped to build what was to become one of the largest and most complex computer systems yet designed, SRI, on January 28, 1952, contracted to develop, construct, and test a pilot ERM. Beise still planned, once SRI had demonstrated a working prototype, to sell the system design to a manufacturing company.

Phase 3 work on the ERM was to involve completing the logical design of remaining operations; constructing a pilot model; testing the model at a Bank of America branch; and finishing and installing the machine at a local branch. The bank was to pay SRI no more than $850,000 over four years, plus an additional $25,000 to cover subcontracts. (Although expenses were never released, most engineers estimate that the final cost was in excess of $5 million.)

Once SRI had the mandate to develop the system, Morrin and colleagues Jerre Noe and Oliver Whitby — referred to by the few bank employees who knew about the project as the "whiz kids" — began working as technical advisers on the creation of a prototype. Conroy moved to Palo Alto to supervise the project and work with the team. Monthly review meetings with Beise were held at bank headquarters. Design and operation of the ERM were fairly well defined by the fall of 1952. The primary system was to consist of four centrally located, 30,000-account capacity ERMs linked by (in some cases, flying) messenger services to approximately twelve branches. Each ERM was to be operated by ten or twelve bookkeepers and handle both bookkeeping and proofing functions.

SRI had begun in 1952 to develop a system for encoding electronically readable customer, bank, and account information on checks to support automatic proofing. A magnetic ink bar printed on the backs of checks was selected as the best solution to punched-card approaches. Encoding project manager Kenneth Eldredge developed a system to form the magnetic ink into Arabic characters that could be read by humans as well as computers. This magnetic ink character recognition (MICR) system, successfully developed and tested in the summer of 1954 on Bank of America's traveler's check program, proved a superb showcase for advances in machine reading and paper handling; by June 1955, more than 300,000 traveler's checks had been scanned through the system.

SRI launched a wide-ranging technology search for components, visiting companies in the United States and Europe to observe and assess willingness to develop products for the ERM. Meanwhile, SRI engineers had set to work on the logical design of the system. A major design choice was to develop electronic logic using tubes and wired programs, leaving open the possibility of transistorizing the final ERM.

Organizing for Automation

On December 23, 1950, just as SRI had begun work on phase one design of the ERM, Al Zipf, an operations manager in a Southern California branch, received from Bank of America president L. M. Giannini a letter marking the former's fifteen years of service. Zipf, a high school graduate, joined the bank as a night clerk and worked his way up to assistant branch supervisor, along the way securing four patents for inventions and improvements in banking machinery and systems. He responded with a detailed letter encouraging the president to automate bank activities. "If we are willing to take an active part in the engineering development of new machines," he wrote, "I am confident that it is possible and economically practical to accomplish the virtually automatic performance of such tasks as the sorting, listing, and commercial ledger posting of near-standard paper checks." He closed the letter with "my best wishes for Seven Million Dollars, less staff, and more machines."[6] Giannini gave the letter to Beise, who invited Zipf to San Francisco. Impressed by his energy and recommendations, Beise asked Zipf to join the innovation team on a confidential basis to explore alternatives to the SRI approach and instructed that he receive Frank Dana's copies of SRI reports and meeting minutes.

Encouraged by Beise and Dana to evaluate the applicability of current technology to banking, Zipf, on leave at UCLA to study electronic systems during the spring of 1952, began searching for equipment and ideas under the guidance of pioneering computer designer George W. Brown. Zipf visited computer-using manufacturers and firms to observe management and service problems and evaluated the banking potential of more than a dozen suppliers' systems. In a letter to Dana, he observed that there "were enormous opportunities in electronics" and suggested that the bank form a systems and equipment research group. In late 1952, over Morrin's protestations that the ERM could be expanded to support all the bank's data processing, Zipf persuaded Beise and Dana that it was important to begin a computer acquisition appraisal to gain experience with computers for improving bank operations beyond the automation of check handling.

Zipf returned to Bank of America in the summer of 1953 and in October was promoted to assistant vice president with responsibility for managing the newly created Systems and Equipment Research (S&ER) Department. He began with one secretary and a mandate to establish internal systems capability, evaluate suppliers, and pursue potential economic applications of general-purpose computers. Zipf, on the basis of an analysis of two general-purpose computers, the UNIVAC I and IBM 702, decided that IBM could deliver better support and reviewed the latter system's potential with Beise. A tentative order, authorized in October 1953, called for delivery of one IBM 702 to San Francisco in September 1955 and a second to Los Angeles in June 1956. It was contingent on Zipf's providing detailed analyses of costs and benefits with profit objectives by the fall of 1954. The implementation effort was to parallel the ERM project to gain experience in the management and operation of general purpose computers in non-check-processing operations.

Discussion of the Searching Phase

The management team had acquired perspective on the state of electronic technology and the means of applying the technology to banking. They knew it was critical to capture information electronically as soon as possible to take advantage of the speed and economics of electronic processing. In addition, for efficiencies, the more information printed in accessible electronic form, the better. Automating with IT was profitable for certain paper-based systems. Planning is most important prior to designing a system because it is essential to perform a careful analysis of exactly what is desired in the process so as not merely to automate existing procedures but to redesign to improve the entire process. Planning is time consuming and iterative with involvement of systems analyzers and knowledgeable bankers. There are no absolutes, but trade-offs must be made between costs and service requirements. The role of business leadership is to make those trade-offs. In addition, some seemingly obvious processing activities, such as on-line access to memory, are not possible at this point but may be in the future.

The team also gained a broader set of insights into the overall impact of electronic automation. To really gain significant cost reductions, old methods had to change dramatically, not incrementally. There existed no paper-processing standards, and each manufacturer had its own set of codes and designs for the proofing and bookkeeping procedures. The manufacturers intent on incremental inventions in their present systems to maintain and grow market share were unwilling to risk a leap to a totally new system. To obtain such a system, significant capital would have to be invested and the banks would have to change their procedures. The push for that change could come from a knowledgeable banker with persistence and capability. Since he knew it was just as difficult to learn banking as it was to learn systems, Beise decided to lead.

Building IT Competence: 1954–1956

Zipf was faced with three immediate challenges: deciding which tasks to automate, designing and developing programs to automate these tasks, and selecting and training a team. He immediately set about recruiting a group of knowledgeable systems analysts and programmers. An internal personnel announcement of an opportunity for training in computer programming drew thirty-four responses from experienced bank officers. After all were carefully screened, four senior managers were selected to attend, with Zipf, IBM's 702 programming school in Poughkeepsie, New York. There Zipf met and hired the bank's first data-processing "professional," Harry Kahramanian, a graduate of Grace Hopper's UNIVAC program. Hopper, a computer pioneer, had developed the first production-control system for a computer and the elements of a systematic approach to programming computers. When they completed the course, two teams were organized — one in Los Angeles and one in San Francisco — to analyze existing operations and determine where computer automation would be most profitable.

Zipf believed that the computer's greatest potential was for improved management reporting but recognized that the cost of large-scale computing could not be justified on that basis alone. With management reporting as the ultimate objective, he and his team of newly trained programmers searched for areas of bank operations characterized by high-volume, repetitive clerical activities.

In 1954, the American Bankers Association, concerned with the explosive growth of float owing to the cumbersome sorting process, appointed a committee on the mechanization of check handling; Harold A. Randall of the First National Bank of Boston was its chairman. In early 1955, Randall appointed a technical subcommittee of operating managers who were the leaders in using electronic process in their banks. At the time, eleven banks were actively pursuing the use of computers, ranging from the suburban County Trust bank in White Plains, New York, to the Mellon Bank of Pittsburgh.[7] Most were automating loan processing and two were testing punched-card checks.

The committee was chaired by John Kley, leader of the White Plains effort. He selected his committee from innovative IT managers at innovative banks.[8] Zipf, a member of this group, gained access to leading users of IT and the opportunity to be exposed to manufacturers' proposed solutions. The committee met regularly twenty-two times over a three-year period to define a standard that would allow automatic sorting of checks and proofing the sort. At these meetings they heard proposals for the standard from all the major manufacturers, including IBM, NCR, Burroughs, and Addressograph-Multigraph. In July 1956 the subcommittee recommended, with ABA committee approval, that the Bank of America's MICR be the standard for U.S. check processing. One year later it approved the present bottom right-hand corner location, which was consistent with the electronic recording machine (ERM) design. The Bank of America was assured that it was developing the standard check-processing system not only for its customers but for the entire U.S. banking system.

By November 1954 programs for real estate and installment-loan accounting were sufficiently defined to permit evaluation of the functionality and economics of the IBM 702. The program design provided a basis for detailed evaluation of the potential savings from converting existing manual operations to electronic processing. The comparison showed early losses owing to conversion, with a profit beginning in the second year and leveling off at $189,364 in the third year as a result of staff reductions. On Beames's death in the spring of 1953, Howard Leif became controller and assumed responsibility for the ERM project. Beise, Dana, and Leif reviewed the analysis with the management committee and in early December 1954 Zipf confirmed the order for delivery of the first IBM 702 to San Francisco. Each group then proceeded with full-time IBM 702 programming of the system it had analyzed — San Francisco for installment, and Los Angeles for real estate and loan programs. They began to automate operations.

Even without a computer, S&ER had grown to twenty-five people by June 1955. Its two development projects, the SRI ERM and the IBM 702, were at the forefront of computer technology with the first operational large-scale computer applications in banking. The ERM was to be announced and begin servicing the San Jose branch, and the 702 was to be delivered to San Francisco in the fall of 1955. Zipf, having learned during his trips to other companies of the anxieties that introducing a computer could generate, had encouraged the bank in the spring of 1955 to launch a training program to further develop bank employees' understanding of computer systems and mitigate their apprehensions by emphasizing the joint man-machine nature of data processing. The message promulgated to bank employees was that although the IBM 702 (nicknamed BEAST for *B*ankamerica *E*lectronic *A*ccounting *S*ervice *T*ool) was to take over dull work, it would require strong personnel support to function well.

Beise, Leif, and Zipf, growing restless as experimental costs continued to rise, declared the design of the ERM complete in the spring of 1955. They had shifted their goal from building an operational system to building an "as is" prototype for a September 1955 demonstration, with adjustments to be permitted afterward.[9]

Completing construction within the bank's time frame proved challenging; engineers were working in around-the-clock shifts as September neared. When existing paper-handling systems were deemed too unreliable to support proofing, the ERM became exclusively a bookkeeping machine. Checks were to continue to be proofed at branches and sent to the ERM centers. SRI's earlier hope of combining high-speed sorting and bookkeeping into a continuous process also proved unfeasible in the time allotted, relegating the SRI sorter to postprocessing sorting of checks to customers.

When, in the spring of 1955, Beise diverted his team's attention from construction to a grand public announcement, the bank's public relations office, deeming ERM too technical sounding and potentially intimidating to customers, introduced a name change. To the considerable dismay of the engineers, who requested the more scientific-sounding FINAC (for financial accounting), the Marketing Department rechristened the machine to the more appealing ERMA (Electronic Recording Machine Accounting).

Bank of America designated September 22, 1955, ERMA Day. To avoid leaks, the press was bused from San Francisco to SRI's Menlo Park headquarters, the site of the announcement. S. Clark Beise, by then Bank of America president, and Thomas Morrin conducted the presentation. Beise spoke of the great contribution the machine would make to Bank of America and the banking community in general; Morrin emphasized the magnitude of the engineering accomplishment and demonstrated the system. Neither named the firms that had collaborated on the project nor the costs incurred. Bank of America had invited an impressive list of journalists — including the financial editors of newspapers and wire services, California business syndicate writers, and writers from *The New York Times, Life, Fortune, Newsweek,* and *Business Week* — which paid off in a barrage of articles lauding its accomplishment.

The same month that ERMA was announced, the bank's first IBM 702 was installed in a new computer room in San Francisco. The installment loan system was brought up on the San Francisco computer within three weeks, followed in November by the Los Angeles–developed real estate loan program, to which 90,000 loans had been converted. An S&ER implementation audit of the installment and real estate loan operations compared estimated with actual costs to verify the savings and justify to the management committee purchase of a second 702 for Los Angeles. Increased machine costs were attributed to necessary system modifications and the high labor costs of variable run times. Scheduled five-hour jobs could be stretched to eight hours or more by system errors and to as much as twenty hours when unplanned maintenance was necessary at busy times, yet overall potential savings still produced a planned positive cash flow in the fourth year and a net profit from labor savings in the fifth. Although machine and labor costs were found to have exceeded expectations by $6,373, or 23 percent, Beise, on the basis of analyses that suggested that the loan system would eliminate 200 man-years of clerical activities, approved the second IBM 702 for delivery to Los Angeles in June 1957.

In 1956 Zipf appointed a number of bank managers who relied on the IBM 702 or were interested in automation to an advisory council charged with appraising bank procedures and suggesting automated-processing improvements. Potential plans were reviewed with this council, which also suggested new applications to Zipf. The annual progress summary for 1957 noted forty-three suggestions, a number of which were incorporated into 1957 activities or a 1958 plan. These included such improvements as five new services for Timeplan loans, automated automobile insurance renewal, and discontinuation of delinquent loan notices, for which the new system had eliminated the need by focusing on collection procedures.

Discussion of Building IT Competence Years

Senior and systems management developed a set of habits that gave the bank technological leadership in the use of computers in banking. The members initiated technology scanning of competitors and suppliers and perfected it with experience. They moved quickly to invest in research or early developments, often in parallel, to ensure that their approach stayed at the leading edge and better understand its strengths and weaknesses. They naturally brought these discussions into the management committee and assumed quarterly reviews and full-scale analyses of new technology standard procedures for running a bank. For 1955, this was a unique bank. In this process, they became competent at managing the complexities of computer systems to reduce costs and provide differentiated service.

The bank's senior management had begun to understand the need for changes and the significance of cost savings in automating paper processing with computers. The costs of processing loans had been reduced and accuracy improved by the 702 system, with a base for doubling volume at marginal increases in cost. For a fixed investment, working computer system costs were, up to a point, independent of changes in volume. However, the fixed-cost structures were complex. There were significant up-front costs for training and programming as well as for equipment. Further, the state of development of electronics and programming made precise estimates of functionality difficult. It was essential to set objectives, deadlines, and cost guidelines and trade off among the three. Eventually, however, the deadline had to be adhered to, and functionality was restricted to control cost. The managers learned that at the current state of the technology, computers were not necessarily cheaper than punched cards and were more rigid and costly to maintain.

The bank's management team and system staff gained an understanding of how to design and build computer systems. On the positive side, they learned what applications would reduce operating costs and how to design systems to improve reliability and accuracy. To obtain this benefit, they learned the nitty-gritty essentials of computer-based systems and the importance of redundancy and reliability. They developed a strong sense of the state of the art in electronics and the reasons the current technology was expensive and unreliable. They learned about emerging technologies, the problems these innovations might solve, and those areas which remained significant uncertainties. This perspective, rooted in a pragmatic systems approach of considering cost versus speed and capacity, evolved into an appreciation for the art of the possible, economically as well as technically. The SRI's learning-by-doing development of ERMA had alerted them to the importance of comprehensive planning for a computer center.

The ERMA experience provided the team perspective on all aspects of implementing a computer system and the necessary lead time required to meet deadlines. It was able to plan and construct a fully operational environment that allowed its 702 to roll in and start up quickly, while at least one bank took delivery on a computer before beginning to build the space. The 702 experience convinced the bank management that programming was time consuming and required considerable testing. In addition, it discovered the importance of exchanging information to learn of problems and solutions as it went along. It initiated and practiced a team approach to system development. It learned that programmers had to provide complete documentation and that running and maintaining systems required well-defined operational procedures. Beise and Dana learned the necessity of management analysis. Careful planning was essential to building cost-effective systems. Most important, the team learned the value of knowledgeable, well-trained people who can solve complex problems quickly.

The SRI experiments tempered the management's expectations about the reliability of electronic systems: they failed unexpectedly. The operation was highly dependent on quick, responsive actions by alert individuals. Repairing breakdowns took time and usually required restarting of the entire procedure. Because banks depend on overnight processing for knowledge of their cash positions at the start of the following day, it was essential to finish processing every night. The development of backup procedures and emergency actions was an early concern of the team. Finally, Beise and Zipf concluded that it was equally important to mold the computer systems to their needs, and that existing technology could not completely satisfy those needs. By the fall of 1955 the team consisted of relatively sophisticated computer managers.

At the time, several banks had automated loan processing and two large banks were experimenting with alternative check-processing systems. The Chase Manhattan Bank was working with the MIT Laboratory for Electronics to design and build a system — a computer referred to as Diana, the "Goddess of the Chase." The First National City Bank was collaborating with an International Telephone and Telegraph subsidiary in Antwerp, Belgium. Both projects relied on slave systems, with checks placed into transparent pockets for sorting and with human encoding at the input stage. The subsequent proof process was electronic. A few banks, including the County Trust of White Plains, were experimenting with books of punch-card checks. Following the announcement of ERMA, all shifted to planning for MICR-type processes.[10]

Finally, they had initiated management procedures for dealing with system issues within a small clique of managers. This group knew how to deal with the technology in terms of costs, risks, and rewards. The ERM experience had shown the value of carefully tracking the system-development process and phrasing questions in bank-processing terms. They appreciated the trade-offs between function, access speed, and cost, realizing that the use of computer technology was in constant, rapid change. The 702 implementation had demonstrated the learning required to achieve technical competence in developing and operating a system and gave them the confidence to expand. The traveler's check project confirmed the value of printed information and taking a system point of view.

Expanding IT Competence: 1956–1958

By the fall of 1956, data processing at Bank of America had grown from one IBM 702 in an air-conditioned room in San Francisco to two full-fledged data centers, one in San Francisco and one in Los Angeles, each with an IBM 702 and a thirty-person support staff, plus thirty temporary staff to handle data conversion. The bank's seasoned systems-development and programming staffs had established proven track records and were growing at the rate of 30 percent per year.

The close ties to senior management that resulted when Zipf was promoted to vice president reporting to Dana enabled S&ER to develop a broad research and development program within its charter to "function as an internal consulting group [with] authority to initiate studies and projects in instances where a preliminary evaluation of an application suggests it is justified."[11] For any project it undertook, Systems and Equipment Research had responsibility and authority for economic evaluation of the application, systems design, evaluation and selection of equipment, site preparations (if required), and installation, conversion, and daily operation until a stable routine was established — essentially complete control of the system-development life cycle.

S&ER maintained a list of potential applications that would provide significant payback, and Zipf sequenced these to reduce expensive infrastructure development. An example was the complete rewrite of tape files, which was embedded in a project to convert all credit applications. The high marginal returns covered the investment in infrastructure. Zipf met with Dana regularly to review progress, and both met with Beise to keep him informed. Quarterly, Zipf discussed a portfolio of projects with the operating committee of senior managers; annually, he submitted a proposed budget and longer-term program plan to the management committee for approval. He generally provided a two-year program of work, which always included two or three research projects such as remote input or modification of standard machines.

Manufacturing ERMA

Following the announcement of ERMA, Bank of America faced the task of selecting a qualified manufacturer to build thirty-six of the machines for use throughout California. A bank team outlined four criteria by which to judge prospective manufacturers: technological ability, financial stability, reputation and size, and cost of the proposed system.

The approximately thirty companies that visited Stanford Research Institute to observe the prototype and submit some form of proposal ranged from such predictable contenders as International Business Machines (IBM) and Remington Rand to companies as remote from electronics as General Mills and United Shoe Machinery. By late November the bank had arrived at a short list of four manufacturers, each of which was invited to make a presentation.

Three of the four finalists: IBM, Radio Corporation of America (RCA), and Texas Instruments (TI) were expected contenders. General Electric (GE), a newer entrant, had experience only in military computer systems. The companies' final proposals were submitted to the bank in February 1956. IBM, although a logical choice, was suspect relative to its intentions (a 1971 report suggested that IBM might have been planning to shelve the technology). RCA, although in the final list, also was not considered seriously, leaving TI and GE.

Texas Instruments' plan was to provide the requisite functionality through staged development of a transistorized computer. Payment to Bank of America for patents and rights ranged from $5 to $17 million over six to eight years, in addition to which it was anticipated that the bank would realize $135,000 in annual savings. TI strongly recommended that the automatic input system be developed with SRI.

General Electric, the dark horse in the competition, had no publicized digital computer experience and no organized unit-developing computer systems. GE's proposal encouraged advancing SRI's system and using transistor circuitry wherever possible. The proposal showed how new technology could increase reliability and speed while reducing processing costs, and a work program called for GE engineers to collaborate with SRI engineers on the initial design stage.

SRI engineers overwhelmingly favored Texas Instruments because of its demonstrated technological know-how and interest in extending a number of SRI innovations. The bankers, however, favored General Electric, whose $30 million proposal was considerably lower than any of the others and specified a million-dollar default to be paid to Bank of America if the machine was not produced. Because TI's more costly proposal specified a down payment, the bank was concerned by what it perceived to be the company's shaky financial circumstances. Ultimately, the bankers prevailed, and GE was awarded a $30 million contract to build the thirty-six ERMA computer systems. The contract called for a detailed design proposal by December 31, 1957.

PROPOSALS AND COUNTERPROPOSALS. Once GE recovered from its surprise at being awarded the prestigious contract, Bob Johnson was recruited from its Schenectady electronics laboratory to form and lead a development team. Owing to severe time constraints, Johnson and his team decided to design and develop the hardware logic, assembler language, and control program in three parallel efforts — incredible goals that were nevertheless realized. The team set three objectives: design a reliable computer that could perform necessary functions without strain, given existing capabilities; write assembler programs to perform the necessary banking functions; and develop peripheral hardware to create sorted input tapes. The bank was to design the latter jointly with NCR.

In parallel with the GE effort, Al Zipf and his team, under assistant vice president of systems Reg Carlson, had been making a detailed analysis of check processing in the Los Angeles area, the fastest-growing customer base. Believing that GE needed more systems guidance, in September 1956 the bank gave GE a counterproposal that detailed check-processing activities at the branches and added proofing to the system. The bank believed that paper handling was key to check-proofing operations; simultaneously proofing and sorting checks to their sources in account order and generating a dollar amount control tape would reduce paper processing to a minimum, as checks would have to be sorted to tape only once, after which all processing would be from magnetic tape.

Proofing, which had been in the original, was lost in the final SRI system design. S&ER's proposal restored it, causing a flurry of meetings among the bank, GE, NCR, and SRI. Although GE and NCR were concerned about the extra cost and complexity of adding proofing, all recognized the market value of doing it, and discussions focused on how best, not whether, to implement the function.

The interest and demonstrated flexibility of the vendors led Beise and his team to conclude that GE would probably fulfill its contract, and Zipf was asked to develop for the bank's board of directors a proposal identifying the costs and benefits of the proposed system (Table 3-1 compares expected cost for the GE ERMA with competing systems of the day).[12] Analysis was favorable due, in part, to recovery of cash from systems depreciation, expected growth in processing activities at relatively constant cost, and projected labor savings from the new system of 51.4 percent direct clerical labor hours, or $46,566 per month, for the Los Angeles branches. The proposal was subsequently approved.

PREPARING FOR ERMA. Planning for the implementation of ERMA began in late 1956 and continued throughout 1957. ERMA systems were to be installed every other month during the first year and every month during the second year. The first system was to be installed in San Jose by December 31, 1959, the thirty-sixth in San Diego County on February 28, 1961. Each would require a trained staff of seventeen and total training time of 221 man-months. With ABA specifications finalized in March 1958, following more than two years of discussion with manufacturers, the bank continued rollout of its standard MICR checks for nearly two million accounts. Over the following five years, Bank of America spent more than $3 million teaching other banks and printers how to print MICR checks and test the quality of printing for character definition and signal strength.

THE FINAL PUSH TO COMPLETION. In the fall of 1958 the GE–Bank of America team hunkered down to develop a working model of ERMA. All components were in the process of being debugged, with connection planned by year end. A working system for December 31 handling of 100 accounts proved that the system could process checks. Zipf accepted the ERMA system from GE as meeting the contract requirements on December 30, 1958. But a contract that spelled out no functions, only the processing of a specified number of checks at a set price, was open to varying interpretations. Zipf and Mel Gienapp, manager of the bank's data operations, recruited a team of thirty seasoned operations managers to be trained as ERMA programmers to serve as backup. Starting on the 702, they switched to the emerging ERMA language. An off-contract compromise on proofing needs, reached in late February, called for GE to expand the core of the main computer hardware to allow the bank to move quickly to automate proofing as the systems were deliv-

TABLE 3-1   Summary of Financial Elements in Proposals Submitted by Prospective Manufacturers of ERMA

	Texas Instruments				General Electric				RCA		
	Plan A		Plan B		Target Prices		Ceiling Prices		Alternative A		Film Prices Alt. B
	Unit Price	Total (36)	Unit Price	Total (36)	Unit Price	Total (36)	Unit Price	Total (36)	Target Prices	Ceiling Prices Alt. A	
Base Price	635,000	22,860,000	685,000	24,660,000	639,000	23,004,000	796,000	28,656,000	29,201,000		25,464,000
Cost of 60 Add'l Sorters	32,500	1,950,000	32,500	1,950,000	30,400	1,824,000	37,900	2,274,000	1,356,000		1,356,000
	667,500	24,810,000	717,500	26,610,000	669,400	24,828,000	833,900	30,930,000	30,557,000		26,820,000
Assume Excise Taxes @ 8%	53,400	1,984,800	57,400	2,128,800	53,552	1,986,240	66,172	2,474,400	2,444,560		2,145,600
Total Equip. Costs	720,900	26,794,800	774,900	28,738,800	722,952	26,814,240	900,612	33,404,400	33,001,560		28,965,600
Installation Costs	15,000	540,000	15,000	540,000	61,052	2,197,872	61,052	2,197,872	1,330,000		2,180,000
Gross Cost to Bank, Installed	735,900	27,334,800	789,900	29,278,800	784,004	29,012,112	961,664	35,602,272	34,331,560	RCA will not quote ceiling prices for Alt. A	31,145,600
Less Tax Savings on Depreciation @ 55.84%	(410,926)	(15,263,752)	(441,080)	(16,349,281)	(437,787)	(16,200,363)	(536,993)	(19,880,308)	(19,170,743)		(17,391,703)
Net Cost After Taxes on Depreciation	324,974	12,071,048	348,820	12,929,519	346,217	12,811,749	424,671	15,721,964	15,160,187		13,753,897
Less: Payments to B of A											
a) Minimum, Guar., after taxes	nil		(200 sales)	(1,779,000)	(50 sales)	(2,396,789)		(2,861,273)	(441,600)		(441,600)
Net Cost				11,150,519		10,414,960		12,860,691	14,719,217		13,312,297
b) Maximum, after taxes					(200 sales)	(8,000,000)	(50 sales)	(4,600,000)	(662,400)		(662,400)
Net Cost						4,811,749		11,121,964	14,498,417		13,091,497

		(1,779,000) (200 sales)	(5,600,000) (50 sales)	(4,600,000)	(662,400)	(662,400)
c) Estimated Probable, after taxes	nil					
Estimated Net Cost, after all taxes	12,071,048	11,150,519	7,211,749	11,121,964	14,498,417	13,091,497
Credit for cost savings on early deliveries	(1,322,766)	(1,322,766)				
Adjusted base for comparative purposes	10,748,282	9,827,753				

Notes on Financial Arrangements

Col. 1: All prices firm. Under Plan B, we receive $2.5 mill. flat, with 20% down and bal. in insts. @ 3% interest. All patents tfrd. under either Plan. Progress payments required, up to limit of $2.5 mill. outstanding (loss of interest = $100,000 + after taxes).

Col. 2: Using prime costs (excl. G & A and Profit) as a base, 100% of cost reductions from ceiling to target will be refunded to us; below target, we share 50-50. Patents tfrd. GE will expedite completion of Erma 1. No progress payments required.

Col. 5: Under Alt. A (Erma), if actual costs are *below* target, we share 50-50; if over, renegotiate. Firm prices will be set when order is half completed. Alt. B (Bizmak) prices are firm. Licensing fee of $1 mil. minimum and $1.5 mil. maximum to be paid us under either plan. *We retain patents.* Progress payments req'd: 75% of insured factory costs; no upper limits.

Maint. & Parts, per year, after taxes (est. subject to revision downward)

		(1,779,000) (200 sales)	(5,600,000) (50 sales)	(4,600,000)	(662,400)	(662,400)
	766,927	766,927	1,062,190	1,062,190	724,626	947,497
Space requirements	1000 sq. ft.	same	1,625 sq. ft.	same	2,600 sq. ft.	4,000 sq. ft.
Power requirements	25 KW	same	20–25 KW	same	47 KW	82 KW
Years to pay out through savings of $2,781,345 (after taxes) per year	5.39	5.00	3.36	5.06	6.45	5.83
Date of first delivery	Oct. 1957	same	Oct. 1958	same	Oct. 1958	Apr. 1958
Date of last delivery	Aug. 1960	same	Nov. 1960	same	Nov. 1960	Jan. 1960
Penalties for late deliveries	$10,000 per month per system on first six deliveries		$10,000 per month per system on first six deliveries, up to limit of $200,000		$10,000 per month per system up to limit of $200,000	

(Tax Rates: 55.84% normal, 28.84 Capital Gains)

Source: Bank of America, internal report, 1957. Reprinted with permission from Bank of America.

ered. Bank of America was to provide most of the programming support needed to code the applications.

Organizational Learning during Expansion

The maturing of the bank's organization is evident in its ability to develop two complex system expansions and at the same time continue a research program and provide new services. The need for detailed, long-range planning for a service-oriented computer system was well understood as a prerequisite to guiding implementation and conversion of computer-supported processing. The management committee recognized that human planning was at least as important as preparing for equipment and buildings.

The bank's experience demonstrated the importance of involving key senior management in reviewing future system developments. Senior management was a part of the ongoing process, which could become intense when important decisions were to be made. Planning never stopped. The state of current demand, future demand, and expected alternatives was reviewed at least quarterly. Tracking outside developments was a full-time activity. Senior managers continuously developed a portfolio of computer-based product services to meet and influence customer needs. This had evolved naturally from early reviews of customer needs and was refined with the rollout of the 702 and ERMA. Monthly, senior management monitored exception to plans on the status of equipment and applications of new developments, always considering cumulative savings and new adaptations of existing systems.

Equally important, management developed the complementary assets to nurture and support systems and gained perspective on the lead times required to develop support. Space, training, utility support, and backup procedures all had to be planned, maintained, and factored into the "cost" of the system. Management's acquisition of pragmatic competence led it to appreciate the necessary level of detail, the lead times, and the importance of people to the success of the system. Charles Conroy's early difficulties in securing suitable printing made the team conscious of how broadly a new system affects existing practices. Initially, printing seemed a minor detail, but it proved to be a major problem that had to be solved for the system to work. SRI and bank employees became printing experts and that knowledge became a competitive edge. The success of ERMA was due in no small part to the bank's effort in training independent check printers.

As technology managers they had fashioned an evolving technology strategy. They managed a broad spectrum of external sources while continuing an internal inventive activity that expanded process and product design efforts. They had also acquired an understanding of and skill in developing specialized IT with ERMA. They tracked their competitors, learned new ideas, and confirmed their policies with regard to the importance of investing in people. They formulated a program to expand the scope of applications with the 702 and began to gain experience in general as well as special-purpose systems. They had developed an efficient electronic banking factory and moved to operational dependence on IT.

Establishing the Banking Industry Dominant Design: 1958–1964

In late 1958, Systems and Equipment Research progressed from automating to include exception reporting, trend analysis, and notice of time-dependent actions, a move to informate as they automated. IBM 702 use was expanded to increase management support for loans and mutual funds and add such functions as bond investment, branch clearings reconcilement, accounts receivable, and corporate trust. The trust system was developed to provide timely information on due dates, coupon requirements, and other operational activities of portfolio management, including inventory management and accounting and analytical investment portfolio evaluation. An S&ER program initiated the same year to develop standards, due dates, and cutoff points for exception reporting on overdue loans helped managers identify out-of-control situations by tracking actual results rather than merely identifying exceptions for management analysis. Most loans were being tracked by 1959. S&ER clearly had progressed beyond the automation of existing procedures to utilizing programmed procedures on electronic data to improve customer service and deliver new services to the branches and credit offices.

Meanwhile, an S&ER team working with the bank's credit manager for retail businesses developed a design for a timely exception-reporting system that would build upon the new systems. By the end of 1959, the bank had extended exception reporting to all loans, balances, and payment procedures, and a number of analytic packages supported trust and loan officers in portfolio management. Management of large commercial accounts and automation of the general ledger were untouched. Commercial banking did not seem appropriate for inclusion, as it would yield no cost savings, and in any case, managers continuously reviewed their credit accounts to provide personal service to their clients.

In April 1959, twenty newly trained programmers and three seasoned IBM 702 programmer-managers began working with the GE team to test the production ERMA system. With an August completion date for bringing up the San Jose system and a parallel installation of a second ERMA system under way in Los Angeles, activity became intense. A bank team headed by Tom Russo, a systems manager, had developed a proofing system and set of procedures for implementing the bank's proposed operations, which were tested and implemented in San Jose in the fall. Against all odds, and in the face of Stanford Research Institute's initial skepticism and the stormy start of the Bank of America–GE relationship, GE produced ERMA on time and within budget, a matter of great pride to those working on the project.

ERMA was a far different machine from the computer SRI had constructed three years earlier. The state-of-the-art, programmed computer with automatic check sorting and magnetic character recognition input took advantage of progress in many areas, including transistorization and the latest data-processing techniques. The central processor's command structure and peripheral equipment were especially designed for Bank of America's accounting system.

A 1959 analysis of ERMA's economic impact showed savings increasing at a faster rate than cost, owing partly to a greater than expected volume of processing resulting from higher than projected numbers of customers and increases in check usage. Original estimates were for 1.98 million accounts; by the time the system was implemented, there were 2.3 million. More accurate check processing, coupled with the elimination of 2,332 bookkeepers, helped to reduce float and expand the customer capacity of branches and variety of services.

Opening ceremonies for ERMA, held in 1960 at three different locations connected by closed-circuit television, were hosted with great fanfare by Ronald Reagan of *General Electric's Masterpiece Theater*. With the installation of the last ERMA in June 1961, 13 ERMA centers, employing 32 computers, were servicing 2.3 million checking accounts at 238 branches. Conversion of the bank's 2,382,230 savings accounts was begun on January 11, 1962, and completed on February 23, 1962.

Exploiting an All-Electronic Base

Shifting data processing to an all-electronic base had opened a new set of opportunities. There was no longer a crisis to solve, only economy of scale and experience in providing systems to build upon. Over the next seven years Bank of America, under the leadership of Clark Beise and Al Zipf, expanded the domain of information technology to link to customers, support the introduction of new products and services, and improve management control. IT support became a means to market expansion, not just a way to achieve cost savings, and the availability of up-to-date information fostered more effective control throughout the bank.

Believing that with ERMA he could economically open more branches in smaller communities than had previously been possible, Beise aggressively pushed branch growth, acquiring and converting small banks to branches. Branches grew from 617 in 1957 to 871 in 1964, with a peak addition of 81 in 1961. Bank of America owned 40 percent of the branches in California, which accounted for a 44 percent market share (because its branches could serve more customers). At a board of directors review of ERMA on July 19, 1960, Zipf presented a detailed cost analysis of the 1958 proposal for savings for 1963 with a 1960 analysis based on two years of actual experience. Compared with the former manual system, the cost would have been $15,880,000 versus an expected total of $9,775,000 or a $6 million–plus saving, as shown in Table 3-2.[13]

Since the internal supply of available and interested bankers could not keep up with demand for systems personnel, a new approach was adopted — recruiting from engineering schools and training the beginners for a career in systems. The key ingredient was not the electronic boxes, but capable people who could use the boxes effectively. Zipf, Gienapp, and Herb Swenson of S&ER personnel carefully worked the bank's bureaucratic personnel system to make their job classifications of systems personnel equal to middle-level loan officers or branch managers so as to maintain externally competitive salaries. They developed career paths from operations to programming systems to analyst and eventually to manager. Although the bank's system development organization was growing rapidly, the operations organization provided faster promotions for professionals. Gienapp, the human resource leader of the group, creatively documented the functions of the new jobs in order to substantiate salary levels and job titles competitive with

TABLE 3-2 **Comparison of Net Operating Savings Year 1963[a]**
Proposal October 1958 vs. Proposal June 1960

	Proposed Oct. 1958	Current Estimate June 1960	Increase/ decrease	%
Proposed Operating Expenses				
Salaries (Staff Costs)	$2,748,817	$4,072,980	$1,324,163	48%
Rent (inc. Taxes & Upkeep)	158,880	197,232	38,352	24%
Janitor	139,944	208,392	68,448	49%
Telephone	95,040	73,200	−21,840	−23%
Power	259,200	252,600	−6,600	−3%
Stationery & Misc. Supplies				
Stationery	310,401	407,706	97,305	31%
Post Printer & Encoder Ribbons	104,760	93,895	−10,865	−10%
Hi-Speed Printer Ribbons	158,760	168,000	9,240	6%
Flexowriter Tape	2,758	(See Note)		
Magnetic Tape	90,720	86,000	−4,720	−5%
	$667,399	$755,601	$88,202	13%
Check Encoding				
Bank Printing Unit	646,668 (Encoding	523,750	−122,918	−19%
Outside Printers	813,528 Only)	1,027,161	213,633	26%
Maintenance				
Air Conditioning	50,160	50,160	0	0%
Post Printers & Encoders	121,480	153,433	31,953	26%
ERMA (not accelerated)	2,520,920 (1959)	2,460,831 (1959)[b]	−60,089	−2%
Total Proposed Operating Cost	$8,222,036	$9,775,340	$1,553,304	19%
Total Present Manual Cost	$12,715,800 (1963)	$15,880,038 (1963)	$3,164,238	25%
Net Operating Saving	$4,493,764	$6,104,698	$1,610,934	36%
Operating Savings After Taxes	$1,819,974	$2,443,943	$613,969	34%

Note: Flexowriter tape is used in the conversion phase only and should not have been included in operating costs in the 1958 estimates.
[a] 1963 was chosen because in the 1958 proposal this was the first full year of operation at capacity.
[b] Reduced by the agreement of January 15, 1960.
Source: Bank of America, internal report, 1965. Reprinted with permission from Bank of America.

outside employers. However, while individually rewarding the creation of a two-culture environment — fast-track techies and traditional bankers — who required much longer to be promoted — began to isolate systems personnel from other bank employees.

The Credit Card Saga

With S&ER overloaded during the ERMA and IBM 702 projects, Howard Leif, asked by Beise to identify other services that might benefit from the processing potential of the new computer systems, had contracted with Arthur Andersen for an analysis of alternatives.

Among other projects, Arthur Andersen had suggested introducing a credit card. Western Union had issued credit cards as early as 1914 but succumbed to expensive operating costs and credit losses. Since the computer could potentially reduce costs and provide tight credit control, Leif recommended that the bank introduce a credit card; a program was initiated in 1958 under the direction of the assistant controller. Development of system design was subcontracted to an outside supplier, which created a debossed card system (depressed versus raised character). The system was to be tested in Fresno in 1959 and, if successful, gradually rolled out to other branches. The plan was to move city by city, issuing credit cards to the bank's better customers, beginning with the valley cities of Sacramento and Redding and refining the system before taking on the large metropolises.

As Bank of America prepared to enter Sacamento, the First Western Bank of San Francisco announced its intention to issue a credit card statewide. With Beise overseas at the time, Leif and the management committee decided, on the basis of a trial, to preempt the competition by immediately rolling out Bank of America's card statewide, beginning in Los Angeles and San Francisco in early 1960. Expansion continued throughout 1960 and into 1961, but when delinquent account losses for the former year were found to exceed $10 million, Leif halted the expansion and changed management. On taking over the credit card program, Jack Dillon initiated a crash development effort with S&ER that was to employ an embossed card and incorporate a credit tracking system. He subsequently brought in Ken Larkin from corporate lending to manage the revised system, which was subsequently installed throughout the branches to replace the existing credit cards. Statewide reissue was completed in late 1961. A follow-up project revised the IBM 702 system to create invoices and account for payments. The new credit card became a solid product and source of strong earnings.

The market popularity of Bank of America's credit card attracted the attention of banks throughout the country. The bank exchanged its credit card system with Mellon Bank of Pittsburgh for a loan portfolio management system and, after Marine Midland of upstate New York bought the system and three other banks expressed strong interest in it, decided to franchise the product. Larkin actively marketed the credit card service nationally and internationally. But when federal banking authorities threatened to sue for illegal interstate banking, Bank of America decided to divest its out-of-state credit card operations. It subsequently sold its non-

California franchises to the founders of Visa and shifted its emphasis to overseas expansion.

Organizational Adaptation

The introduction of the IBM 702 and ERMA systems occasioned fundamental changes in Bank of America's operations. Traditionally, each branch manager had reported to the president as the personal representative of Mr. A. P. Giannini and his successors. Credit granting and various financing instruments were subject to strong functional control, which had grown with the bank. Central credit staffs in Los Angeles and San Francisco had line responsibility for large statewide and national accounts and functional control of branch credit products such as home and consumer loans and Timeplans. Each branch had a manager, an operations officer, a loan/credit officer, and depending on size, a range of positions focused on such customer areas as retail, small business, and home loans. Branch managers operated fairly independently, occasionally visiting the central office and being visited by specialists. They tended to focus on the banking needs of consumers and small retailers and worked to be identified with the community. Branch managers who routinely exceeded project objectives and expanded market share were given greater autonomy and rewarded with promotion to larger branches.

Clark Beise realized when he launched the automation project with S&ER that the organization would have to decentralize. His first step was to create four functional field staffs — in credit, personnel, operations, and business development — that would exert control over the branches from the center of each region. Field representatives of these staffs served groups of geographically adjacent branches.

The automation effort also shifted roles at the branches. The position most affected was that of Operations officer, traditionally the second in command, with the greatest number of direct reports and responsibility for maintaining fiscal integrity. With expansion of its services into operations and loan procedures, S&ER often met with branch operations officers to assist with developmental activities and training. As automation transformed the branches, Operations lost clerical duties and gained increasing responsibilities related to new systems, staffing requirements, training in standard procedures, and managing support for new products. The latter responsibility drew Operations officers into business development and marketing activities, and its strong link to S&ER made it an important presence in the branch.

The result was a shift from laissez-faire independent branch management of a constant product line with functional staff guidance to an ongoing marketing program orchestrated by S&ER through the introduction of new procedures and products. Gradually, through system-development studies and continual search for new applications, S&ER became the dominant influence in the branches.

As S&ER grew, Al Zipf assumed more control over field operations, first by managing the development and implementation of IBM 702 applications and later in deploying the ERMA program. He assumed formal control of operations in 1959 and extended his authority to personnel and bank operations in 1960. Branch managers then had two bosses — Zipf with his area managers and the president with his regional credit managers. The objective was to make every branch officer a business developer with a focus on customer service. Although it was officially a dramatic change, the bank had been moving in this direction since the introduction of the IBM 702.

A New Hardware Base

Customer and application growth created a capacity problem sooner than anticipated, but rapidly changing technology fortunately made it less expensive to upgrade than to continue with existing capacity. The bank's experience with the IBM 702 installation and observation of other banks' experiences suggested a two-year lead time for planning and installing new equipment. Russell Fenwick, an early programmer who became S&ER's system planner, annually forecasted capacity demand four years out, which was in excess of 15 percent per year. By 1958 applications growth resulted not only from the opening of new branches but also from accelerated growth of applications and management reports. Fenwick's projection showed that the bank could exceed the capacity of the IBM 702s by 1960 instead of the planned 1962–1963 date.

IBM had announced its 7000 family of computers in the summer of 1958. Its initial offering was the 7070, a fully transistorized, core memory machine that was less expensive, significantly more powerful and reliable, took up less floor space, and required less air conditioning than the IBM 702. Moreover, the 7070 was to be easily upgraded to take advantage of rapidly changing transistor technology. In the spring of 1959, S&ER ordered two 7070s for delivery in early

1961. Analysis of costs predicted substantial savings from the 7070s, and 7070 assembly language promised a significant improvement in programmer productivity over the constrained machine language and standard IBM programs of the 702. The management committee approved a proposal that documented the value of buying rather than leasing the systems, at a saving of more than $5 million before taxes, assuming a five-year life expectancy.

New accounting systems for the 7070s, completed in 1960, used an exception-based management reporting procedure for branches, credit cards, and trusts. The San Francisco–based systems group moved into a new building in February 1961; the two machines, installed and tested in March, were running production applications in fewer than ten days. Soon thereafter, most of the other programs were upgraded, and those remaining began to be converted from the 702, a complex task that required subtle system modifications to enable their taking full advantage of the 7070s. Conversion was complete by the end of 1961.

New Markets

The IBM 7070 provided excess computer capacity that Zipf and his team believed could be used to expand services to customers outside the bank to earn real income. S&ER subsequently formed a business service group under Hugh Dougherty, a founding member of S&ER, to provide computer-based services to retail stores and professionals. As Bank of America was already linked to the stores through its credit card, it had an established customer list. It began by offering payroll for stores, doctors, and other professionals. Pricing its services competitively enabled the team to gain market share quickly and break even, with a positive cash flow in the second year. The second step was to expand the product line to include professional billing and freight payments.

In late spring 1962, Zipf discussed with the management committee the need to expand computing capacity, noting that the IBM 7070s could process the existing workload until 1968, but that new applications in planning and development, including personal trust, accrual loans, and business services, would require greater capacity. Technological changes, he pointed out, would allow significantly lower per unit costs while adding capacity, with essentially no conversion expense, since the new 7074 was compatible with the 7070. In December 1962 Zipf recommended and the management committee approved conversion to IBM 7074s.

Expanding the Communications Function

Awareness of the importance of communications as an aspect of information processing had led Zipf and S&ER to assimilate the communications functions and actively begin to manage the cost and form of service. Spurred partially by the need to service a broadly distributed branch banking service, the move quickly led to consideration of how communications might be employed to improve service to customers.

By 1959 Bank of America boasted a complete internal communications service, with a new switchboard in Oakland and an expanded service switchboard in San Francisco. Two years later it had the equivalent of an 800 number dial-in service for customers in the San Francisco area. The bank continued to expand its direct-dial switchboards throughout the state and initiated a program to purchase standard telephone equipment for all branches at quantity discounts. A later study of the feasibility of using private point-to-point microwave links between locations in Fresno led Bank of America to file for a license to become one of the earliest private microwave operators. By 1963 the bank was operating its own telephone service throughout California.

Linking computers over telephone lines had reduced transportation costs and permitted information to be processed in a more timely fashion. The trend generally was to centralize processing and develop electronic means for collecting and distributing information. One important set of technological projects concerned communications between ERMA and the IBM 7070s; S&ER developed a magnetic tape conversion method for transferring information from one system to the other. Building on competence gained from working on the 7070-ERMA link, S&ER was able to select an input or remote processing system on a cost-effective basis and plug it into existing communication systems.

Discussion of the Dominant Design Era

The confidence gained in the expansion period fueled Beise's appetite for new IT products, and as his team expanded into the new technology, he and Zipf found a real leap in productivity owing to the new solid-state reliable system. The team realized enormous cost savings on the operation side, and new storage capacity led to the opening of an entirely new set of products. The team shifted to product expansion and new services in addition to automating and informating old systems. Their visions began to grow to services founded on their existing competencies and customer base. Their payroll and payable services were expanding with the rollout of ERMA. Bank of America was changing from an automate/informate focus to a market–new product service strategy. Its economic scale allowed it to make money at lower costs than small customers could realize independently, in proving its reliability. An entire new market based on existing relationships opened up. S&ER, strongly supported by Beise, expanded rapidly, and the cash flow supported this activity.

Beise, who wanted to grow faster to dominate the market, searched beyond his maestro for new ideas, partly because Zipf was wedded to automating, informating, and then expanding on that electronic base and partly because Zipf's team had a great deal to do. Beise wanted to move to new markets. When the credit card venture was proposed, S&ER was overloaded and Beise recruited an inexperienced team to evaluate and introduce a new IT product without involving the credit organization or S&ER. That team became a classic example of enthusiastic product champions who expect a system to be successful without their taking careful steps to prevent problems. They did not institute a trial, nor did they really want to understand what their market was telling them, namely, that the system was cumbersome to use and card impressions were not readable. They wanted success quickly. The resilience of the existing organization demonstrated the value of competence in systems and the ability of experienced line managers to quickly use the systems to bring the product under control.

The maturing of the organization is evident in its ability to move to an all-electronic base as a means to expand its customer base and product line. In addition, the managers continued to experiment and provide new services. They had clearly mastered the art of detailed long-range planning for a service-oriented computer system. In the entire rollout of ERMA, the most serious glitches were caused by weather-related construction delays. Giving as much attention to human planning as to system development and implementation building is an art several companies ignore today.

A second aspect of planning that is evident is the timing and involvement of key individuals. It was a process that became intense as important decisions had to be made. They never stopped planning. They reviewed the state of demand, future demand, and expected alternatives at least quarterly. Involved staff tracked outside developments and senior managers continuously reviewed the needs of their customers. They did it naturally, as they had started this process in the beginning and refined it with the installation of the 702 and ERMA to enable the 7070 decision as a normal banking investment.

They combined their technological scanning with constraint reviews of capacity and how bottlenecks might be alleviated with new technologies. When none existed and they saw a real need, they confidently invented a system. Their analysis of technology was always based on capacity and cost: How much per unit of service? was the criterion. At this point they were experienced users of transistor-based assembler-programmed computers. They were clever in organizing the input/output functions to increase throughput. In short, they had learned to adapt existing technology.

Zipf and S&ER had become aware of the importance of communications as an aspect of information processing. Among the first to assimilate the communications functions, they began actively to manage the cost and form of service. This was to some extent due to their real needs of servicing a broadly distributed branch banking service. It quickly led them to consider how they could provide better service to customers.

Strategically, the most important lessons were how to use the systems competitively. The following quotation from Zipf's letter recommending the new focused services documents his insights:

Bank of America's leadership in pioneering the development and application of electronic processing techniques to internal bank accounting activities today yields a competitive advantage from a standpoint of quality and accuracy in existing deposit account services. However, today's advantage is largely, if not entirely, a question of lead time over competition, for with the passage of time, our competition will achieve the same benefits from the plans they now have under way. It is therefore clear that if we are to maintain our position of leadership and the attendant competitive advantages, we must set out now to establish new variations in service that will enable us to preserve our present margin.[14]

Sustaining an Evolving IT Strategy

The group worked to stay ahead in systems in order to stay ahead in services, not as an end in itself. During this era it gained in competence and understanding of the intricacies of operating a growing complex system. On average, 2 million checks were processed and more than a million customer transactions were handled each day. In addition, it was expanding services and attempting to link new services to old to provide better customer service, making the processing more interrelated. At the end it had the lowest cost in the industry and broadest product line through information technology. The group was secure in the belief that its future lay with new technology.

The group had not made any significant shift in the commercial side of the bank other than in trust, owing partly to the personal nature of corporate banking and partly to the lack of scale economics in its customer-relation activities. It converted loan accounting but did not change the loan negotiating process or strive for innovations. Nor did it try to move overseas with its retail computer competence or work with any affiliate. The leadership and Zipf's competence was focused on California retail banking. This concentration influenced the evolution of computing at the bank.

Clark Beise felt that technology was a force which could be managed to meet market needs. The bank was managing an IT-based strategy through which to support market growth. Evaluating the technological risks as well as the market risks was customary. Beise and Frank Dana reviewed the progress of projects under way and approved new proposals quarterly. For large project proposals, full discussions were held with the management committee. The multiple-year plan, which documented cumulative savings to date, and market progress of new services or products were reviewed annually. Special emphasis was placed on these areas and on significant research projects, such as credit card or microwave communication. Beise presented the business case; Zipf handled the technology costs and risks.

With greater understanding of the potential of systems, S&ER's organizational structures changed to fit the bank's new needs. In the early days an operations group to run the computer and a programming team and analyze and create programs was sufficient. Later a standards and control group, which defined operations and programming standards, was created. Soon thereafter a maintenance group to work on released programs was created.

The 702 conversion had driven home the importance of standards not only for input data but for procedures in creating and maintaining programs, operating systems, and files. The value of moving to a standard system to gain overall economies of system development was demonstrated. As the system-development organization grew, working software development standards evolved. The group was subsequently split to accommodate different customers' needs, a change accompanied by a commitment to maintain well-trained individuals familiar with those requirements.

The S&ER managers combined technological scanning with a review of capacity and how bottlenecks might be alleviated with new technologies. Real needs, unmet by existing technology, were dealt with by inventing a system. The GE experience had taught them a valuable lesson as to the importance of defining the necessary functions of a system before searching for alternatives. Bank processing was considered to be in its elemental steps of input, memory access/ size, processing steps, future processing needs, and maintainability requirements. Technology was analyzed on the criteria of capacity and cost: How much per unit of service? As experienced users of transistor-based assembler language programmed computers, they devised clever solutions to organize the input/output functions to increase throughput. In short, the bank personnel had learned to adapt existing technology to their business needs. They were confident they could make things work, and they did.

Senior management grew more and more confident that its systems expertise was a real competitive advantage that would allow it to stay ahead. Continual reviews were held on system progress, alternatives, and new market opportunities for system use. Considering complex investments in research and development became routine. Management had learned to appraise and evaluate the risks of an R&D decision, for example, the Stanford Research Institute overrun and the occasional mishaps with General Electric and IBM. A tradition had evolved of annually reviewing the three-year technological plan that identified major applications and hardware system changes. Zipf was convinced that technology was an engine of growth. Beise felt that technology was a force which could be managed to meet market needs. They were managing an IT-based strategy to support market growth.

Management worked to stay ahead of the competition in systems, not merely as an end in itself but to stay ahead in banking services. Beise, as president, led the management team and was supported by Dana, his operations chief. Together with Zipf, they were the overall designers of IT systems, continually scanning for new technologies. A common tactic was to invent a new service system, then find someone to develop it for them, sharing the risks, as in the credit card. New product services and processes were designed as extensions to existing systems. System support was expanded throughout the value chain to retail store customers, other banks, and the Federal Reserve.

("Buck") Rodgers of IBM believed that the bank was at least two years ahead of all other banks and even further ahead of most financial service companies.[15] Maintaining the bank's lead required confidence in the system and a well-trained staff. A resilient support system had been developed during the implementation of ERMA. The bank managers comfortably assumed that computers were reliable and never failed to deliver on time. By 1962 an extraordinary competence had evolved to develop new products and operate mainframe computer systems in support of banking activities. The largest distributed private-sector system had been installed economically, and on time. The bank was on the top of the mountain, confident and aggressive in its intensions.

Losing Momentum: 1964–1968

In early 1964 S. Clark Beise became chairman of the board and Rudolf A. Peterson, a former bank employee who had been CEO of a Hawaiian bank and had experience in international banking, became president of Bank of America.[16] With California banking opportunities growing well and further expansion within the United States thwarted (A. P. Giannini's dream of U.S. expansion had been denied by the Congress and the Federal Reserve, and there was considerable pressure to divest Transamerica), Peterson's charge from the board was to expand overseas.

That summer Zipf sent Peterson a plan outlining personnel expansion as an introduction to systems planning. The summary, highlighting recent growth in demands on central office systems, which in 1964, with 114 fewer people, was handling 51 million items, an increase of 1 million since 1962, called for increasing administrative staff by 195, with 90 additional people in Business Services, 74 in Trust, and 31 in Systems and Equipment Research. The rationale was to build programming support for an intregrated branch accounting/management system and further expand Business Service's product line by introducing a professional billing service. In lieu of a strategic discussion with the CEO, Zipf received a note from Peterson, who was traveling abroad, to proceed. Peterson, focusing on overseas expansion, delegated all information technology responsibility to Zipf.

The spring 1964 planning review had convinced S&ER management that business service expansions and increased volume would soon exhaust the capacity of the IBM 7074s. IBM had just announced its 360 series to replace all its prior series, including the 1401, 1074, and 7094 computers, and Burroughs, Remington Rand, and General Electric had recently announced new computer models. Analysis of eight different systems convinced S&ER that the IBM 360, with its operating system COBOL support and massive disk storage capacity, was the only true third-generation system; an IBM 360 could replace a 7074 and increase capacity while reducing costs. S&ER subsequently ordered one and initiated a cost-benefit analysis.

Zipf and his team were eager to convert to a higher-level language such as COBOL. Heralded as the programming language of the future, COBOL held the promise of standardized, machine-independent programming, which would minimize the amount of recoding required in moves to subsequent generations of hardware. S&ER was maintaining more than 400,000 lines of assembly code running 2 million machine instructions and adding approximately 80,000 lines of code per year. S&ER personnel would have to convert all these programs, reformat hundreds of millions of tape records into disc format, and learn new operating techniques. The longer S&ER waited, the greater would be the cost to change, which made moving to COBOL a prime objective.

The first step was to bring up the IBM 7074 data-processing programs. Concurrently, planning could begin for conversion of the ERMA system, which would be more complex, its master account file having grown to twenty-two tape reels and become an operating nightmare for daily posting. Tape failures were causing occasional delays in providing the branches with necessary balance information before opening. Russell Fenwick and his colleagues believed that mass disc storage would eliminate existing cumbersome procedures and improve reliability. Although ERMA would have to continue to rely on card-to-tape data capture and tape-to-printer operation, a parallel tape operation was expected to speed the process. The biggest challenge would be running both systems during the transition.

On November 30, 1964, the management committee approved $3,643,100 for the acquisition of two IBM 360/50s to replace the IBM 7074/1401s. Existing 7074 programs would have to be converted from assembler to COBOL, and 7074 tapes to 360 tape formats. On the basis of its 702 and 7070 conversion experience, the bank decided to subcontract a large part of the effort to reduce the hiring hump and allow development to continue.

Consolidating the Hardware Base

In the spring of 1965, IBM announced the details of its operating system for the 360/65, which with greater disc capacity and more upward growth potential than other 360s promised "more bang for the buck." Four IBM 360/65s could replace all the ERMA processors and provide the same overnight service, as well as acccommodate the 7074 workload and planned expansions during daytime processing, thus supplying a consistent computer architecture and the potential for economy-of-scale operations.

Moreover, the 360/65s promised multitasking (i.e., simultaneous input, printing, and computing), which would reduce elapsed processing time, and supported random-access secondary disc storage, which was much faster than serial-access magnetic tape. Existing bank operations were tape and printing bound, and processing growth was pushing the twelve-hour turnaround window for delivering accurate, up-to-date balances to branches each morning. At more than a million transactions per day, the bank was at the upper limit of a tape-based system. The primary operating appeal of the 360/65 was that it would allow consolidation of all operations into two centers with remote inputs and concentrated operations. This would permit the bank to reduce operations personnel, concentrate support at two sites, and keep running up to a seven-day workweek.

To provide background for the IBM 360 decision, S&ER developed the "Impact of Automation," an economic analysis dated November 8, 1965, and discussed it at a management committee meeting called to review the progress of automation. The analysis, based on the number of employees the bank would have to hire to support its current business at standard manual times for processing tasks, concluded that the existing 2,862 system employees would have to be increased to 4,478. Adjusting for differences in higher system salaries, the annual savings for ERMA would be $4.6 million. Furthermore, actual head count in check processing was decreasing as volume was increasing. Bank of America's profitability continued to rise with expanded service and efficiency enhancements, and processing costs per transaction had fallen by more than 7 percent per year for the past four years. But the bank was approaching a limit to growth within the existing ERMA system. The new computer promised an opportunity to continue striding foward.

A careful cost analysis of alternative systems of comparable capacity, including utilization of the ERMA for its full operating life versus switching to the IBM 360/65, demonstrated operating expense savings of $12 million from converting ERMA and the 7074s to 360/65s. Growth and dramatic improvements in technology had led Zipf to make this request four years earlier than he had anticipated. The management committee, after some discussion, approved a $14.22 million proposal (considerably less than the $32 million it took to build the GE ERMAs) to replace ERMA with two IBM 360/65s and substitute two more 360/65s for the 360/50s.

Converting ERMA

Zipf and his team planned to begin converting ERMA and IBM 7074 programs to the 360/65s after scheduled delivery in June or July 1966. Check processing was to be done at night, most normal data processing during the day. Existing 7074 procedures were to be tested on the 360/50 over the winter and spring of 1966 and converted to the 360/65s on their arrival in the summer. Conversion was to be completed by December.

The ERMA conversion was to be a massive task. Fenwick estimated that approximately 500 man-years of programming, data conversion, and testing would be required to convert all bank systems to a COBOL-based disc system. Existing systems would not only have to be converted, but also relieved of accumulated patches made over the years and improved to take advantage of disk access. The S&ER staff was to be augmented with IBM system developers and a number of consultant programming groups. In fact, there were to be as many outside as inside staff reprogramming and building new systems during the transition period. The IBM 360/50s were to be installed on delivery and replaced by the 360/65s as soon as the latter became available.

EARLY DISILLUSIONMENTS. The first IBM 360/50 arrived in San Francisco in September 1965, the second in Los Angeles in October. By mid-November it had become apparent that IBM's operating system was not functioning effectively and was highly unstable except in running jobs one at a time. Gloom spread through the S&ER group, but programming continued, one job at a time being debugged with sample data. Conversion plans had to be revised considerably because of the instability of the IBM software. On the basis of conversations with senior IBM executives, S&ER members were convinced that they would be able to begin heavy-duty conversion efforts by summer, and a personnel plan was implemented for training and placement of ERMA workers to be transferred to other jobs later that year.

In January 1966, S&ER informed the management committee of a revised plan that deferred the start of the conversion until August 1966. They warned of the possibility of further delays, citing a faulty operating system and unstable tape and disc drives. S&ER estimated the cost of system failure and lost work at between $70,000 and $100,000. Capacity restrictions soon began to influence operations. Business Services, which had been growing at 15 to 20 percent per year, believing that it could not deliver, stopped soliciting new business and terminated several of the projects it had under way, such as loan flooring, which promised a 200 percent return on investment. Worse, contention surfaced in job scheduling for on-time delivery. Growing demand from both new market services and volume expansion among existing customers exacerbated the problem and delays persisted.

On December 9, 1966, S&ER informed the management committee that the conversion of IBM 360 programs was deferred once again as a result of IBM's continued delay in providing a multitasking operating system. IBM informed the bank that "no other large scale business user . . . approaches [the bank's] level of complexity of multiprogrammed systems."[17] The additional expense of delay, estimated at $364,000, was due to the cost of maintaining parallel systems and a loss of programming effectiveness stemming from operating system failures. Data-processing and ERMA programs were converted to a IBM 360 assembler, with some COBOL routines, using IBM service center 360s and the bank's 360/50s.

By late December 1966, the operating system seemed stable and it was decided to try to convert the mutual fund package, which relied on a massive tape file of the Los Angeles and a smaller file of the San Francisco customer bases. Conversion, scheduled to occur over the New Year's holiday, went as planned in San Francisco. But in Los Angeles, where the entire twenty-reel customer master file had to be updated to finish the conversion, the new high-speed tape systems proved inoperable. Fenwick was called away from a New Year's party at Zipf's home to try to expedite the conversion. After three hours, he called IBM's Buck Rodgers, the company's banking industry executive, who flew a team of IBM tape specialists and system engineers in from Denver to mount a massive changeover effort, which failed. But at least all then understood the scope of the problem: the size and sophistication of the application was pushing the IBM 360/65 to the limits of its capacity. IBM's hardware support was good, but its lack of strong software had hurt the effort.

END-OF-CONVERSION CRISES. Frustration at the lack of progress and delays in bringing up new systems generated a storm of criticism from members of the management committee in the spring of 1967. Zipf felt compelled to defend his decision to proceed with the IBM 360; on May 10, 1967, he dispatched a letter of explanation to Peterson in which he noted that

> 1966 was the first disappointing year since the group was created in 1954. Disappointing because the delays in converting to the 360 systems did not permit us to achieve the operating economies that had been forecast. Having acknowledged responsibility for what have proven to be unrealistic conversion schedules, I should not like to think my error in judgment will reflect unfavorably upon a competent, dedicated staff who worked ceaselessly in an attempt to achieve the impossible.[18]

On May 25, Zipf reviewed with the management committee a plan that had been prepared in late March, but delayed because of improvements in systems stability and the addition of more core memory. The plan, developed by Fenwick, suggested that S&ER was finally seeing light at the end of the tunnel. The department had regrouped, summarized its progress, and generated a more positive plan with demonstrable results. Morale, which had been terrible, had picked up and the group's "can do" spirit returned.

Although only 35,000 of 400,000 BankAmericard and 504,000 of 2 million Timeplan accounts had been converted by March, the group gained momentum during a stable and productive April; by May it had completed the conversion of BankAmericard, Timeplan, and one of the largest ERMA products. The group had developed new fail-soft procedures and through strenuous efforts with IBM had stabilized the tape subsystems. An additional ray of hope came from the successful start of the demand deposits conversion, the bank's largest ERMA application. With the transformation secure in the spring, Zipf, in a presentation to the management committee, emphasized that not only had other banks followed its leadership to similar systems, but the others' shifts vividly demonstrated the Bank of America economy of scale, as shown in Table 3-3.[19]

However, the delay had entailed serious costs. A staff analysis

TABLE 3-3 **Deposit and Loan Volume**
Bank of America and Principal Competitors System Comparison

No. of Accounts	Bank of America	Wells Fargo	UCB	Crocker Citizens	Security Pacific
Checking	2,695,000	600,000	350,000	650,000	1,300,000
Savings	3,033,000	650,000	450,000[a]	600,000	673,000
Installment Loans	1,130,000	125,000	300,000	500,000	250,000
Real Estate Loans	263,000	75,000	13,000	25,000[a]	40,000
Total	7,121,000	1,450,000	1,113,000	1,775,000	2,263,000
Equipment	(4) 360-65s	(2) 360-65s	(1) 360-65s	(2) 360-65s	(2) 360-65s
Del'd or on order	(2) 360-30s	(8) 360-30s	(5) 360-30s	(2) 360-50s (2) 360-40s (6) 360-30s	

Source: Memorandum from A. R. Zipf to R. A. Peterson, Samual B. Stewart, F. M. Dana; subject: Computer Systems — Third Generation, Burroughs vs. IBM, May 5, 1967. Reprinted with permission from Bank of America.
[a] Approximations.

suggested that conversion delays for some of the services, such as the flooring program, had had a direct economic impact on profits of $1,471,000 and that delays in developing new products for Bank-Americard and providing more automated support for mutual funds and trust had significant negative impacts on earnings. Total impact was estimated to be in the millions of dollars, offset, according to the report, by IBM's contributions, which increased paying all equipment costs, providing professional help valued at $2,700,160, and maintaining an account balance of more than $14 million.[20]

The inescapable conclusion was that the massive conversion effort had failed because of software problems. The report reviewed all the decisions, including the new plan and the cost of the bank of programming and outside help. By May the total direct reprogramming effort was estimated at 167 man-years at a cost of $1.65 million, of which at least 37.4 man-years, valued at $363,834, had been lost — a costly effort.

Discussion of Stagnant Period

The IBM 360 conversion debacle could not have happened at a worse time. Senior management had just shifted from an operations orientation with long experience in systems to a credit orientation with no systems experience or interest. Promotion of key architect

Al Zipf to a wider venue had diluted his influence and diminished reliance on his expertise. Dialogue among senior members of the group about systems development ceased and nothing formal replaced that interchange. System managers, overwhelmed with the conversion, could devote little time or energy to promoting general understanding of what was happening, and the technicians, because the system they had chosen was not working, were constrained in their explanation.

The systems group, which over time had become isolated from the rest of the bank, was nurturing managers from within. It had enjoyed a history of rapid growth and quick promotions; managers in systems were promoted in about half the time and garnered higher salaries than managers in operations, causing resentment in some quarters (for example, Russell Fenwick at thirty-one became Bank of America's youngest vice president ever). Tension between the two cultures continued to grow.

Unfortunately, what the new senior managers believed they had learned was that trying new technology is risky and unnecessary, that the only safe move is to use "tried and true" technology. Moreover, they came to believe that computer suppliers, IBM in particular, were not to be trusted. Senior management reached these conclusions as observers, not as active participants in the events or from hands-on reviews of system development efforts. With no one but Zipf competent or interested, IT development was no longer a senior management topic. IT had become a tough sell, and Zipf, who also had a retail banking agenda, had to select his topics carefully. Ultimately the lessons of the IBM 360 conversion were absorbed only by the technical, not the senior, managers. They moved from a strategic use of IT as their engine of growth to a support IT strategy.

The systems group soon learned the terror of unreliable systems and disgruntled customers. As long as the group was pushing the limits of the technology, any change in the system could and did result in system crashes. Because S&ER took the blame, regardless of the source of the crash, the group became conservative and tested very carefully. Group members became, by some accounts, highly cautious noninnovators.

Lacking senior management support and unable to deliver new services, the systems group quickly lost any remaining support among its active practitioners, who began to use the chain of command to secure priorities rather than work within the system planning process or take leadership from S&ER. The long-term effect of the two-culture environment and conversion debacle was to turn S&ER's once docile customers into aggressive, shortsighted cost savers.

Finally, four years of seven-day workweeks and eighteen-hour days had exacted a toll on the health and morale of the group. The IBM representatives noted that when the conversion was finally complete, the exhausted group received no compliments from users, who had waited impatiently to get on with their work and viewed the job as long overdue. In the wake of the strenuous effort, the systems group faced the development backlog with little enthusiasm. It had learned both the frustration and sadness of failure.

A more fundamental impact on the bank's IT orientation resulted from the lack of shared vision or understanding between Rudolf Peterson and his maestro. Peterson viewed Zipf, whom he trusted implicitly in the dual role of line officer and maestro, as automating retail banking while expanding market share and adding new products. The CEO neither believed it to be his role, nor was he inclined to explore new avenues for IT. Peterson's interest, encouraged by the bank's board, was in expanding commercial banking overseas, a pursuit for which he saw no relevance for IT.

In hindsight, it would have been wiser to experiment with the 360/50 in connection with the delivery of the less time-dependent customer-oriented services. But with the opportunities so great and the risks seemingly so modest, Zipf had boldly struck out. Falling back and regrouping was not considered. No other senior executive had any interest or competence in IT, and IBM's marketing branch was unaware of how far behind schedule development of the multitasking operating system had fallen. Quite simply, both the vendor and the customer had underestimated the complexity of the project.

The Cost-Minimization Era: 1968–1978

Events returned somewhat to normal during 1968. The IBM 360 conversion, despite an enormous backlog of work, was under control, but urgent priorities arising from failures of outmoded systems interrupted other activities. Changeover of the general ledger had to be aborted to deal with a number of operating systems crises, and continued conversion demands delayed almost all requests for support and new products.

Although the S&ER leadership believed that the conversion, because it had resulted in the development of a modern, stable platform as a basis for growth, had been worth the effort, senior management was skeptical. A. W. ("Tom") Clausen, who replaced Peterson as CEO in late 1969, continued to emphasize credit and overseas expansion. Zipf, the only management committee member with operations or computer experience, was promoted to executive vice president in charge of the California bank in the spring of 1970. He was charged with reorganizing retail from a functional to an area structure, and given responsibility for marketing, credit, operations, personnel, and profit of the retail bank. Fenwick became the operational leader of S&ER, reporting to Samuel Stewart, a lawyer in charge of administrative functions. With a backlog of system work, Fenwick and the S&ER team focused inward.

The S&ER management process had changed from an annual three-year planning discussion and follow-up annual budgeting session with quarterly program review with the management committee to an annual budgeting session oriented toward short-term payoffs. Despite a severe backlog and more work than staff, expansion of S&ER was not considered. The new senior management, preoccupied with expanding overseas and managing California retail operations for cash flow, did not perceive any overseas opportunities for IT, and the recent conversion experience had shaken its confidence in technology.

S&ER continued to grow apace with overall volume expansion but lost its leadership role. The early 1970s were devoted to catching up with systems work and improving existing services. S&ER's experience was in large mainframe systems and batch processing; its technicians had little experience with and no means to test on-line processing with database technology. Such an implementation would have required a complete rewrite of existing systems, a task for which they had no enthusiasm. S&ER had slipped behind a full generation of computer software, and its systems effort was not in strategic mode. The group had come to be viewed and managed as a production factory, driven by low cost and timely processing, not product or service innovation. Its broad presence in California and efficient service continued to sustain a growth in retail banking into the 1970s.

Expanding Abroad

By the 1970s Bank of America had eighty-eight overseas branches in eleven countries. With the credit market abroad growing faster than that in the United States, management focused on expanding such markets to gain economy of scale. Overseas system development began in 1968 with a London accounts receivable project that was quickly extended to provide a comprehensive analysis of overall accounting needs.

Development of a new loan-reporting-and-accounting system was led by S&ER's Bruce Foster, an experienced systems developer. The design selected after an extended proposal process called for a central site with distributed minicomputers in the branches. In August consideration was given to means of improving vendor maintenance response to machine failures, which had become common. At the same time, more horsepower was applied to printing, disk storage was expanded, and commitments were made to rapid response. Still the systems failed, so in spring 1975, Alvin Rice, senior vice president of the International Division, demanded a "high noon" review of international support. This resulted in the transfer of international computer support from the central group to Rice's organizations. With international development fragmented in Europe, Asia, and South America, Bank of America's systems groups lacked the coherent image that Citibank and other competitors had fostered. However, electronic banking had not become a force, and Bank of America's markets were growing rapidly owing to the bank's presence and breadth of product line.

Management Succession

In the early 1970s the four systems groups (S&ER, Centralized Operations, Business Services, and Management Science) had reported to Stewart and coordinated with one another, maintaining close ties to Zipf. When Stewart retired in 1973, Zipf assumed responsibility for the computer groups, but being deeply involved in managing the California bank, delegated day-to-day activities to Fenwick. Gradually the systems organizations drifted apart, Business Services creating its own development group. As it became completely independent and forsook technology sharing, Business Services' income growth began to erode and costs increased.

When illness caused Zipf suddenly to retire in 1975, Tom Clausen selected Stan Langsdorf, a former comptroller, to be responsible for all administrative systems, including S&ER. Langsdorf, a relatively passive manager, allowed the three remaining systems groups to continue to coordinate domestic development. In 1975, after receiving permission from the comptroller of the currency, S&ER experimented with ATMs. Fenwick proposed, but the head of branch operations vetoed as too expensive, risky, and counter to the bank's tradition of personal service, a statewide introduction of ATMs.

Bank of America was growing faster overseas than in California, where it had begun to lose market share. Its share further declined as Security Pacific and Wells Fargo rolled out ATMs and other competitors aggressively introduced new loan products. By 1978 Bank of America was being outstripped by all its major competitors and losing market share per branch. This loss was due to a variety of factors, growth of competitors, increased price and product competition, and lag in systems development significant among them. The bank's decentralized, branch-oriented full line of banking emphasized loans as the prime source of income; in IT services the bank lagged considerably behind those of the competition. Senior management in retail banking had a strong bottom-line profit orientation with no in-depth understanding of the economics of systems development. Twenty-six executives had to agree to the acquisition of a significant computer system for the California division; consequently, there had been no major improvements in several years.

Organizational Learning during the Declining Years

The seventies marked a continued shift in Bank of America's strategy from focusing on California to focusing on the international scene and on loans rather than on retail banking. This change was pushed by capable credit managers with no experience or interest in computer technology; stylistically they were delegators rather than hands-on managers. They inherited a split voice for systems: Stewart's pleas for caution and cost control and Zipf's thrust to stay technologically strong.

The ability of Zipf to lead actively was encumbered by his responsibilities in managing the largest retail banking operation in the world in a time of increasing competition and continued population growth. Although he maintained close contact with S&ER, adhering to his retail banking agenda was a severe challenge, and he could spare only modest energies to focus on systems. Further, Stewart's formal authority limited Zipf's influence.

Systems continued to grow to keep pace with the overall volume expansion but lost its new processes leadership role. The early seventies were devoted to catching up on systems and improving existing services. S&ER's experience was in large mainframe systems;

developments in distributed systems were producing innovations in which the group had little practical knowledge. Although it had developed a large, mainframe-based branch support system on the latest IBM equipment, it began to gain experience relatively late in 1972. The system effort was not in a strategic mode — at best it was considered a production factory and managed as one. S&ER was driven by maintaining low cost and timely processing, not innovating products or services. Because it delayed its decision on space, as well as concern for not being first in a computer technology, the bank was a late converter to the IBM 370. This limited its opportunities to move to on-line query and remote processing. Part of the problem was the massive rewrite of existing software that would have been necessary and S&ER's reluctance to undertake that task.

By the end of the era management had lost all its managerial and system competence to effectively guide the development of competitive information systems. The conversion to the 370 absorbed S&ER. Only system managers were concerned with innovative systems. There was a complex set of reviews: any proposal that required investment and new technology generated tension. Hugh Dougherty retired when the environment ceased being fun. Fenwick left, not merely because he did not get the promotion, but also because of the continued hassles the job entailed. They were the last of the old-guard managers, although most of the programming efforts were still run by experienced system managers. In five years the bulk of the innovative talent in the organization in both the systems and management groups had dissipated. Joe Carrera, an effective comptroller, was experienced in solving operational problems but had no familiarity with computers. Having observed the 360 debacle, he wanted to distance himself from the problem.

The fundamental cause of this dramatic loss of technological leadership was lack of concern in maintaining an edge. The new management did not have an understanding and perspective of managing technology. It was composed of credit-oriented bankers when systems had not yet become a powerful force. Leadership must be nurtured to be sustained.

The Long Climb Back: Building Competence

Clausen, who began to recognize the problem in 1978, appointed John Mickel senior vice president in charge of systems.[21] Mickel, the former CEO of Decimus, one of Bank of America's most profitable subsidiaries, had a strong product-line marketing focus. He was charged with staunching the loss of market share by reviving the competitiveness of the bank's computer systems with newer technology in the branches. With Clausen's sponsorship, Mickel recommended two critical projects that seemed essential to providing a basis for electronic banking: statewide rollout of ATMs and shifting the demand-deposit accounting system for checking to an on-line database system, which would provide easy access to data and support more rapid development of new products and services.[22] Both projects received full funding for a two-year implementation. Mickel recruited teams of experienced systems managers and outside consultants and hired Peter Hill from IBM to provide guidance in developing a distributed system. Twenty-six ATMs tested by the Santa Clara branch were subsequently deployed statewide. In 1981, eighteen months into both projects, Clausen went to the World Bank and Samuel H. Armacost became CEO. Worldwide banking was in a credit crisis and U.S. banking was in the process of deregulation. Bank of America's loan and credit portfolios were mismatched and its decentralized organization was ill prepared to meet demands for rapid response.[23]

Armacost embarked on a reevaluation of Bank of America's systems strategy, recruiting Max Hopper from American Airlines to restore momentum in retail banking — Mickel had left to start a telecommunications business — and forming a senior retail banking advisory committee.[24] Discussions between Armacost and Hopper about how to make the bank a competitive systems user became a daily ritual, and a vision for the future emerged. Hopper recruited Bruce Fadem of IBM Systems to run Retail Banking and Joe Ervin to head Operations and Technology. This team, with Hill, analyzed the bank's need to develop an overall architecture, which was discussed with an expanded advisory committee.

With the help of Hill, Fadem, and Ervin, Hopper initiated the development of a high-capacity, bankwide communications system and centralized policy to create an overall bank view. Recognizing that enormous investments would be required to bring the bank's structure up to competitive standards, he initiated two major system-development projects — BankAmerica Systems Engineering (BASE) and BankAmerica Payments Systems (BAPs) — to provide the essential architecture for the future. As a member of the management committee, Hopper was involved in discussions of why these systems were essential to establish bankwide standards and support the eventual integration of information and payments.

Armacost had recruited Tom Cooper, an early ATM proponent, an experienced computer user, and a cost-oriented banker from Mellon Bank, to the International Division for the worldwide rollout of BAPS. They developed a program to integrate overseas and expand the product line with BAPS. When Bank of America subsequently experienced a series of earnings pressures that made expansion unpopular and cost cutting important, Cooper pressed to reduce system costs and slow the transition, while Hopper believed it was essential to continue. When Armacost sided with Cooper, Hopper returned to American Airlines and was replaced by Lou Mertes of SeaFirst of Seattle, a Bank of America subsidiary.

Armacost and Cooper charged Mertes with controlling systems costs, establishing a business-oriented planning process, and developing a bottom-up planning and budgeting process that would provide an economically sound basis on which the management committee might evaluate systems investments. Mertes emphasized a detailed, analytical economic planning discipline as the core of systems planning and worked to streamline and reduce the size of the systems organization. When he left a year later after a series of system problems, Hill and Fadem became acting managers of information technology.

Clausen, returning to Bank of America in 1986, assumed personal responsibility for restoring the bank's leadership position in IT. His search for a strong IT manager produced Mike Simmons of Fidelity, who subsequently launched an aggressive integration of electronic banking in Credit and Retail worldwide. Dick Griffith, hired by Clausen from the Federal Reserve to manage Wholesale Banking, brought with him Bill Ott, the architect of the Federal Reserve system. With this new team, which possessed more than a hundred years of systems development experience, and the competent technical managers Mickel and Hopper had hired, the systems function regained its intellectual base.

Simmons, charged with demystifying the technology and encouraging users to support expansion, worked with Clausen to better understand users' requirements. Finishing the implementation of BASE and BAPS, they were early marketers of a personal computer-based treasurer's system. Simmons artfully described the impact of IT programs in customer terms and organized a user committee of senior managers that met regularly to review a portfolio of proposed projects and establish priorities.[25] He also rejuvenated Hopper's experiments in future technologies and created a lab to test, among other products, a new smart card. Most important, his team produced reliable, money-making services and products on time and within budget.

Hopper's communications network capitalized on economies of scale by consolidating all systems at the four existing sites into one overseas system in London (for Asia and Europe), all national accounts in San Francisco, and South American accounts in Los Angeles. This network, coupled with a coherent hardware design consolidated around a few vendors and software systems with consistent operating systems, lent Bank of America a modern bank architecture. At Clausen's retirement in 1992, Richard Rosenberg was named CEO. When Simmons subsequently moved on to First Boston to continue rebuilding, Rosenberg hired as his new maestro Marty Stein of Paine Webber, who was later promoted to vice chairman.

Diversion cost it twenty-two years, but Bank of America has regained its leadership position and is building momentum. The next dominant design for information processing in banking, if it is not originated by Bank of America, will quickly be appropriated by the bank.

Discussion of Decline and Regaining Momentum

The gradual demise of Bank of America prowess in IT was masked by its incredible economy of scale and competence in retail banking. The California bank was a classic cash cow as it allowed its technological competence to decline. Had it rolled out ATMs, the bank might have moved into other new technologies. Technological brass rings appear but quickly pass the hesitators. Senior IT line leadership is essential to sustain appraisal of the art of the possible. These investments require an understanding of both the potential and the risks of emerging information-processing innovations. Had the bank been experimenting with minicomputers along with its competitors, management might have understood the future trend in IT architecture and the need for ATMs. Management has to appreciate the market impact of emerging IT innovations within an evolving IT strategy. Few unique innovations cause a strategic shift, but the fast pace of change in the underlying chip continually causes potential services to appear. To judge the innovation effectively requires a shared vision of how the organization could function as well as how to merge new technologies and move the organization. The bank leadership lost the planning process and thereby sowed the seeds of its eventual loss of leadership.

The ensuing saga demonstrates the momentum an IT strategy creates and the ability to obtain short-run profits at the expense of long-term gains. As Richard Vietor has pointed out, IT was a contributing factor to the mismatch of the bank's loan- and interest-generating portfolios. Whether that was a direct result of not continuing improvements in management control is not clear. However, lack of an integrated overseas system hindered the bank in understanding its overall international portfolio and allowed individual managers to pursue different policies. Domestically, the bank not only fell behind but extended an outmoded technology, creating a more costly renovation project.

The Bank of America had lost its apparent technical competence and ability to frame technological investments in business terms acceptable to the line managers. Whether the loss was real or apparent is irrelevant because the IT group could not arrange a productive hearing of the issues and opportunities. A dialogue is essential to maintain the ability to perceive the impact of new technologies on the market and to believe in the economics of the investment. In large part, innovating with IT is a matter of faith created by experience. A key issue is to perceive how an innovation will affect the organization as well as the market. At their peak, Beise and team could review an idea and instantly perceive the impact on their markets and costs, for example, of the credit card. The technological glitch arose from lack of experience in developing and implementing the system and failing to involve S&ER.

The long climb back to competence documents the deep, implicit nature of an IT strategy. Management's attentive curiosity to the art of the possible and willingness to experiment depends upon IT leadership. Information processing typically impacts not only procedures and services but also the management process and organizational structure. The line managers during the decline of IT at the bank realized that they had to rely on IT and wanted to sustain it within their purview. They gradually created a strong control system to maintain the status quo — a typical response, as IT causes change that can threaten roles, the experience base of individuals, and power bases. Creating a vision that includes how the organization could function and the growth potential is a salient facet of IT strategic planning.

The long road back required not only rebuilding technology but also perspective on the competitive value of IT. Clausen saw the need and moved but did not weave the effort into the bank's processes. Armacost, who recruited and empowered Hopper, again, had not embedded IT as a vital element of strategy. When Clausen returned, he realized the full court-press effort required to regain momentum and effectively built upon former efforts to forge an IT-based strategy. The saga documents the ease of slipping and the expense of regaining momentum.

Notes

1. Detail references can be found in A. Weaver Fisher and J. L. McKenney, "The Development of the ERMA Banking System: Lessons from History," *IEEE Annals of the History of Computing*, 15, no. 1 (1993): 44–57.

2. SRI memo, G. B. Gibson to J. Noe, December 6, 1954.

3. A proof machine totaled and sorted by bank, branch, or general category batched checks submitted by tellers. The machine operator checked individual totals against adding machine tapes supplied by the tellers and the total of all sorted checks against the total of all the tapes. Batched checks transferred between sort stations were accompanied by printed tallies of individual amounts and totals until the final sort to customer account. Automating proofing inferred that the operator would enter check amounts and the system would read encoded customer identification information, eliminating subsequent manual activities.

4. Frederic C. Lane, *Andrea Barbarigo, Merchant of Venice, 1418–1449*, Johns Hopkins University Studies in Historical and Political Sciences, Series 62, no. 1 (Baltimore: Johns Hopkins Press, 1944).

5. "A History of the Electronic Recording Machine (ERM)," SRI, Menlo Park, Calif., June 1, 1955.

6. Letter from A. R. Zipf to L. M. Giannini, December 27, 1950.

7. The others were Bank of America, Portland National Bank (Oregon), First Wachovia (Winston-Salem), Fletcher National (Indianapolis), Salt Lake National, First National Bank of Chicago, First of Dallas, Republic National (Texas), Chase Manhattan, and First National City Bank of New York.

8. Other members of the technical subcommittee included Herbert A. Corey of the First National Bank of Boston, which was a leader in the use of proofing machines and had an excellent cost system; C. M. "Mac" Weaver of the First National Bank of Chicago, which used bar-code traveler's checks; and Loren Erickson of the First National City Bank of New York, which was implementing a slave check-processing system. Later, Raymond C. Kolb at Mellon Bank, who had installed one of the first computers in banking, joined the committee; David Hinkel, also of Mellon, replaced Weaver. Edward Shipley, the auditor at the Wachovia Bank and an enthusiastic computer user, joined the committee in the second year.

9. The ERM was designed to automate the bookkeeping details of 50,000 checking accounts. The computer and drum memory were used to determine whether checks exceeded account balances (the memory stored only account numbers and current balances), with proofing and sorting performed on supporting systems. Account numbers, names, addresses, checks by amount and date, and current balances were retained on magnetic tape, from which was printed monthly a record of all account activity, including calculated service charges for each account. The computer, which comprised 8,200 vacuum tubes, 34,000 diodes, 5 input consoles with electronic reading devices, 2 magnetic memory drums, a check sorter, high-speed printer, power control panel, power plant and maintenance board, 24 racks holding 1,500 electrical and 500 relay packages, 12 magnetic tape drives, each able to handle 2,400 foot tape reels, a refrigeration system, and more than one million feet of wire, weighed a hefty 25 tons and occupied 400 square feet.

10. J. L. McKenney, "Developing a Common Machine Language for Banking: The ABA Technical Subcommittee Story," HBS Working Paper 92-061, 1992.

11. Memo from F. Dana to A. R. Zipf, October 27, 1957.

12. Cost justification to GE ERMA, board presentation, November 14, 1956.

13. Summary of board of directors' presentation, July 19, 1960.

14. Letter to S. C. Beise, December 10, 1962.

15. T. P. "Buck" Rodgers, interview with author, March 12, 1992.

16. See J. L. McKenney, and A. Weaver Fisher, "The Growth of Electronic Banking at Bank of America," IEEE *Annals of the History of Computing* 15, no. 3 (1993): 87–93, for reference details.

17. Rodgers, interview.

18. A. R. Zipf, letter to R. A. Peterson, May 10, 1967.

19. A. R. Zipf memorandum to R. A. Peterson, Samuel B. Stewart, and F. M. Dana, May 5, 1967; subject: Computer Systems–Third Generation Burroughs vs. IBM.

20. During the conversion IBM had invested 66 field engineer man-years and 10 tape specialist man-years to make the subsystem operable. At one point an IBM 360 production team had been flown in from Poughkeepsie to "make the system work." After the conversion, IBM accepted the GE equipment as a trade-in, allowing credit for the remaining book value of the ERMAs. A first for IBM, the allowance was kept confidential to avoid starting a trend.

21. McKenney interviews with Clausen, May 17, 1990, October 22, 1992.

22. McKenney interview with Mickel, October 22, 1992.

23. R. L. Vietor and J. M. Lynch, "Bank of America Corp. (A), Case No. 9-390-176" (Boston: Harvard Business School, 1990).

24. McKenney interview with Hopper, October 5, 1992.

25. McKenney interview with Simmons, September 18, 1992.

Chapter 4

Rattling SABRES: American Airlines and the Reservations System Revolution

A large cross-hatched board dominates one wall, its spaces filled with cryptic notes. At rows of desks sit busy men and women who continually glance from thick reference books to the wall display while continuously talking on the telephone and filling out cards. One man sitting in the back of the room is using field glasses to examine a change that has just been made high on the display board. Clerks and messengers carrying cards and sheets of paper hurry from files to automatic machines. The chatter of teletype and sound of card sorting equipment fills the air. As the departure date for a flight nears, inventory control reconciles the seat inventory with the card file of passenger name records. Unconfirmed passengers are contacted before a final passenger list is sent to the departure gate at the airport. Immediately prior to take-off, no-shows are removed from the inventory file and a message is sent to downline stations canceling their space.[1]

Growing passenger volumes and expanding flight schedules had made these activities of American Airlines' Chicago reservations office circa 1954 the norm for large airline reservations centers. Space to seat sales agents with a clear view of congested reservations boards was limited by the twenty-two-by-twenty-two-foot distance between supporting columns in most buildings, hence the gentleman with field glasses. A typical personnel tally for such a center would be sixty reservations clerks and forty follow-up clerks and board maintainers recruited and trained by the managers responsible for maintaining the pace of operations.

Since the 1930s, American Airlines had based its reservations system on decentralized control of seat inventories maintained at a flight's departure point. This request-and-reply system required agents to communicate with inventory control — two messages — before confirming passengers' reservations — a third message. Passenger-specific data (name, telephone number, and itinerary) were recorded at the time of confirmation on a passenger name record card and subsequently transmitted via telephone or teletype to inventory control.

In 1939 American's Boston reservations office determined that until a flight was 80 percent sold out, agents could sell space freely and report only the sales, allowing passenger requests to be accommodated quickly and halving message volumes. Inventory control monitored sales, and when available seats decreased to a prescribed level, broadcast a stop-sale message to all agents. This "sell and report" system required maintenance of a cushion of seats to allow for the effect of sales reports in transit at the time a stop-sale message was issued, the size of the cushion determined by the length of the pipeline. On receipt of a stop-sale message, agents reverted to the request-and-reply system.

These largely manual systems were time-consuming, requiring from several hours to several days to complete a reservation. Moreover, they were cumbersome and unreliable, plagued by lost names, reservations made but not confirmed with travelers, and inaccuracies in the passenger lists held at boarding gates, with the result that most business travelers returning home on a Friday would have their secretaries book at least two return flights.

Widespread awareness of the value of flying and the larger, faster aircraft that followed in the wake of World War II had substantially boosted both airlines' passenger carrying capacity and demand for that capacity. The air trip from New York to Los Angeles, which had taken three days in 1931 and twenty-one hours in 1934, took only eleven hours by the mid-1950s and seven by the late 1960s. Over this same period, the number of passengers per flight had increased from a handful to more than a hundred. In light of these circumstances, the ability to process passenger reservations assumed increased importance. Given the highly perishable nature of the airlines' product, reservation personnel needed to have rapid access to seat availability, be able to register customer purchases instantly, and in the event of a cancellation quickly recognize that a valuable item of stock had been returned to inventory and was available for resale.

The Searching Years: 1943–1951

Charles E. Ammann had joined American Airlines, an amalgam of carriers flying an assortment of planes, during World War II and begun to analyze its sell-and-report system and, more broadly, the airline's reservations problem. A systems analyst with an affinity for electronics and communications, Ammann decomposed the reservations process into three steps: determining the availability date of space, adjusting the inventory, and recording passenger names. Recognizing the limitations of candidate technologies and the perishability of the basic product, Ammann concluded that seat availability and inventory control should be tackled first. Solving the passenger name problem would benefit from the experience gained developing a rudimentary availability system. To be successful, Ammann decided that such a system would have to meet at least the following criteria:

- Make American's product immediately available to agents without inducing eyestrain or fatigue.
- Record sales and cancellations as they occur and maintain an accurate running inventory.
- Reduce the airline's dependence on large, auditorium-type spaces for reservations offices and employ existing communications facilities to make available to ticket, satellite, and other offices all the information available in the reservations office.
- Retain a record of the last operation until it is manually cleared or another transaction is entered.
- Automatically advise other stations as necessary when a flight is sold out.
- Accomplish the foregoing accurately and economically and be capable of being expanded.[2]

To Cyrus Rowlett ("C.R.") Smith, who had learned of the potential for using electromechanical technologies to control aircraft capacities while deputy commander of the Military Air Transport Command during World War II, Ammann's priorities made sense.

President of American Airlines since 1934, Smith envisioned substantial growth for the airline on returning to its helm after his war
service; he is said to have remarked when American was flying
eighty-five planes, the largest U.S. fleet at the time, "Any employee
who can't see the day when we will have a thousand planes had
better look for a job somewhere else." Though his projections were
exaggerated, by the 1950s Smith was preparing American for the
jet age, his competitive strategy to buy a bigger, faster plane and
buy it first. "We're going to make the best impression on the traveling public, and we're going to make a pile of extra dough just from
being first," he observed.[3]

A hands-on manager who prided himself on knowing every employee, Smith spent most of every week visiting stations on the
airline and staying in touch with managers via phone or memo. His
functional, airport-based organization of American situated the bulk
of personnel in operations. Large meetings were rare, as Smith preferred to meet with key managers on specific issues, typically with
Marion Sadler, his customer service and sales manager, on marketing and organization issues and with Bill Hogan, financial officer
for fiscal control and overall planning, on cost issues. Sadler, who
became Smith's heir apparent, focused on operating the airline
while Hogan nurtured capital and equipment acquisitions.

Encouraged by Smith to find a supplier that might produce an
electronic system to perform airline reservations functions, Ammann quickly discovered that inventory control problems had received little attention in the veritable frenzy to satisfy accounting-
oriented needs. The system requirements were poles apart; whereas
accounting applications revolved around one person's need to access many hundreds of records, American needed to ensure access
to a specific item in inventory by hundreds of geographically distributed people. Exhibit 4-1 lists the key events in the development of
the American Airlines design.

The Reservisor Project

Manufacturers seemed disinterested in developing new machines
to meet American's requirements. Resigned to solving his own
problem, Ammann approached the design of a new system with
an open mind. He retrospectively listed American's advantages as:
"Knowing the problem, not knowing how it could not be solved,
and a limited group of one person working on it."[4] Ammann
mocked up an electrical system that could track and maintain inven-

EXHIBIT 4-1 **Development of the American Airlines Dominant Design**

Year(s)	Event	Significance
1930s	Request-and-reply system	Policy for maintaining invento- ries at point of departure in re- quest-and-reply system; two messages/reservation
1939	Sell-and-report system	Installed availability boards and policy of "sell and report system" when 75 percent full; one message/reservation until stop cushion reached
1943–46	Smith supports Ammann's development of passenger- name-record system	The first electromechanical system; demonstrates po- tential
1946–52	Ammann explores use of IT with a drum memory	Demonstrates the value of on- line storage
1952	Magnetronic Reservisor	Drum memory for inventory control
1953	C. R. Smith meets B. Smith	American's reservations prob- lem becomes focus for IBM's SABER project
1954–57	Creation of joint AA-IBM proj- ect to develop objectives	Compromise needs to fit tech- nology to seat availability
1958	System objectives defined	Realization that traditional ap- proaches were inadequate and that a fully mechanized system offered scale econo- mies
1959	American accepts IBM pro- posal	C. R. Smith bets $30 million on a teleprocessing system
1964	SABRE fully implemented	PNR system becomes domi- nant design for internal reser- vations processing
1968	First PARS systems imple- mented	Easy adoption of PNR capabi- lity
1970	American selects Eastern- based PARS as foundation for updated SABRE	American's technical slide re- versed
1972	PARS-based systems the in- dustry standard	Enhanced dominant design for reservations processing

EXHIBIT 4-1 **Continued**

Year(s)	Event	Significance
1972–74	New management team at American	American regains focus and innovative will
1974–75	JICRS study	American gains intimate knowledge of travel agent requirements
1976	Marketing automation established; travel agents seen as key constituency and driver of functional specifications	Commitment to transform SABRE from passenger services system to sales distribution system
1978	Deregulation	SABRE's role as a sale distribution system supplies market intelligence at a time of extreme industry uncertainty
1982	Regulatory scrutiny	Power of American's dominant design for the deregulated environment attracts charges of unfair competition

tories of seats by flights in visual columns. Smith, on seeing the project demonstrated in 1944, approved funds for further development. A working model was shown to the Teleregister Company of Stamford, Connecticut, which agreed to construct a pilot system.

Installed in American's Boston reservations office in February 1946, the Reservisor system marked the first time an airline had adapted electronic discoveries to reservations handling. A one-year trial found Boston serving an additional two hundred passengers daily with twenty fewer people. Although they recognized that other changes had contributed to the productivity improvements, Smith, Sadler, and Ammann concluded that this type of electronic equipment was economical and enhanced revenue.

Discussion of Progress in Searching Phase

C. R. Smith believed in the competitive advantages of being first. C. E. Ammann learned that being first in automated reservations processing was going to require that American invent its own solution to its problems. Neither man was dissuaded by the complexity of the processing challenge or the ineptness of existing technology. Performance improvements in the Boston reservations office inspired American's senior management to adopt a long-term perspective in acquiring automated reservations capabilities. Smith saw that Ammann could deliver a working system and that the design was sound. However, the design was known to be incomplete, addressing only seat availability, one of the three steps in the reservations process. For operating precision, inventory control was required. Executives like Marion Sadler believed that quantum advances in customer service would come only when the third step, electronic recording of passenger names, was incorporated in the system. In essence, the Boston Reservisor whetted management's appetite for further exploration of the potential of electronics.

Building IT Competence: 1951–1954

Despite its virtues, which stemmed from its merits as an availability system, the Reservisor suffered considerable delays in adjusting inventories. It took time to move the passenger name record card from the sales agent to the inventory agent, who then posted the sale; the agent was responsible for recognizing when the cushion was reached and inserting the plug in the master control board to establish the stop-sale condition. The logical next step was to address the inventory control problem, which was as much economic as technical. The challenge was storage costs. The publicity received by Howard Aiken at Harvard University made magnetic drum memories look promising. Still, American's requirement for absolute accuracy and reliable twenty-two-hour-a-day operation required innovations like duplexed hardware, which obviously doubled the amount of memory. Ammann's solution, a magnetic drum–based Reservisor, built by Teleregister and installed at La Guardia Airport in 1952, reduced both cost per reservation and personnel and further improved service, much to the satisfaction of Smith, who tracked its progress through installation.

The outgrowth of this line of inquiry was the Magnetronic Reservisor, again designed with the help of Teleregister and installed at La Guardia in 1952. Ammann was learning the importance of considering the reservations agent in his system designs. Therefore, considerable ingenuity went into the design of the agent sets. An important sales advantage of the system was to allow an agent to recommend an alternative flight should a passenger's original choice be fully booked. This increased the requirements for rapid interaction between the agent and the system. After trials with special keys, buttons, dials, rolls of paper, and loops of 35-millimeter film, Ammann thought of the "destination plate." Small metal plates, later cards, for each flight were inserted into agent sets to query the system quickly. Notched edges on the plates triggered a series of snap switches in the agent set, returning seat availability for a particular flight as well as alternate flights if the passenger's first choice was sold out. In the event of a booking or cancellation, the agent could adjust the inventory on the drum memory by pulling a lever on the agent set.

In 1956, a larger and faster Magnetronic Reservisor was installed in American's reservations office in the New York West Side Terminal. Where the 1952 system could hold inventories for 1,000 flights for a period of ten days, the 1956 version accommodated 2,000 flights for a period of thirty-one days. Average response time fell from one second to one-half second. In addition to availability and inventory information, the enhanced system also included flight schedules and was equipped with counters to record the number of availability requests, sales, and cancellations for each circuit and for the system as a whole.

In keeping with Ammann's appreciation of the human component of his systems, the 30,000-square-foot reservations office was redesigned to take advantage of the power of the new system. A total 362 seating positions were wired to accommodate reservations calls from the general public, with a subset of 40 dedicated to travel agents and large business accounts. Another 140 positions were for service functions to the airline, acting as a hub for American's private telephone network connecting reservations offices in fifty cities. Forty supervisors occupied the remaining positions, monitoring the load of incoming calls, which averaged 45,000 per day.

While working on the Magnetronic Reservisor, Ammann did not forget that he was targeting only a partial solution to American's reservations processing problem. So, beginning in 1954, Ammann began to consider the third step in the reservations process: passenger information. Automating the availability and inventory steps highlighted the inadequacies of paper-based handling of the passenger name record (PNR). Working with IBM, he developed the Reserwriter and tested it in Buffalo in 1956. The machine read cards keypunched with passenger data and determined whether messages had to be sent to downline stations and whether those stations were with American or another carrier. It then prepared a paper tape with the appropriate routing codes and automatically transmitted the messages through American's teletype system. This marked the first time a reservations agent in one city could directly sell or cancel space based on flight information stored in another city. By late 1958, Reserwriters had been installed in key sites throughout American, greatly increasing the speed and accuracy of distributed reservations processing.

Successive improvements notwithstanding, American's early reservations systems suffered from problems of inadequate processing speed and data inconsistency. Approximately 8 percent of all transactions were in error, an unacceptable proportion for an airline that prided itself on its customer service. Moreover, because the early automation projects affected only a subset of the total reservations process, completing a round-trip reservation between New York and Buffalo still required the efforts of twelve people, involved at least fifteen procedural steps, and consumed as much as three hours. Growing numbers of flights and passengers per plane adversely affected productivity, with the number of passengers boarded annually per reservations employee declining from 5,100 in 1950 to 3,100 in 1958.

Further, during reconciliation of seat availability inventory with the manual file of PNR cards, an imbalance between the two files was common. If the number of confirmed seats exceeded the number of PNR cards, American's policy was to reduce the confirmed seat count, making those seats available for sale. This created the possibility of finding missing PNR cards and thus unintentionally overselling the flight and aggravating customers. If the number of PNR cards exceeded the number of confirmed seats, American adjusted the seat count upward, but then ran the risk of rejecting customer requests for seats, underselling the flight and needlessly driving customers to competing carriers. Processing errors, such as failing to log passenger cancellations, which delayed "reopening" a flight, also contributed to underselling. When passenger inquiries necessitated reference to the master inventory files, significant delays were common, resulting from lost records, manual file searches, and the unavailability of file agents during times of peak volume.

Discussion of Building IT Competence

American learned three important lessons during this period. First, stored electronic information exponentially increased the speed of reservations processing. Second, the working definition of a "system" had to include the people who worked with it and the layout of the facilities where they worked. Finally, and perhaps most significant for what was to happen next, Smith and Ammann knew about the confines of a partial solution to the reservations processing problem. As long as passenger information remained disjoint from seat inventories, progress would be limited. As passenger volumes grew, these deficiencies became increasingly acute. Fortunately, Smith was convinced of the benefits of persistence in searching for solutions that stretched the bounds of conventional technology.

The SABRE Project — Expanding the Scope of IT: 1955–1959

American had begun planning for jet service in 1952. The additional seating capacity of the thirty Boeing 707s it had ordered in 1955 for delivery in 1959 heightened the importance of control over seat inventories; the 707s accommodated 112 passengers, the airline's DC-7s had 80, and the jets reduced travel time over transcontinental routes from ten hours to five or six, depending on direction. The jets' travel time exceeded the pace at which the airline's existing reservations systems could transmit messages about them, rendering pointless manual inventory adjustments to passenger lists for last minute additions or no-shows.

Smith was already acutely aware of the shortcomings of the Magnetronic Reservisor system when, on an American flight from Los Angeles to New York in 1953, he engaged in a casual conversation with Blair Smith, an IBM sales executive. This chance in-flight meeting culminated in an invitation for Blair Smith to visit American's La Guardia operations, where the prototype Magnetronic Reservisor was operating, in the fall. IBM sales executives had been cognizant of American's relationship with the Teleregister Company since the original Reservisor was installed in Boston in 1946, and Blair Smith, following his tour, alerted IBM president Thomas Watson, Jr., to the opportunity for significant collaboration with American. Watson, concerned about IBM's slow entry into the market for electronic computers, was then highly receptive to new initiatives. IBM had several important technologies under development, notably interactive remote terminals, teleprocessing, and disk files, and a project, code-named SABER (for Semi-Automatic Business Environment Research), to find business applications for them. Perry Crawford, a member of the Product Planning group, identified the airline reservations problem as an ideal focus for the SABER project, and his team developed a proposal for American.

APPORTIONING RESPONSIBILITY. James Birkenstock, director of product planning and market analysis, with Watson's approval presented IBM's proposal to C. R. Smith and returned with a memorandum of understanding for a joint development program. At this early stage, the effort involved only three people, IBM's Crawford and Pete Luhn and American's Ammann, head of the airline's new Advanced Process Research Department. By 1956, the three had framed a sufficiently clear definition of the problem — an automated, integrated marriage of passenger name to seat reservation — to merit a major research project.

The proposal IBM submitted to American on September 18, 1957,[4] described an "electronic data processing system for airline customer service functions" that would integrate reservations, ticketing, passenger check-in, boarding, air cargo, and management reporting under a centralized teleprocessing design philosophy. At American, responsibility was given to Marion Sadler, vice president–Customer Service. C. R. Smith saw control of seat inventories as foremost a customer service issue and the fledgling SABER system as a marketing initiative. In keeping with this view, Sadler took day-to-day responsibility for the project away from Ammann and assigned it to Roger Burkhardt, director of training for customer service. Sadler was impatient with Ammann's tinkering ways and believed the project was more likely to reach fruition under Burkhardt. On his appointment as director of Reservations Special Projects in July 1958, Burkhardt had a mandate to determine whether the project, which by then was five years old, was worth pursuing further. Burkhardt refined the system's functional requirements and worked with IBM to identify prevailing deficiencies in computer processors, peripherals, communications facilities, terminals, and approaches to system design and development that might impede its implementation.

JUSTIFYING THE SYSTEM. The joint development project convinced Smith, Sadler, and Burkhardt that no substantial improvements in the efficiency of reservations processing could be expected from incremental improvements to existing methods. More important, economies of scale could for the first time be expected in reservations processing, provided that a fully automated system was implemented. This was in stark contrast to projections that costs for the

FIGURE 4-1 **Annual Projected Operating Costs Magnetronic Reservisor vs. SABRE**

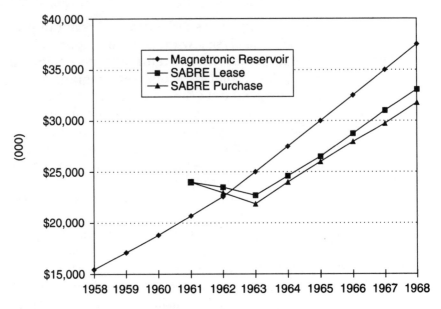

Source: D. G. Copeland, "Information Technology for First Mover Advantage: The U.S. Airline Experience" (DBA diss., Harvard Business School, 1990).

Magnetronic Reservisor would rise at a rate equal to or greater than the rate of growth in passenger volumes. (See Figure 4-1.)

In March 1959, IBM presented to C. R. Smith a second proposal to build a system that could

- accurately control seats for all American flights;
- enable all locations to sell and cancel seats instantly;
- automatically and continuously ensure that seats sold balanced with names stored;
- store immediately and until no longer needed, and make available instantly to all sales locations, all passenger information (e.g., names, contacts, continuing seats, time limits, and so forth);
- automatically request space from other airlines;
- automatically process outstanding requests, time limits, and so forth;
- automatically accommodate schedule changes and make available records of affected passengers;
- store and make available to all sales locations fares for most

commonly used routings (this function was ultimately deferred because of its excessive storage requirements).

Accompanying the proposal was a document describing the findings of Burkhardt's Reservations Special Projects group. Smith's concerns were more pragmatic than visionary; he believed that the solution to American's reservations problem lay in the use of electronic equipment but worried about hardware reliability, given the passenger service implications should it fail. He was also bothered by costs, suspecting that IBM's equipment lease rates were intended to pressure American into purchases. "We do not have the money for that," he stated flatly.[5]

Smith passed the proposal and findings to Hogan, who assigned Fred Plugge, director of Corporate Financial Analysis and Budgets, to perform a business investment evaluation. Plugge concluded that American's return on investment would be between 5 and 16 percent, depending on assumptions about passenger volumes, wage rates and technical configurations. He deemed the proposal to have merit, but because neither he nor anyone in his department had experience with investments in computers, advised that American seek a second opinion. Hogan, distrustful of engineers because of his experience negotiating the design and purchase of aircraft technology, and suspicious of technology in general and IBM in particular, engaged Arthur D. Little, Inc. (ADL), to work jointly with Burkhardt's and Plugge's departments and Harvard and MIT professors to devise ways to improve the project's return on investment.

Plugge's report reveals remarkable insight into the impact of automation. In assessing deficiencies in the statement of objectives for the proposed system, Plugge observed that

> the installation of a major automatic system should almost always provide for far more than direct transfer to machine of the manual operations of a single department. The automatic system will normally have capabilities both for eliminating some processes necessary in the manual system and for efficiently conducting work outside the original cognizance of the single department. Furthermore, the machine system will normally provide means for doing things that previously could not be undertaken. While it is quite proper — and often necessary — to approach automation with a step-by-step process, the full potential benefits, including those outside the original scope of single department objectives, should be considered in reaching any conclusion to go ahead.[6]

ADL's July 1959 report concluded that neither IBM's nor Burkhardt's proposals possessed the necessary balance between service standards and cost, and as a result, the project was "not a good business risk in its present form." The report suggested that reducing the cost of the agent sets — which accounted for nearly 70 percent of total equipment costs — would enable American to achieve a 25 percent rate of return for the project. The report also alerted the airline to the challenges it would face if it decided to proceed.

Cliff Taylor, the member of Burkhardt's team responsible for the financial aspects of the system, by paring proposed functionality and reducing implementation time was able to strike a balance between Sadler's customer service requirements and Hogan's financial hurdles. But in the end it was the value of accurate reservations data and the promised displacement of 1,100 clerical personnel that provided the basis for justification. The system was scheduled for a phased installation beginning in 1961. Installation costs were estimated at $2.1 million, and capital expenditures for hardware between 1961 and 1968 were to be $37 million.

American's board of directors approved a revised proposal from IBM on October 29, 1959. The reworking of estimates and performance covenants accepted by IBM notwithstanding, the airline's decision took courage. Smith was accustomed to assuming risk in the purchase of expensive aircraft, and the board was receptive to new technologies that could improve passenger handling, but an untried teleprocessing system which utilized agent sets that cost $16,000 apiece represented a new kind of corporate commitment.

The task of naming the new system fell to Burkhardt, a man who "despised acronyms with a passion." After rejecting approximately a hundred suggestions, Burkhardt still had an anonymous system on the day a name was needed for inclusion in the official press release. Leafing through a magazine that day, Taylor noticed an advertisement for a 1960 Buick LaSabre; "Let's call it SABRE," he suggested, figuring that reversing the order of the last two letters would yield a less acronymic name. Burkhardt agreed and the name stuck.[7]

Discussion of Expanding Scope

American's capacity to search for technical solutions to business processes had grown to a level of sophistication in the 1950s where parallel, overlapping explorations became the norm. For example, simultaneously in 1955, the capacity of the Reservisor was being enhanced by the addition of magnetic drum memories, distributed inventory control was being pursued with the Reservwriter, and Ammann was working with IBM's Crawford and Luhn to conceptualize the integration of passenger data with seat inventories. Implicit in this approach was an understanding of complementary life cycles for problem domains and applicable technologies. Significantly, this understanding permeated the management hierarchy. Even Hogan, an avowed skeptic of technology, appreciated the benefits of contracting ADL's skills when American's internal technical judgment was stretched beyond its limits.

The maturity of Smith's understanding was demonstrated by Smith's assignment of Sadler, a marketing man, to take responsibility for what was ultimately a marketing project, despite its reliance on state-of-the-art technology. Burkhardt, under Sadler, and Plugge, under Hogan, challenged IBM to propose a system that met organizational, not just technical, requirements. American's multifunctional management team expanded the system's domain as it saw that it could restructure the airline by centralizing the reservations function while providing timely support to a range of other business processes. Integrating the airline with the emerging system provided an entirely new means of conducting business in the airline industry.

SABRE Development: 1954–1963

Two weeks after American's board approved the IBM proposal, Plugge, as director of American's Technical Reservations Systems Department, was assigned overall responsibility for the SABRE project and charged with making reservations a paperless process. Smith authorized him to hire people as necessary. A recent graduate of the Program for Management Development at Harvard Business School, Plugge was familiar with SABRE concepts and jargon from having worked with the IBM proposal, but his principal qualification for his new assignment was his record as an able financial administrator who was familiar to C. R. Smith, Marion Sadler, and Bill Hogan. Smith's marching orders to Plugge were succinct: "You'd better make those black boxes do the job, because I could buy five or six Boeing 707s for the same capital expenditure."[8]

To integrate seat availability and inventory data with passenger name records required rapid access to large databases, and the random nature of inquiries dictated the direct access capabilities of disk files. Solid state logic components gave IBM's 7090 processor, which was to be the heart of SABRE, a 500 percent improvement in central processing unit performance and memory cycle time over its vacuum tube predecessor for only a 33 percent increase in price. Equally important, access to records via random access disk storage was faster by two to three orders of magnitude than sequential magnetic tape storage.

Hogan, with the encouragement of Mal Perry, continued the relationship with ADL to maintain a check on IBM and retained Dick Heitman, an experienced ADL systems engineer, as a resident professional. Plugge hand-picked a team to define the SABRE system's detailed functional requirements and associated decision processes.

To bolster internal data-processing skills, American invited interested personnel to take IBM's programming aptitude test and interviewed for the SABRE project those who earned an A grade. Interest was particularly heavy among reservations and customer service employees. Ultimately, 28 of more than 350 applicants were selected. Everyone involved with SABRE, including project managers, underwent some technical training. Most attended an IBM programming class that introduced participants to the systems development process and sought to instill in them an appreciation for what computers could and could not do.

American's programming staff was built around a nucleus of ten programmers, each with a minimum of three years' experience with IBM computers, recruited from outside the airline. Notable among them was Perry, who was to become American's manager of systems and programming, hired from Ramo Wooldridge, the forerunner of TRW. Perry was a rare combination of brilliant conceptual thinker, problem solver, and consummate programmer. His understanding of the subtleties of managing a systems project and ability to transfer his knowledge to apprentices fostered within American a consistent approach to systems management. The dictum that all programs be logically segmented in blocks of 500 instructions or fewer, with minimal interprogram cross-referencing, was Perry's way of eliminating the need to know a program's ultimate storage location and isolating the effects of subsequent changes.

The conversion plan called for American's reservations office in Hartford to begin using SABRE in parallel with the Magnetronic Reservisor system in May 1962, but software bugs delayed full cutover until November. The on-demand nature of a teleprocessing system, with its random inputs and operations, prompted speculation that the system could never be debugged. Programmers suspected hardware deficiencies; hardware engineers faulted the software. Moreover, to support a network entailed planning for data transmission, which necessitated establishing for the first time working relationships with telephone companies. Smith's penchant for short-notice visits to the SABRE data center at Briarcliff Manor in Westchester County, New York, heightened tensions; the president's support was much appreciated by the project team, but his prideful demonstrations to visiting dignitaries magnified system testing problems.

IBM, which was contractually responsible for SABRE's performance, believed that only 10 percent of the 7090's processing capacity was being utilized throughout development and testing at American. Perry's concerns about the machine's capacity were brushed aside with assertions that it was not possible to saturate a 7090, that any throughput problems would arise from disk inputs and outputs. But when the April 1963 addition of the New York reservations office slowed response time to thirty seconds — system response time not to exceed three seconds during peak-volume periods had been specified in the contract — forcing the flagship office to be taken off-line after only two weeks, the main memory of the 7090s was doubled. Perry replaced the latest version of the control program with a new one that incorporated the segmented, structured programming techniques he had established as a standard for American's application programs.

Perry's action might have been viewed as an affront to IBM, as the project's formal division of labor held the vendor answerable for the control program. However, the project team's sense of purpose and persistence in devising a systems solution to the reservations problem let technical competence dominate political concerns. Twenty-eight years later, Plugge and Taylor credited Perry's remedy with saving the SABRE project, which, following delays, aborted conversions, health emergencies among project team members, and hardware modifications, became fully operational in December 1964 with the addition of the airline's Cleveland reservations office. American admitted that both it and IBM had underestimated the complexity of the job.

Organizational Ramifications

As SABRE's development gained momentum, Marion Sadler, whose responsibility for customer service included the reservations center, initiated personnel planning. The immediate implication of the conversion to SABRE was the elimination of entire sets of manual procedures required to process passenger reservations. Sadler delegated to Roger Burkhardt the job of transforming the organization to reflect the shift from the manual system to SABRE.

Two massive marketing and educational programs, one targeted at customers, the other at employees, were launched to prepare for the rollout of SABRE. The former was to promote customer understanding of SABRE's potential, the latter to enhance SABRE's appeal to sales agents.

In parallel with the educational programs, a detailed system analysis of new procedures was conducted. Time and motion studies had refined the physical design of reservations consoles to maximize agent comfort and efficiency. In anticipation of preparing budgets for field installation of agent sets in eighty-nine locations in thirty-nine cities, American reviewed up to a hundred physical requirements for each of its offices. The requirement for uninterrupted operation during physical renovation of the reservations offices necessitated a period of concurrent operation of the manual and SABRE systems. Where local manual procedures were to be completely subsumed by SABRE, the process was expected to be a relatively straightforward cutover.

Sadler, recently promoted to president, announced in January 1961 that all permanent reservations personnel displaced by SABRE would be assigned other jobs within the airline, a policy extended to teletype operators in July 1962. The jobs being eliminated, because they were largely occupied by young women, were subject to high attrition, permitting a dignified transition to an automated reservations process with substantially less human action. Nevertheless, both internal and external public relations campaigns were launched to counter negative union publicity. Models of the SABRE data center and a reservations agent's desk outfitted with SABRE equipment were displayed in major airport terminals, and between August 1961 and March 1962, more than 1,900 American employees, ten to twenty at a time, were briefed about the project in 247 ninety-minute meetings conducted in nineteen cities. The meetings encouraged open discussion in order to dispel doubt and avoid confusion that might hurt morale and lower productivity. Two-week train-the-trainer sessions were subsequently held at Briarcliff Manor for each reservations office.

Although SABRE's seat availability and inventory control operations did not vary greatly from those of the Magnetronic Reservisor,

FIGURE 4-2 **Comparative Load Factors**

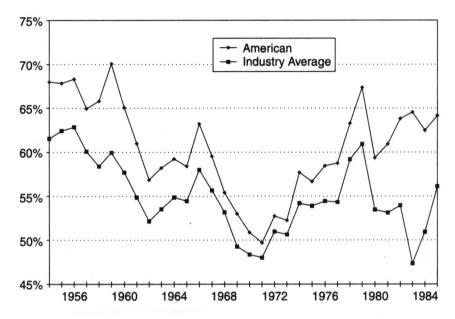

Source: D. G. Copeland, "Information Technology for First Mover Advantage: The U.S. Airline Experience" (DBA diss., Harvard Business School, 1990).

response time was faster. But a more significant improvement was on-line availability; changes in passenger and flight schedules were immediately available throughout American's route network, compressing time and distance and minimizing constraints on airline operations. Instead of reservations records disappearing into a back office, perhaps forever, seat and associated passenger information was immediately sorted, processed, and stored at the Briarcliff Manor data center. When a record had to be retrieved, either to book a return flight or cancel space, any agent at any location could quickly receive a printout by pressing the display record key on the agent set. Most important, agents could perform this and every other customer service task without assistance, greatly improving their efficiency. Moreover, the system was able to sustain its load factor advantage as jet aircraft were added (see Figure 4-2).

With SABRE, American had achieved a quantum leap in processing capacity to cope with daily demands of 85,000 telephone calls, 40,000 passenger reservations, 30,000 interairline seat availability inquiries, and 20,000 ticket sales. Sadler, Plugge, and Perry understood that they had acquired a real-time data-processing foundation — both in technology and in skill — for implementing future applications to improve American's customer service, flight operations, and management control.

Discussion of Using IT to Drive Strategy

The development of SABRE created an IT staff at the leading edge of the technology and a management attuned to exploiting the availability of on-line information. Plugge's acceptance of responsibility was absolute — he was free to hire as necessary, but not free to fail. Recruiting the genius of Mal Perry ensured that he did not. The IT group organized to operate and develop new systems as the system matured and demands for more services grew. Sadler revised organizational routines and began to integrate operation of the airline with the available information. Hogan expanded the system beyond the reservations activities into market and financial planning as the operations, through timely information, were becoming better coordinated. The presence of SABRE itself became the basis of an advertising campaign guaranteeing seats and striving for on-time arrival. All aspects of the organization were influenced by the system; its potential seemed enormous to those involved and a threat to those uninformed or hostile to change.

Emulation–Alternative Designs: 1960–1972

In 1960, Delta's CEO, C. E. Woolman, and chief technologist, Frank Heinzmann, after protracted conversation with IBM, signed a contract with the company to build a reduced version of SABRE. Delta, under tighter economic constraints than American, chose as a base for its reservations system a smaller computer, the 7074, whose cost was about 40 percent that of a 7090. Although Delta completed the contract and took delivery of its computer a year after American had, Heinzmann had been exchanging systems ideas with American's Mal Perry from the start and, with IBM facilitating technology transfer, quickly adapted Delta's PNR design to Perry's modular design. Delta finished its system six months after American, but did not perceive the system improvement as a marketing force and, consequently, did not initially market its advantage.

Pan American World Airways (Pan Am) commenced development of a reservations system a year after Delta, selecting an IBM 7080 computer which, being compatible with its accounting system, could serve as a backup. Although not ideally suited to the reservations function, the 7080 was able to support Pan Am's relatively small fleet and concentrated traffic. Delta and Pan Am's imitation of SABRE was significant because it advanced IBM's experience with alternative functional and technical environments and continued and strengthened the tradition of sharing, or at least emulating, computer systems in the airline industry.

Adapting to Exploit SABRE

Having installed SABRE, American quickly came to appreciate the further challenges and opportunities that stem from an initial technical solution to a transaction-processing crisis. SABRE's centralized database afforded American its first opportunity to provide accurate and timely information; SABRE's contribution to the airline's strategy lay in planning and analysis.

Historical reservations data archives on magnetic tape supported modeling of airline operations to an extent previously impossible and fed demand models that supported new levels of marketing precision. Manipulating reservations data generated management insights unavailable to other carriers. As functional enhancements extended its influence in the organization, SABRE became the dominant design for a reservations system, setting the standard for efficiency and effectiveness in internal airline operations. Acquisition of a PNR system quickly became a managerial imperative for airlines generally.

Less obvious to other airlines was the complexity of integrating such a system with corporate strategy and structure. SABRE's benefits extended beyond improvements in passenger service; planning for ancillary tasks such as crew scheduling and food services became possible with a new level of precision, and the trials endured by Plugge's team were the genesis of a tradition of technical competence in the airline.

Little SABRES, Big SABRES, and Imitators

By 1965, IBM's projects for American, Delta, and Pan Am had demonstrated that real-time teleprocessing was a viable solution to the core problems with passenger reservations. The increased processing capacity of its 360 computers had encouraged IBM to create a standardized airline reservations product that Eastern Airlines subsequently expanded to set a new technological standard for large-scale reservations systems. Both Trans World Airlines (TWA) and United Airlines had tried to build comprehensive custom systems that went far beyond PNR functions, even exceeding SABRE's original goals, but lacking experience with the application and the technology, they had failed.

IBM leveraged the experience gained from SABRE's successful implementation to develop its own Programmed Airline Reservations System. Dubbed PARS, the system was expected not only to promote sales of IBM's new 360 computer to airlines, but also to free the company from the risky, time-consuming business of developing custom reservations systems. To maximize its market appeal, PARS was targeted at the functional requirements and transaction volumes of midsize carriers of up to one hundred planes. In 1965, IBM began taking orders for processors with the PARS software for installation in 1968. With jet service accelerating the pace of operations throughout route networks, PARS's promise of basic seat inventory control was a welcome, if rudimentary, capability that attracted the interest of Braniff, Continental, Delta, Northeast, and Western, among other airlines.

Having concluded that its operations required the functionality of a PNR system, Eastern Airlines had elected to expand IBM's PARS to meet the needs of a large trunk carrier rather than build a system from scratch, a decision influenced in no small part by Frank Heinzmann, who had joined the airline only in 1965. A technical genius who led the development of Delta's early PNR system, he had encouraged IBM to introduce an airline reservations product, and PARS's reliability and performance benefited from both Delta's and American's experience. Despite similar price tags (about $25 million), Heinzmann had urged adaptation of PARS over development of a custom system because he had faith in the IBM product as the basis for a system that could ultimately meet Eastern's requirements.

Other carriers were allying themselves with other hardware vendors, so Eastern's was IBM's only contract with a major carrier. Consequently, the success of the Eastern effort was important to IBM and the project received commensurate support. With the 1968 installation of Eastern-based PARS II in the airline's new Miami data center, the carrier achieved its stated goal of "having the most advanced system for computerized reservations" in the industry.[9]

PARS II was an important chapter in the history of airline reservations systems, setting new standards for performance and reliability in the operation of real-time systems and eroding the dominance of American's SABRE system. Moreover, it proved to be the salvation of airlines that had engaged other vendors to develop custom reservations systems.

In 1965, TWA and United, following American's example, had contracted with Burroughs and Univac, respectively, for the development of custom systems. But recognizing the potential benefits of system linkages across airline functions, both carriers sought vastly more comprehensive information systems than American's.

TWA contracted with Burroughs for a 2,000-terminal system that would, among other functions, automatically encode the names of Israeli passengers on flights passing through Arab countries. United's system, to be built around four UNIVAC 1108s supporting 3,000 cathode-ray-tube (CRT) terminals, was to support reservations, management information, flight planning, ticket issuance, freight billing, market research, and location control for major spare parts. Whereas other data-processing applications reported either through the finance or operations departments, United's Unimatic project was overseen directly by its president, George Keck, a reflection of the industry attention SABRE had commanded.

There are four likely reasons why TWA and United attempted custom systems rather than adopt IBM's proven technical solution. First, IBM's Airline Control Program was designed for efficient processing of "computationally trivial" reservations transactions, not the expanded functions the two carriers sought. Second, American, TWA, and United's viewing one another as principal rivals based on their transcontinental route structures may have made a SABRE clone instinctively unappealing. Third, lack of relevant technical experience blinded the airlines to their hubris. Finally, both Burroughs and Univac, motivated by IBM's experience with the airline industry, had submitted extremely competitive bids.

The airlines' ambitious functional designs eluded technical solutions; neither vendor was familiar with on-line systems, and existing technology was simply incapable of supporting the systems' extensive functional requirements. American had earlier pared its aspiring vision for SABRE to a design that was consistent with the capabilities of available technology. Absent American's experience, TWA and United had tried in the late 1960s to install the sorts of systems that were not realized until the late 1970s.

United concluded in 1969 and TWA in 1970 that they were experiencing classic data-processing calamities. Having underestimated the complexity of their requirements and overestimated the capability of the available technology, they faced the prospect of scrambling to accommodate the passenger volumes of the 1970s with primitive availability systems long deemed inadequate. Forced to seek alternative solutions to their reservations problems, in 1970 both airlines arranged to purchase Eastern's software, helping to offset its development costs, and contracted with IBM for assistance with accelerated installation projects. Both TWA's PARS II and United's version of PARS II, APOLLO, were up and running at the end of 1971.

American's Dilemma

While the foregoing scenario was playing out, American was restructuring its organization around SABRE's capabilities. Recognizing that SABRE had become the basis of efficient operations systemwide — supporting centralized crew scheduling, meals and fuel allocation, improved flight planning, airport customer services, control of bookings to optimize service levels and load factors, and focus marketing strategies — Sadler had directed Plugge and the management team to develop an integrated, SABRE-based management system capable of providing prompt, planned-versus-actual daily reports and retrieving, on demand, historical data on past performance and daily load factors for all flights.

The problem of excessive data was quickly appreciated. Daily reports of load factors for all flights and monthly breakdowns of sales by station, activity, and sales agent could quickly occupy significant space in a manager's office, precipitating the curtailment of many regular reports and initiation of on-demand reporting for exceptions requiring senior management attention.

The shift to request-based management reporting reinforced Sadler and Plugge's appreciation for centralized data and secure, reliable processing facilities. They viewed such an architecture as essential to support the decision making required when, for example, a plane was taken out of service and rapid scheduling of alternatives were considered in light of tangible costs, revenues, and regulatory issues as well as intangible customer service and corporate image factors. The same class of constrained optimization simulation was extremely relevant to long-range planning for operations and marketing strategies. Plugge and Hogan realized that it would take time to achieve the standardization and flexibility needed to support total enterprise simulation. Moreover, they understood that data-processing details and top management processes were complementary.

American added fare-quote capabilities to SABRE in 1968. In 1969, it implemented a passenger-processing system that balanced ten-year traffic projections with service requirements and future needs for aircraft and gates at each airport it served. But despite these advantages, American was experiencing technical and organizational challenges. SABRE struggled to accommodate peak transaction volumes, and Cliff Taylor, as director of Systems, could count on an annual Christmas-inspired need to invent a new jerry-rigged solution. Although American, in light of Perry's conviction that the IBM 360 was a "compromise" not well suited to the reservations application, was considering both General Electric and Univac for possible hardware upgrades, in late 1967 the company added two IBM 360/65s as support processors and six disk file units to expand SABRE's capacity. Additionally, the airline intended to convert gradually to the *de facto* PARS II standard.

But SABRE's centrality to the business of American, although well established in practice, was not reflected in formal structures or procedures. Hogan and Plugge, using new computer-based modeling techniques, had developed effective planning procedures that enabled them to evaluate, for example, the profitability of using particular airframes on specific routes, yet long-range planning remained a process of informal conversations with C. R. Smith. Although American had changed its operating structure, means of analysis, and decision procedures as a result of SABRE, it had neither altered its overall strategic processes nor formally reorganized planning into a ritual of management meetings. Management remained concentrated in Smith and his direct reports.

The Relapse: 1968–1972

With Smith driving American's realignment, opposition was hushed. But his departure in 1968 to become secretary of Commerce in the Johnson administration left a leadership vacuum and opened a window for dissension. Sadler, whom Smith had chosen as his successor only four years earlier, resigned for health reasons and was replaced by the airline's general counsel, George Spater; Hogan retired and was replaced in the top financial post by economist and strategic planner Don Lloyd-Jones; and Perry, the technical energy behind SABRE, succumbed to melanoma. New leaders with new management styles substituted for the dominating — and stabilizing — personalities of Smith, Sadler, and Hogan.

Spater, who sought to manage American by committee, rarely

acted decisively on his senior management's input. Worse, managers would leave a meeting believing they had received formal approval for something only to learn later that it had been revoked because someone who had been absent subsequently voiced an objection. Spater tended to focus on large-scale projects to the neglect of everything else. Internal dissension and in-fighting plagued the airline while a number of strategic issues, including an unfocused venture in hotel ownership, excess seat capacity from aggressive acquisition of wide-body jets, and a proposed merger with Western Airlines, distracted management's attention.

American's investment in SABRE suffered as a consequence. The original SABRE agent sets were modified typewriters with three-second response time that eventually limited agents' productivity and exacerbated capacity problems. In 1969, Spater visited a reservations center of Mohawk Airlines, an upstate New York regional carrier that had earlier adopted IBM's CRT-oriented PARS system. In the face of CRTs capable of displaying a 960-character screen in five seconds, SABRE's fifteen-character-per-second teletypewriters were clearly obsolete. Yet Spater concluded that their replacement would involve a major investment and draw attention to the system's capacity problems.

Lacking an endorsement from Spater, Plugge nevertheless purchased 1,000 CRT terminals, but his efforts to fund their installation were blocked by assistant vice president for Marketing Rod King. King favored a model of air transportation based on lean, decentralized operations to which a systemwide, "Big Mother" concept such as SABRE was anathema. King had Spater's ear, and his influence contributed to the neglect of SABRE. With King voicing Passenger Services' distaste for SABRE, plus tensions between Marketing and Finance unrelated to the system, Lloyd-Jones was free to allocate scarce resources to other projects, leaving SABRE without needed enhancements.

Fortunately for American, the technical managers and staff who maintained SABRE were largely insulated from the changes occurring at more senior levels of management. Paternalistic toward their system and loyal to, if temporarily resentful of, the airline that had supported it, they remained fiercely devoted to SABRE and determined to protect it from harm.

In 1970, Plugge and SABRE director Oliver DeSofi visited Miami at the invitation of Heinzmann to discuss Eastern-based PARS II as a solution to SABRE's woes and Plugge's frustration at lack of support for his incremental conversion to a new technical architecture.

Because its north-south route structure confined its operations to a single time zone, producing the largest peak processing loads in the industry, Eastern's experience was salient to American's problem of peak demand. Plugge and Heinzmann struck a deal that brought Eastern's software to American in exchange for programming assistance with Eastern's fare-quote system and Sabretalk, a high-level programming language developed by American. Nevertheless, the frustrated Plugge, after receiving a commitment that his successor, Jim Welsh, would complete the conversion to the new SABRE architecture, departed American to seek new challenges.

Two years were devoted to SABRE's rejuvenation, much of the effort going into modifying the user interface. Charged with preserving the look and feel of the original SABRE, Art Poltrino, who possessed a consummate understanding of SABRE applications, single-handedly tested every function in the new SABRE to confirm that it remained true to the original. "Polly," as he was known to all, a member of the original SABRE functional design team, had taken it upon himself to look after the users' interests ever since.

Conversion required a dedicated communications mainframe. Master files were flown from Briarcliff Manor to a new data center in Tulsa, Oklahoma, with update transactions arriving on subsequent flights. The first cutover attempt in April 1972 was aborted after eight hours on line. The second, successful, attempt, which took place on June 11, 1972, incurred a scant fifteen minutes of downtime. By 1972, of the ten U.S. trunk airlines, only Northwest, with its UNIVAC-based reservations system, had not adopted the PARS II standard.

Conversion to PARS II elevated the standards for reliability and capacity in reservations processing and established a foundation for enhanced system functionality. Expansion of the passenger record for hotel and rental car reservations, complete flight itineraries, and individual needs typically came first. By 1973, automated fare quotation and itinerary pricing applied to 50 to 80 percent of all domestic flights, computerized ticketing was available at check-in counters in most airports, and automated seat assignment and boarding pass issuance were standard features. Reservations systems had been transformed into passenger service systems, greatly increasing the randomness, complexity, and volume of transactions. "Computers," observed a leading trade journal in 1973, "are changing the character of airline functions as one capability leads to another."[10]

Industry ranking of the "best" systems at the time, which placed United first, TWA second, Eastern third, and American fourth, are based on highly subjective technical and functional criteria and are arguable in terms of specific order. What is clear is that American's preeminence had declined; by the early 1970s, all major carriers possessed stable, reliable internal systems and communications networks that had become essential components of their operations. The second computer-based industry transformation was complete.

Discussion of Emulation and American's Relapse

United Airlines and TWA had experience with punched cards and small accounting machines with their respective computer suppliers but no in-depth experience with programmed computers. Univac and Burroughs, as they were eager for the business and to gain a competitive edge with IBM, encouraged the airlines. Both aspirations were unrealistic and they failed to perceive the real challenges.

This period saw the first fast-second move by Eastern, the costs of not staying abreast of IT technology, and the means of diffusion of IT as a new design dominates competition becoming a necessity. Eddie Rickenbacker, Eastern's CEO, quickly appraised the potential, recruited a maestro, and worked him to catch up and move ahead. Shrewdly, Heinzmann built upon the IBM design and expanded it on the basis of Eastern's needs. The resultant design had more functionality than the original SABRE, thanks to improvements in computer hardware and operating systems as well as Heinzmann's own experience at Delta. The clear lesson for American was that demonstrating the achievement of a dominant design limited instant attempts at imitation.

The organizational infrastructure aspect of IT depends on management leadership to shape the use of the information and reorganize the roles to fit the integration or centralization of functions and roles. In dramatic change periods, a powerful organizational memory must be overcome by those threatened or upset by the change as it impacts their role. Senior management leadership and discipline in usage are essential to sustain momentum and implementation of new organizational processes to exploit the potential of IT. Smith's style did not lend itself to layers of management and he had not institutionalized the rituals of a more centralized style of business. Perhaps if Sadler had persevered American would have sustained its momentum. The incident reinforces the importance of the CEO as the metronome of an evolving IT strategy.

Surrounded by people who did not know that they did not know,

Plugge, prior to resigning from American, issued as a last decision the most consequential one a maestro could make in isolation. By cutting a deal with Eastern's Heinzmann, Plugge ensured that SABRE and the people dedicated to it would have a fighting chance. By updating the technical architecture, and paying for it in a barter arrangement invisible to other American executives, he laid the foundation for a rebirth of the airline that would be possible only with a change in management style and awareness.

Regaining Momentum: 1972 to the Present

The early 1970s finally saw the installation of an effective senior management team at American, the first since the departure of Smith and company in 1968. George Warde, vice president of Customer Service, replaced George Spater as president in 1972, assuming responsibility for day-to-day operations as the latter became chairman and chief executive officer. In March 1972, director of Corporate Financial Analysis and Budgets James Welsh hired Max Hopper, who had been responsible for United's operations system. Hopper had previously advised American Airlines, as a consultant for Electronic Data Systems, Inc., to complete the conversion of SABRE in Tulsa and, more generally, consolidate the architectures and locations of all its information systems. Robert Crandall, who assumed responsibility for TWA's data processing in the wake of its difficulties with the Burroughs system, and made the decision to adopt Eastern-based PARS, joined American in 1973 as senior vice president for Finance, replacing Lloyd-Jones, who left to head Operations. Convinced that computers would be a critical component of the airline industry, Crandall encouraged "what-if?" software design, asking, for functions such as ticketing and yield management, such questions as "What would you do?" and "What would you need?" To let it be known that he was concerned about SABRE and personally in charge, Crandall, on learning of the cache of unused CRTs acquired by Plugge and discovered by Hopper, loudly ordered their immediate installation.

Crandall's hands-on style clashed with Welsh's preference for delegation. In June 1973, seeking a replacement with whom he was familiar, Crandall hired James O'Neill from TWA to head American's Management Information and Data Processing (MIDP) Department. O'Neill had served as a consultant to Crandall when the latter was responsible for the TWA credit and collection function and the carrier was considering establishing its own credit card. Crandall had subsequently hired O'Neill to take charge of the demise of the failed Burroughs system and replace it with PARS II. By the time he left for American, O'Neill had assumed responsibility for all real-time systems at TWA. He accepted his old associate's offer because he knew that Crandall would, and could, marshal the corporate support SABRE needed and because, in O'Neill's words, "SABRE is magic." Reporting to O'Neill in his new role were Hopper, in charge of American's real-time systems, and Nick Magnus, in charge of all commercial systems.

Warde's stewardship ended when Smith returned in August 1973. Trying again for a stable succession, Smith successfully courted Albert Casey, former chairman at Time Mirror and an experienced chief executive with a track record as a turnaround manager. Casey inherited a troubled airline when he took over in February 1974. His first action was to reduce the number of routes American served and temporarily ground the underutilized, fuel-guzzling Boeing 747 wide-body jets.

Next Casey imposed his own philosophy for cutting levels of organization; he was the boss with three direct reports, whom he termed "a production guy, a marketing guy, and a scorekeeper." In August 1974, Casey appointed Crandall senior vice president for Marketing, noting that Crandall's questions to external candidates for the position reflected an understanding of the issues superior to the candidates' own. Crandall was succeeded as head of Finance by Thomas Plaskett, a young Harvard MBA who had been the airline's controller. With his "production guy," Lloyd-Jones, "marketing guy," Crandall, "scorekeeper," Plaskett, and a "corporate garbage can" in corporate counsel Gene Overbeck, Casey had assembled a tight management team that possessed the numbers orientation instilled by financial backgrounds. When Casey asked this team to identify problems, current resource allocations, and key success factors, Crandall highlighted SABRE's poor standing relative to United's APOLLO. SABRE's inadequacies fell into two categories: its functionality as an internal reservations system and the need to "do something" to provide better service to travel agents.

Discussion of the Rebound

Casey selected a strong experienced team and Crandall was empowered to pursue rebuilding IT as a force. The technical team had sustained its core strength and, given adequate resources, was quickly able to regain its momentum. The adroit team of Hopper and O'Neill, with Crandall as surrogate CEO, quickly moved to a leadership role. United's lack of leadership, in part due to the hotel experience of its CEO, provided an interesting opportunity for Crandall, and the three moved adroitly to gain the upper hand. They have sustained their position in their markets ever since by applying the approach pioneered at American during the C. R. Smith era — understanding complementary life cycles for problem domains and applicable technologies.

The Next Dominant Design: 1974–1985

In 1967, when American began to expand SABRE's reach by placing terminals with a limited number of travel agencies and commercial accounts, travel agents sold approximately 30 percent of the industry's tickets. The bulk of retail distribution was through the airlines' ticket offices in major cities and at airport ticket counters. By the early 1970s, the major carriers were selectively distributing reservations system terminals to third-party locations and arriving at varying conclusions about the long-term viability of such a strategy. They subsequently reached a tacit understanding to place a moratorium on further retail expansion so as not to provoke a computer war. Of course, limitations on computer capacity and the avoidance of unnecessary communications costs entered into the decision as well. Moreover, the early 1970s were the nadir of competition in the airline industry, with the Civil Aeronautics Board's (CAB) suspension of new routes and sanctioning of interairline capacity agreements.

Creating a Common Reservations System

Travel agents without access to computerized reservations systems had to rely on printed paper schedules and telephone or teletype communication to determine seat availability and make reservations for customers. Among early efforts to develop a common computerized reservations system for travel agents were the UNIVAC-based Donnelly Official Airlines Reservations System, begun in 1967 but abandoned when the participants could not agree on financing, and the PARS-based Automated Travel Agency Reservations System, intended as an exclusive industry system for airlines and travel agents, for which CAB approval was sought in 1969. The Justice Department characterized the exclusivity feature of the latter system as a *per se* violation of antitrust laws, prompting an investigation into the competitive ramifications of an industrywide system, and the initiative faded.

In 1972 the president of the American Society of Travel Agents (ASTA) approached Control Data Corporation (CDC) to propose a joint effort to develop a common integrated travel agency system. CDC concluded that such an endeavor had become not only technologically feasible, but financially desirable as well. Pending cooperation between CDC and ASTA did not escape the attention of Crandall, Hopper, and O'Neill, who were uncomfortable, as were managers at other airlines, with the prospect of a computer vendor controlling access to travel agents, a small but growing segment of the airlines' distribution chain. According to Hopper, the arrangement would have resulted in carriers' being charged for use of the system by the travel agents, CDC, or both.

THE COMMITTEE APPROACH. In October 1974, Crandall received permission from the CAB to establish a task force comprising carriers, hardware suppliers, and ASTA members to consider development of a Joint Industry Computerized Reservations System (JICRS). Crandall believed automating airline distribution channels would be increasingly important and that advantages would accrue to the airline which got started first, but with money scarce, JICRS offered a less expensive alternative.

When Eastern and TWA refused to make their qualified managers available, O'Neill volunteered Hopper to serve as JICRS's project leader. Following a two-year study of the costs and benefits involved and functions that should be included in a system, the JICRS technical team, on July 15, 1975, issues a report which concluded that a joint system was technically feasible and economical. Based on IBM 370 processors, and assuming for each agency three terminals and one multipurpose printer at a cost of $14,000, the team estimated that the air transportation industry could save as much as $3 billion between 1977 and 1982. United dissented, holding that the projected economics of the system were optimistic and objecting to the committee nature of JICRS, which had one-member, one-vote authority, yet called for development costs to be allocated in proportion to passenger volumes. As the largest carrier, it would shoulder the bulk of the financial burden for what it expected would be the lowest-common-denominator system built to operate at the slowest possible speed. Moreover, United was confident that it would take American three years to bring SABRE up to the functionality of APOLLO.

Hopper's involvement with the JICRS study alerted him to United's dissatisfaction and to the possibility that the competitor might withdraw from the project and make APOLLO widely available. He noted that United was installing new commercial accounts and notifying travel agents that they would not be left without a system, regardless of the outcome of JICRS. American stressed its continued support for an industry approach to automation, but made it known that in the event of a computer war initiated by another airline, it would "respond in a positive and agressive fashion [to] meet and surpass each and every challenge."[11]

In September 1975, Crandall authorized Hopper to prepare American to compete should United withdraw from the joint effort. As head of JICRS, Hopper had visited all the major travel agents and listened to their needs, which were different from those of the airline. He, O'Neill, and Crandall agreed that American's system should be modified to better accommodate these needs. The task benefited from the three-tiered JICRS project organization to scope and design the system and update members. The first tier was devoted to the detailed design of a joint system, the second focused on the functional and technical requirements of travel agents, and the third summarized the components of the second tier for management. To the extent that managers at participating airlines read only third-tier material, the detailed findings became de facto proprietary intelligence for American. One such finding was that the presence of only one terminal would be acceptable to travel agents, with obvious implications for the benefits of being first to automate an agency.

By the end of October, a sixteen-page strategy specifying means and ends, desired functional enhancements, personnel requirements, and an implementation timetable had been devised for American. This preparation subsequently entailed investing in additional equipment and programming for SABRE, using the JICRS findings as a model for the most marketable system, and developing a detailed marketing plan for SABRE's rollout. By December 1975, Crandall was telling Hopper to hire as necessary to compete with APOLLO.

At a final meeting in Arlington, Texas, on January 8, 1976, Ray Smith, ASTA's vice president for Industry Automation, proposed that system ownership be 40 percent by equipment vendors, 20 percent by travel agents and "other investors," and 40 percent by the airlines, whereupon representatives of the airlines withdrew to a closed session.

Even at that late date there was much debate on basic issues. The carriers were agreed that vendor control would not serve their purposes, either then or in the future, but there was no agreement on the economics of travel agent systems. Some representatives doubted that there would be sufficient demand for agent terminals to cover costs and "that individual carrier-supplied reservations systems would result in an uneconomic duplication of hardware and costs." More fundamental was the concern that any form of automation for travel agents would "institutionalize the way that airlines distributed their products," limiting flexibility at a time when airlines were "faced with the possibility of deregulation legislation that would make investments, such as proposed, an extreme risk." In the end, the airline representatives concluded that further studies being proposed by ASTA were pointless and that they would not ask the CAB to extend their authority to discuss the matter among themselves.[12]

THE DARWINIAN COMPETITION APPROACH. United announced its withdrawal from JICRS and intention to make APOLLO available to travel agents and commercial accounts on January 28, 1976. It put the industry on notice that it would begin accepting subscribers' orders in May 1976 for installation beginning in September. Mechlin Moore, United's group vice president for Marketing, claimed that the move was "not intended to close the door on an industry system if an economically viable system can be designed," but rather "to provide immediate automation services to travel agencies that want it."[13] *The Wall Street Journal* warned that United's decision could "touch off a costly industry battle in which carriers will fight to supply the terminal equipment to an agent because of the presumed business advantage in obtaining potential customers."[14]

By making its announcement nine months in advance of delivery, United handed American an opening and essentially forced TWA to make a similar announcement. Crandall publicly decried United's action: "While American Airlines believes that some agents may benefit from this kind of automation, it does not believe that the agency and carrier community as a whole will realize the fullest advantages of automation available now or achieve the ultimate potential that a common system would bring about."[15]

Having anticipated a faster rollout by United, American was positioned to install the first SABRE terminals under its new Travel Agency Automation program. Crandall announced in February that American would provide terminals to cooperative travel agents in April 1976. American's sales effort benefited from the goodwill developed during the JICRS project and the inclusion of a number of agent-oriented system functions with a promise of more to come.

Once committed to a strategy of travel agent automation, Crandall made the structural modifications needed to support it. In mid-1976, he created Marketing Automation. Headed by Hopper, and reporting through Marketing to Crandall, the new unit was responsible for all planning and functional design for marketing systems.

Expecting shortly to resume his responsibilities for real-time systems, Hopper recruited Mohawk Airlines' Richard Murray, whom he designated his heir apparent. One of his first moves being to track the business associated with the newly installed terminals, Murray came to understand early on that putting terminals in agents' offices increased sales significantly more than had been predicted. American had found a ready market; it beat its estimate of two years to reach its initial objective of 200 locations by half, having equipped approximately 130 travel agent locations by the end of the year. When it became clear that its goal would be achieved in fewer than eleven months, funding for an additional 200 installations was quickly arranged. Feedback from a number of large travel agencies that confirmed the worth of the automation strategy and suggested functional enhancements led American to redouble its efforts.

Understanding the benefits and recognizing that the first airline into a large travel agency could secure a loyal distribution channel, Marketing Automation accelerated its terminal rollout. Long hours and frayed nerves were the order of the day, exacerbated by growing resentment on the part of other departments that saw Marketing Automation as a bunch of entrepreneurs with a blank check. Ill will could be ignored, except when it came from O'Neill's MIDP group, which was responsible for designing and implementing the strategies and priorities established by Marketing Automation. This division of labor proved very effective, as Hopper's responsibility for functional specifications permitted him to focus on what to do while O'Neill worried about how to support it technically.

Although the last thing O'Neill wanted was to inhibit Hopper's ability to recruit travel agents, satisfactory technical support was not easy. The transformation of SABRE from a passenger service system with an emphasis on airport locations to a sales distribution system receiving messages from hundreds and ultimately thousands of travel agent locations created both throughput problems and new reliability requirements. O'Neill relied on a dozen systems engineers to devise the necessary enhancements. When a particularly vexing problem arose, O'Neill would take his supertechs to dinner, focus discussion on the problem, and listen for the best ideas. This complement of technical skills was motivated by the "magic" of SABRE, the same enticement that had led O'Neill to join American in 1973. A technical career ladder that "let techies stay techies" was insurance against alienating these vital employees.

In September 1976, United installed APOLLO terminals in four pilot locations to determine what functional enhancements might be required. Any agency that booked $300,000 annually on United or $1 million annually with at least 15 percent on United was eligible for a free evaluation of its automation needs on a first-come, first-served basis.

It took about a year for United to realize that SABRE was preferred by travel agents because it included many of JICRS's "bells and whistles." Moreover, United initially did not place much strategic importance on APOLLO. Marketing duties were assigned as an additional responsibility to United's field sales force, resulting in a relatively low-level promotional effort. Then, in October 1976, United furloughed thirty PARS programmers as part of a 3 percent companywide head-count reduction. The cuts, based on seniority, resulted in the loss of some of the airline's most relevant expertise in data processing. Many of those let go were immediately hired by American.

SABRE's top-down marketing plan targeted large or geographically well-situated locations likely to create local ripple effects in demand. Hopper interacted closely with travel agency managers, while Murray coordinated the ten field representatives who prepared individual travel agents and their offices for conversion.

American was confident that its reputation would make it the carrier of choice for many travel agents, provided its schedules were available to them and SABRE was the system in use. American justified its first 200 locations on the basis of revenue retention, believing that the benefits from "float" (passenger revenues were collected by the airline flying the first segment of a passenger's itinerary) and "breakage" (the carrier collecting passenger revenue retained it unless it was expressly claimed by another) would complement fees charged directly to travel agent subscribers.

During installation of the initial locations, it became apparent to

American that although travel agents leased less hardware than expected, decreasing subscriber fees, Marketing Automation was responsible for substantial revenue generation and retention. The expected contribution of the first 200 installations was originally estimated to be $3.1 million annually in incremental passenger revenues, the return on investment projected to be 6 percent without, and 67 percent with, incremental revenues. Before the installation effort was complete, the estimate for incremental passenger revenues was revised to $20.1 million, resulting in a projected return on investment in excess of 500 percent.[16] The justification for appropriating funds to automate an additional 200 SABRE locations included the following paragraph, which captures the essence of American's experience in early 1977:

> What began as a necessary competitive counter to a precipitous action on the part of a major competitor has now evolved into a project of significant financial magnitude to American Airlines. Further, it is occurring at a time when we are threatened with major regulatory changes which potentially could lead to a situation in which the marketing information provided and even a limited control over the distribution mechanism could prove invaluable.[17]

American's 1977 projections for the profitability of its retail automation effort for the years 1978 through 1980 anticipated a doubling of revenues each year. More important, the ratio of incremental revenues to subscriber fees was projected to be 9:1. By 1980, SABRE was expected to return a net profit of $300.2 million on total revenues of $339.3 million.[18] Although American's expectations inflated incremental revenues by overstating the number of flight segments that were truly incremental, the decision to pursue retail automation aggressively was made easier by the early knowledge that substantial cash contributions were possible.

CO-HOST PROGRAMS. Despite its coordinated marketing approach, by 1978 American perceived SABRE's share of the travel agent market to be lagging APOLLO's, largely on account of the greater breadth of United's route structure. Hopper's response was the "co-host" concept, whereby other carriers' schedules were given preferential display on SABRE for a fee. In an atmosphere of questioning the wisdom of standing interline agreements, Crandall, Hopper, and Murray saw SABRE as a package of services that could be profitably unbundled. Moreover, Hopper saw co-hosting as a "mini-JICRS"; the added completeness of SABRE's listings and programming changes that enhanced the reliability of interline messages benefited the larger travel agents that had nurtured Marketing Automation in its formative stages. By the end of 1978, five carriers had signed co-host agreements with American. Although the fee helped defray the cost of expanding travel agency automation, the primary intention was to increase SABRE's presence in markets American did not serve, particularly those served by United, thereby locking in travel agents and slowing APOLLO's expansion. United immediately introduced its own co-host option.

For an airline without its own retail automation program, co-hosting offered several advantages. In 1979, for example, Western Airlines was alarmed to learn that although its flights dominated the Salt Lake City market, local travel agents largely used APOLLO; the "halo effect" of an APOLLO installation gradually increased United's passenger market at the expense of Western. Moreover, United had access to Western's traffic statistics when reservations were booked through APOLLO. As an affordable alternative to offering its own system in competition with APOLLO, and in an attempt to stem the latter's advance, Western signed a co-host agreement with American and actively promoted SABRE to travel agents throughout the western United States. Delta contracted with United in 1982 to protect its markets from SABRE and promoted APOLLO in the Southeast. For both Western and Delta, promotion of reservations systems owned by carriers whose schedules were relatively noncompetitive with their own was the lesser of two evils.

Deregulation

The Airline Deregulation Act of 1978, and the two years of regulatory reform that preceded it, introduced airlines to an unaccustomed array of competitive threats and opportunities. Although many believed that an unregulated air transport system would "reach something that more or less resembled a competitive equilibrium," there was little consensus on how this would take place.[19] A fundamental expectation of deregulation's proponents, disproved by experience, was that the industry would display conditions of contestability, that is, costless entry and exit at sufficient scale to result in welfare-maximizing industry performance regardless of the number of actual competitors.[20] Advocates of deregulation were "misled by the apparent lack of evidence of economies of scale . . . and by the physical mobility of aircraft, which caused [them] to underestimate the other obstacles to entry."[21] An additional assumption contained in the theory of contestable markets is that all relevant information is freely available to all interested parties.

The airline industry began to feel the effects of deregulation during the latter half of the 1970s. Most notable were the implications for route and fare structures. As airlines added routes in high-traffic markets and dropped those with low traffic, service to city pairs changed rapidly. In the absence of price regulation, carriers significantly increased the variety of fares and the frequency with which they were adjusted. The number of fares in the large reservations systems rose from tens of thousands in a regulated environment to millions, and the rate of fare changes went from semiannually to monthly, semimonthly, and in some instances daily. As the nature of passenger inquiries changed from simple seat availability to price shopping, lengthening the duration of interaction with travel agents, real-time access to the carriers' volatile schedules and fares became a necessity. An independent study estimated that use of a computerized reservations system increased travel agent productivity by 42 percent.[22]

At the same time, some carriers were questioning the cost effectiveness of city ticket offices and looking for ways to control the costs of reservations offices, reservations agents, and internal communications. These factors combined to create a strong incentive for airlines to transfer the reservations function from their own offices to travel agencies, with the result that the percentage of tickets sold through travel agents continued to grow. By the late 1970s, other carriers had begun to recognize the potential market power of reservations systems as they changed from production tools to demand-enhancement systems. The 1978 *Annual Report for Continental Air Lines* conceded that its position as a preferred carrier was threatened when either APOLLO or SABRE was adopted by a travel agency in one of its markets. With 55 percent of its seats sold through travel agents, Continental believed that signing a co-host agreement with American was necessary to ensure the availability of its schedules.

Beginning in 1978, American and United intensified efforts to add to their systems features that would help travel agents manage their business and further improve productivity. United negotiated a restricted software license with a Florida company, Agency Data Systems, which specialized in minicomputer systems for travel agent accounting, but before the contract was finalized O'Neill flew to Florida and bought the company for American.

Another example of an enhancement that had far-reaching implications was travel agents' customer files. Whereas the primary unit of analysis for airlines' reservations needs is the flight, travel agents are concerned first and foremost with the passenger. The larger agencies that counseled Hopper on their requirements suffered from redundant Rolodex files of passenger records. Hopper's response was the SABRE Traveler Automation Records System (STARS), which enabled travel agents to better manage client relations. Later, when Crandall and Plaskett were mapping, on a commissary napkin, the programming flows needed to implement the industry's first frequent-flier program, they combined STARS with SABRE's PNR records and a program for post-departure passenger list reconciliation. The result, AAdvantage, was introduced in 1981 after a secretive six-month development, creating customer loyalty in a viciously competitive market where airline seats were becoming a commodity, with all the pricing implications that entailed.

The expense of creating reservations systems that were responsive to the competitive environment precluded all but the largest carriers from participating in the travel agent automation arena. By 1978, the processing complexity added by the co-host programs, the increase in the size of the fare database, and the added features and transaction volumes associated with usage by travel agents, not to mention the demands of supporting a private communications network with its attendant remote hardware, were straining processing capacity. Marketing Automation's success at attracting travel agents was taxing SABRE's capacity. New subscribers were forced to wait for the installation and connection of their SABRE terminals. Quick-fix solutions, such as defragmenting disk drives, were no longer adequate.

The industry's tradition of cooperation to resolve common problems enabled O'Neill to enter American into a cooperative study with United, Eastern, and TWA to explore ways to relax constraints on processing capacity. American donated the machine time, Eastern two key architects, and all contributed programmers. The SABRE Network of Attached Processors (SNAP) project resulted in the development by 1979 of a system that supported on-line sharing of the processing load among multiple computers operating simultaneously in an Airline Control Program environment. Project participants freely shared the necessary code, further distinguishing the systems capabilities of the "Big Four" airlines. By 1980, a new travel agent subscriber could be connected to SABRE within one week of signing a contract with American.

To this point, a carrier's willingness to invest in retail automation had been more significant than its capacity to invest. But as the stakes climbed and the largest systems approached nationwide coverage, scale economies began to determine airlines' ability to participate in the substantial returns available. In 1980, for example, American estimated that its SABRE locations collectively generated $78.5 million in incremental passenger revenues. In 1981, SABRE's nine domestic co-hosts contributed $6.9 million in fees to American. Obtaining such income, however, required financial support. American's 1982 budget for retail automation called for spending at an annual rate of nearly $20 million, justifying the expenditure with a projected return on investment still in excess of 500 percent. More significant, American's assessment of SABRE's position in 1982 reveals that its 1977 goal of "limited control" over distribution had been emboldened by success.

> With the establishment of such a large and sophisticated industry distribution network, American has been able to increase its influence over the flow of passengers through the air transportation network in a manner most beneficial to American. In addition, recent (functional) enhancements . . . have resulted in increased utilization and dependence by agents on SABRE for virtually all aspects of travel services thereby increasing SABRE's foothold and dominance as an industry-wide distribution system.[23]

American's objectives in 1982 were to (1) display American's products preferentially at the retail level, (2) maintain SABRE's superiority among automated reservations systems, (3) receive revenue from every booking made by subscribers to SABRE, (4) increase the amount paid by third parties, and (5) receive a satisfactory return on investment without consideration of incremental passenger revenues. The financial returns on these technological developments compared with those of the competition are summarized in Figure 4-3.

In 1983 American reported that it had invested $170 million in its travel agency automation program to capture 27 percent of automated travel agent locations. United's investment to that time reportedly exceeded $150 million and had garnered the airline an 18 percent share. By way of comparison, the 1983 shares of the travel agent market for the systems of Delta, Eastern, and TWA were 3 percent, 5 percent, and 10 percent, respectively. Of the revenues booked through the systems by travel agents, SABRE accounted for 43 percent, APOLLO for 27 percent.[24]

FIGURE 4-3   **Financial Contribution (assuming 80% contribution from incremental revenues)**

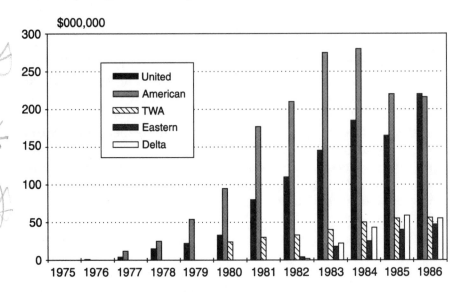

Source: D. G. Copeland, "Information Technology for First Mover Advantage: The U.S. Airline Experience" (DBA diss., Harvard Business School, 1990).

American Airlines, under Robert Crandall and Max Hopper, continues to lead the industry. It has developed sophisticated yield-management systems that have enabled it to maximize revenues through variable pricing and terms, routinely tracks market segments, and is pursuing worldwide links with other carriers. In the early 1990s, American launched an aggressive campaign to market its analytical and other IT-based services worldwide, with the result that cash flow from these services has at times in recent years exceeded that generated by its airline operations. No airline is better positioned to dictate future permutations of the dominant design of information processing in the industry.

Discussion of the Next Dominant Design Shift

With the talent in place, American embarked on an innovative binge that transformed its systems, its strategy, and its structure. As functional enhancements transformed SABRE from a reservations system to a passenger service system and ultimately into a sales distribution system, the system was the catalyst for changes to

American's strategy and structure. JICRS supplied the airline with industry-sponsored R&D. Hopper's Marketing Automation group, formed to assert control over the industry's distribution channel, amounted to quasi-forward integration, while the growing Decision Technologies Department brought the principles of operations research to bear on SABRE's databases to produce information-based competitive advantages. Once secured, the system and structure enabled an information technology strategy that allowed American to thrive in a deregulated environment, effectively subverting public policy that was supposed to place it at a severe disadvantage relative to industry entrants.

The interdependencies in American's strategy are clear. Information captured by SABRE was put to multiple uses spanning functional departments in the airline. Only through regular face-to-face interaction between Crandall and Hopper, as well as other members of senior management, could this strategy evolve. Furthermore, American's tradition of successful IT innovation made it natural to consider information-based solutions to business problems. When Crandall assembled his executive team for its regular Monday morning meetings, all participants, regardless of their functional titles, considered SABRE's potential, with Hopper in a position to inform them of the degree of technical difficulty and thus the time and resources required to implement their initiative.

Notes

1. Duncan G. Copeland and James L. McKenney, "Airline Reservation Systems: Lessons from History," *MIS Quarterly* 12, no. 2 (1988): 352. Originally from "American Airlines Sabre (A)," Case No. EA-C758 (Boston: Harvard Business School, 1967), 6.

2. Charles E. Ammann, "Airline Automation: A Major Step," *Computers and Automation* 6, no. 8 (August 1957).

3. "The Cautious Pioneer," *Forbes*, June 1, 1956.

4. Ammann, "Airline Automation."

5. C. R. Smith, memorandum to C. A. Rheinstrom, executive vice president-Sales, April 9, 1959.

6. Fred R. Plugge, "Evaluation of Proposed SABER System: Appendix II — System Objectives."

7. D. C. Copeland interview with Fred Plugge and Claude Taylor, Tulsa, Oklahoma, March 1, 1991.

8. Fred Plugge letter to D. C. Copeland, March 23, 1992.

9. Eastern Air Lines, Inc., *Annual Report*, 1968.

10. *Aviation Week and Space Technology*, October 22, 1973.

11. T. J. Ross, Jr., *American Airlines Bulletin*, November 19, 1975.

12. "Minutes of Industry Task Force Meeting re: Joint Reservations Systems," U.S. District Court, *Continental Airlines v. United Air Lines*, Case #CV86-0696 and 0697 ER (MCX), Exhibit 19281, January 1986.

13. "United Offers Agency Automation; American and TWA Reluctantly Follow Suit," *Travel Management Daily*, January 29, 1976.

14. "American Airlines, TWA to Offer Travel Agents Automated System," *Wall Street Journal*, February 2, 1976.

15. American Airlines, Inc., press release, January 28, 1976.

16. Thomas G. Plaskett memorandum to A. V. Casey, January 17, 1977, U.S. District Court, American Airlines documents AA080713-AA080714.

17. U.S. District Court, January 1986, American Airlines document AA080717.

18. "SABRE Pro Forma," U.S. District Court, January 1986, American Airlines document AA035416.

19. Michael E. Levine, "Airline Competition in Deregulated Markets: Theory, Firm Strategy, and Public Policy," *Yale Journal of Regulation* 4 (1987).

20. S. Morrison and C. Winston, *The Economic Effects of Airline Deregulation* (Washington, D.C.: Brookings), 1986.

21. Alfred E. Kahn, "Surprises of Deregulation," AEA *Papers and Proceedings*, 1988.

22. D. Saunders, "The Antitrust Implication of Computer Reservations Systems (CRS)," *Journal of Air Law and Commerce* 51.

23. Appropriation Request AR 901-566-5-8, U.S. District Court, January 1986, American Airlines document AA072613.

24. American Airlines, Inc., *Annual Report*, 1983; *Aviation Week & Space Technology*, November 28, 1983; United Airlines, Inc., *Annual Report*, 1982.

Chapter 5

How the Pioneers Transformed Information-Processing Technology

Historical analysis of the management activities and tactics of Bank of America and American Airlines reveals a common shift in focus and management concerns that is both cumulative and expanding in nature. Both firms' CEOs recognized an impending information-processing crisis and launched a search for a technological solution. Both settled for partial solutions that the technology was capable of supporting. These initial trials provided valuable insights into the costs, benefits, and management issues associated with developing innovative information technology (IT) systems.

These CEOs and their maestros developed IT-based concepts of their businesses, moving adroitly when the technology was able to satisfy their firms' broader information-processing needs. Their sequence of projects expanded their competence and provided insights into a larger spectrum of business needs and the unrealized potential of IT. The information-processing designs they created fundamentally changed the basis of competition essential to their industries.

Confirming the Model

Analysis of information technology usage at Bank of America and American Airlines further reveals similarities and differences in the development, introduction, and evolution of IT as a competitive force. Both companies faced formidable information-processing crises, had access to equivalent technology, and were run by CEOs inclined to pursue solutions through that technology. On the other hand, the management styles of the CEOs differed considerably, as did the companies' organizational structures, procedures, information-processing requirements, and the function of information in their respective industries.

Both companies' CEOs actively involved themselves in all important company matters. At once pragmatists and visionaries, they perceived IT as a means to more economical services leading to greater market share in a period of rapid growth, but accepted partial solutions within the limits of existing technology. Gaining confidence from their limited successes, they empowered their managers and marshaled their resources in repeated trials that gradually expanded the domain and functionality of IT within their organizations. These ultimately yielded a new design for information processing.

On the other hand, the two companies were markedly different. Time is money in banking, and speeding collections and payments reduces float and improves profits. Bank of America, an enormous presence in California, already profitable and expanding in a growing market, had very deep pockets, enabling it to move quickly to invest in creating needed technology. Its organizational strength, together with a tradition of systems analysis dating from the 1920s, enabled the bank to create a system team of experienced bankers able to select, develop, and implement profitable computer applications in 1955. Bank of America's CEO could concentrate on strategic issues because he had a strong management team overseeing branch banking growth, and relevant competencies in an experienced systems analysis division, a senior systems manager, and a broad range of managers schooled in bank systems.

Geographically distributed American Airlines was part of a regulated industry in a state of flux. The assimilation of jet aircraft posed an enormous capital drain and threatened a rapid increase in supply. Although it was a tight organization with only modest slack, in pilots and flight support to ensure safe operations, American's earnings were not keeping pace with capital demands. Its CEO retained no direct staff support, nonoperations staff were considered overhead, preferring to coordinate and cheerlead in the course of regular visits to field personnel.

The technology of the era met the needs of the bank for a large proportion of its immediate processing needs, and it could use commercially available computers profitably for its repetitive calculations in large numbers of accounts. The airline could reduce cost but had to develop partial solutions to shape the technology to meet its unique needs to access a computer file of seat status. Both compromised their requirements to test the potential of IT. In the process, both began to appreciate the potential of electronically stored information as well as the state-of-the-art and emerging technologies. From the start, both recruited and worked with outside suppliers while continuously appraising other suppliers' alternatives. They continued such surveillance throughout their developing periods.

CEO, Maestro, and Technical Team

Despite their differences, the CEOs of Bank of America and American Airlines were their organizations' metronomes — top-level executives who guided and wedded changing IT functions to market shifts. Pioneers in a time of relatively inept technology and rudimentary systems engineering that demanded heroic efforts to succeed, they recruited maestros who were capable of sharing their visions and assembling, in turn, a technical team capable of realizing those visions. We look briefly at the individuals and groups that filled these three key roles at the bank and the airline, then examine the effect of their participation in each of the five phases of the cascade.

THE CEO. S. Clark Beise and C. R. Smith represent the epitome of Joseph Schumpeter's aggressive innovator who destroys an existing organization and transforms an industry through new uses of technology. Both had an instinctive sense that information technology afforded a means to resolve a particular crisis and initiated and guided a research and development effort aimed at employing it toward that end. In so doing, each learned to exploit the potential of IT and effected a concomitant change in strategy to gain competitive advantage. Beise and Smith were persistent risk takers who bet on their teams' abilities and the advantages of being first. They attended to details while sensing the gestalt. Dynamic leaders and visionary strategists, they forged innovative teams that created radically new IT designs.

Beise, by all accounts, was an extraordinary executive who possessed vision and an ability to deal with a broad range of issues. He involved himself in all important projects by scheduling debriefing meetings with involved managers and holding periodic review sessions with the management team. The culture of the bank engendered, and Beise fostered, a strong emphasis on service and innovation. Determined to expand the bank's horizons, within an eight-year period he initiated an R&D effort, groomed a maestro, partnered with various suppliers, and implemented innovative IT systems that changed 500 years of banking tradition.

Smith, a tireless, hands-on manager dedicated to making American the premier airline in the world, was a hard-driving, person-to-person CEO who prided himself on knowing every employee. He set objectives in one-on-one meetings and insisted on being kept up to date by telephone, memo, and occasional meetings. Smith ran a flat organization, his direct reports working in tandem to keep operations on track, and maintained involvement with individual projects, helping them to pass financial muster and guiding them to completion.

Both CEOs recognized the information-processing crises that faced their companies, but their responses varied with the nature of the crisis, their personal management styles, and the available technology and competence of their organizations. Smith empowered an experienced R&D manager to determine what would be required to maintain an up-to-date, remotely accessible inventory of 100,000 passenger seats. He settled for a remedy for immediate problems of poor inventory management, overbooking, and lost reservations. Beise engaged an R&D firm to explore possibilities for automating check processing and only later recruited and groomed a maestro to pursue one of these.

However different their styles and approaches, the CEOs engaged in five common activities. They incubated research and development projects, recruited and groomed maestros and technical teams, courted business equipment manufacturers that might be able to accommodate their companies' needs, evolved strategies of IT use, and integrated IT management into the normal course of doing business.

THE MAESTRO: IT STRATEGIST AND CHANGE AGENT. An effective maestro creates jointly with the CEO a vision for an IT-based solution to the firm's crisis and then, with the senior executive's commitment, recruits and manages a technical team competent to implement that vision. The maestros at the bank and airline employed technology to transform existing information-processing activities into competitive information systems, in the process altering organizational functions and means of managing. They learned by doing. Their proposals to build entirely novel systems for which no precedents existed reflected enormous self-confidence. They believed in themselves, in their ability to learn new concepts, in their ability to get the job done.

The maestros were able managers — energetic, charismatic, in essence their organizations' IT intelligence officers, alternative generators, and IT marketers. They could build strong technical teams capable of developing working systems on time and within budget by instilling in their managers a pragmatic business perspective on the bottom-line impact of their efforts. They were the architects of the information infrastructures their firms developed and consummate systems analysts who could perceive new processing designs. The CEO was their client, the management committee their purse strings; to be effective, they had to deliver to both.

Al Zipf's track record in the use of technology was impressive: four patents and a reputation for creating innovative paper-processing systems. Bank of America's troubleshooter, he had successfully transformed three money-losing branches into solid profit performers. Zipf's enthusiasm for the potential of IT turned his interview with Beise from an exploratory talk into a planning discussion.

When Smith discovered him, Charles E. Ammann *was* American Airlines' system R&D organization. Impressed by his concern about the crude system in place and his analysis of the airline's reservations system needs, Smith encouraged Ammann to search for suppliers and keep him informed. A thoughtful and innovative engineer, Ammann diligently sought out appropriate technical partners and advised Smith of the limited capacity of state-of-the-art electronics relative to the airline's processing needs.

An evolving IT strategy depends to a large extent on the ability of the manager charged with developing and implementing systems to create an innovative IT infrastructure. This involves not only conceptualizing a new processing system, but also devising means to implement both the system and attendant organizational changes. Ammann and Zipf, in the course of resolving the information-processing crises identified by their management, had to deal with power struggles, limitations of the technology, and demanding personnel requirements. Although they went about their tasks differently, according to their varying circumstances, personal styles, and relationships with their CEOs, both could be characterized as effective technological entrepreneurs, tough, bottom-line managers, organizational change agents, leaders of competent technologists, and creators of strategic planning processes for IT.

THE TECHNICAL TEAM: THE CRITICAL RESOURCE. Management of the technical teams was discussed in the bank and airline histories only with reference to the services they developed and sequences of innovations they pursued. The systems they built and operated are compelling evidence of their competence. The precise art they performed, beyond the normal management of professionals, is unique in that it is continually changing with the development of new systems at the frontiers of the technology while remaining constant to support and nurture the several generations of systems in place.

A technology team faces three significant management challenges: to maintain reliable service that continuously adapts to changes in the underlying technology; to deal with the firm's growing dependence on technology for management as well as for operations; and to diffuse the technology throughout the organization and to customers and suppliers. These challenges call for strong leadership to support flexibility in organizational roles, job rotation, careful career management, and significant investments in training. Key to programs for meeting these challenges is an understanding of the likely impact of shifts in IT on the system and the organization. Critical issues include sustaining an innovative, service-oriented group that can maintain and adapt a firm's entire set of services and related systems, old working systems being as important as new ones.

Such strong and effective leadership works. The ingredients seem to be a flexible approach to organizing, recruiting, and maintaining professional competencies, developing organizational procedures that fit IT needs, staying involved with development and implementation, promoting and sustaining user involvement, and adapting planning and organizational procedures to stay ahead of the issues. Success builds a track record. At the bank and the airline, innovative, maestro-supported managers scoped the nature of these activities and implemented programs that successfully nurtured the competencies necessary to meet their organizations' requirements for timely and useful information delivered efficiently.

The expertise implicit in an organization's technical team includes the ability to evaluate and adopt or adapt new information systems and technologies; design and implement a portfolio of systems;

maintain and incrementally improve existing systems; troubleshoot and resolve problems expeditiously; evaluate and test commercially available software and work cooperatively to adapt vendors' systems to local needs; operate a flawless, twenty-four-hour service-oriented IT system. An organization enjoys these capabilities to the extent that its technical managers possess the requisite knowledge and skills and can manage implementation effectively.

The bank and the airline sagas clearly illustrate the range of skills and knowledge required to support an organization's information systems needs. These range from attention to detail to a passion for perfection in routine, day-to-day operational activities; to understanding of and appreciation for the information users require and sensitivity to their training needs; to drawing on vendors' broad range of knowledge; to the programming and project-management skills associated with supporting simultaneously system design, development, implementation, and training; to maintaining several generations of systems; to a broad understanding of how hardware and software evolve and the significance of the changes they occasion in organizations.

Bank of America, American Airlines, and many other organizations organize the information services activity into four functions: evaluation and testing of emerging technologies; management of the development and implementation of IT services; operation of a reliable network of computers and communications services; and liaison with the suppliers who provide and customers who use the information systems. The groups responsible for delivering these services are typically R&D, Project Management, Operations, and Customer Services, respectively.

Navigating the Cascade

Within an organization, the strategic process develops with management's understanding of the broader potential of IT and how, with accompanying changes in organizational structure, it can be applied to resolve business crises. A new information-processing design is seldom well understood in the beginning. Understanding comes with experience, as the management builds competence and accumulates knowledge of how to innovate with technology in a way that broadens its scope and horizons. Further, as the technology is continually expanding its processing capabilities, the team must envision new procedures that exploit the emerging potential, a process we have termed the "cascade." As the technology con-

EXHIBIT 5-1 **Bank of America Cascade**

	CEO	Maestro	Technical Team
Phase 1 Information- processing crisis and search for an IT solution 1950–1954	Perceives magnitude of and engages SRI to help combat, check- processing crisis; re- cruits Zipf as maestro; approves IBM 702 project	Selects credit as trial application and IBM as system vendor; sys- tem analysis projects profit; orders IBM 702 and launches system design	Schedules training for bank managers at IBM computer school; or- ganizes into teams; analyzes loan system
Phase 2 Building IT competence 1954–1956	Reviews design of and contracts with SRI to build ERM; develops IT plan for bank; alters structure of branch organization	Pursues IBM 702 proj- ect with credit users, ERM design with SRI; installs 702s in Los Angeles and San Fran- cisco; builds internal communications system	Designs routines with users; programs sys- tems and trains users; substantiates system savings
Phase 3 Expanding the scope of IT 1956–1958	Arranges demonstra- tion of SRI ERMA; con- tracts with GE to build production model; ex- pands branches and approves credit card system	Participates on ABA committee formulat- ing check-processing standard; expands ap- plication portfolio for 702; establishes user group and creates three-year IT plan	Initiates communica- tions services; ana- lyzes trust systems; establishes exception reporting; develops detailed ERMA plan
Phase 4 Developing plans to exploit dominant design; IT driven strategy 1958–1962	Sees in ERMA rollout opportunity to serve smaller cities; lever- ages 702 to expand product line; develops IT strategy	Is invited to join man- agement committee; saves credit card sys- tem; promotes user portfolio; offers com- puter services and pro- poses upgrade	Continues growing IT organization; installs credit card system and undertakes mas- sive training and con- version effort
Phase 5 Competitors emulate Continues evolving 1962–1968 1968–1978 1978–1991	• Mellon Bank, First Chicago, White Plains, Country Trust, FAST second • Within five years, 85% of checks on MICR • 1964—Federal Reserve Bank requires MICR checks • Decline; bank focuses on cost • Start through cascade. CEOs: Clausen, Armacost, Rosenberg; maestros: Mickel, Hopper, Simmons, Stein		

tinues to evolve, strategic use depends upon staying abreast of changes and the flow of innovation opportunities. This allowed Bank of America and American Airlines to ride the wave of innovation in IT to attain strategic advantage. We now examine, in light of the model elaborated in Chapter 2, the salient actions of the two companies' management teams as they progressed through each phase of the cascade. (See Exhibits 5-1 and 5-2.)

PHASE 1. PROCESSING CRISIS AND SEARCH FOR AN IT SOLUTION. The first condition for our model is a crisis of sufficient proportions to capture the attention of senior management. The early 1950s found Bank of America poised for dramatic growth; already preeminent

EXHIBIT 5-2 **American Airlines Cascade**

	CEO	Maestro	Technical Team
Phase 1 Information- processing crisis and search for an IT solution 1946–1950	Recognizes and real- izes that commitment to jet aircraft will exac- erbate reservations- processing problems; finds in Ammann both maestro and solution	Has reservations needs analysis in hand; prototypes electronic system; engages Teleregister; recruits technicians	Works with Teleregis- ter on system design
Phase 2 Building IT competence 1950–1956	Encourages Ammann to develop idea and find manufacturer; approves Reservisor; reviews needs with Ammann and ap- proves magnetic Reservisor	Oversees installation and testing of and evaluates Reservisor; proposes magnetic drum Reservisor to ac- commodate volume	Works with Teleregis- ter to build Reservisor system; trains system users
Phase 3 Expanding the scope of IT 1956–1959	Contracts with IBM for expanded functional- ity SABRE system; engages ADL as watchdog; appoints Plugge maestro	Oversees development and implementation of magnetic drum Reser- visor; works closely with ADL on IBM con- tract	Performs system cost analysis; studies on- line system needs; pushes technology to limit
Phase 4 Creating design to drive strategy 1959–1966	Molds organization to exploit SABRE; mar- kets SABRE broadly	Reinforces technical team; oversees devel- opment of and transi- tion to SABRE; estab- lishes links to airports	Builds, tests, and re- vises SABRE system; creates new operating system; routinizes sys- tem operation and user training
Phase 5 Competitors, emulation by all 1966–1968	• IBM builds 100-plane SABRE; 50 airlines adopt • EAL's Heinzmann builds 400-plane SABRE; gains lead in IT • UAL and TWA fail to build; buy EAL • Crandall regains momentum; sustains evolving IT strategy		
Continues evolving 1973–present 1968–1972 1972–present	• SABRE rollout; exploit system • Spater stops investing in IT; Plugge sustains IT momentum • Crandall restarts evolving IT strategy		

in California, and constrained by banking regulations from entering other states, it expanded its branch banking facilities from 495 in 1945 to 574 by 1955 and was increasing its customer base faster than the state's 8 percent population growth. (See Figure 5-1.) This rapid expansion accompanied burgeoning check use nationwide, which threatened to overwhelm the banking industry's paper-based check-processing systems. Float was increasing, as were amounts of unknown deposits and obligations, and control was expected to wane further with continued growth. Clark Beise, then a senior vice president, recognizing the magnitude of the impending crisis and unable to interest business equipment manufacturers in developing an automated bookkeeping system, acted on his belief that electron-

FIGURE 5-1   **Bank of America and California Growth**

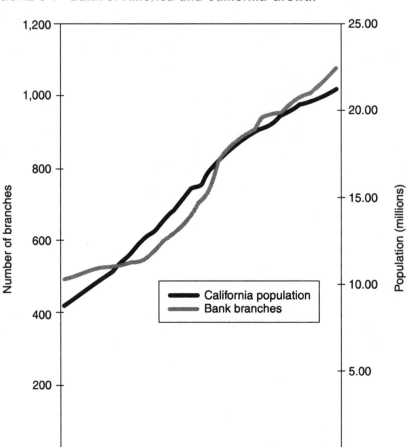

Source: Bank of America, annual reports, 1945–1975.

ics held the key to Bank of America's, and banking's, survival. He quickly responded to the invitation of Stanford Research Institute (SRI) to explore an electronics solution, engaged the research firm to frame a proposal, and authorized a project targeted at finding a solution.

Beise found his maestro in Al Zipf, who in turn assembled a competent technical team. Together they acquired considerable knowledge of the state of electronic-processing technology and the means of applying it to banking. The core of their competence in the development and deployment of IT was the ability to appraise opportunities systematically and revise the process to suit the capabilities of proposed systems.

Beise and Zipf understood that automating existing practice would miss productivity improvements, that entire processes had to be redesigned to take advantage of electronic processing. Consequently, they performed detailed analyses of required functions and invented electronic means to provide those functions. This analysis and design was time consuming, often iterative, and highly dependent on the availability of knowledgeable bankers and systems analysts. The bank's leadership recognized and executed its responsibility to make trade-offs between system and operating costs and service requirements as it sought solutions.

For American Airlines, the crisis was seat reservations. Booking reservations for 100,000 available seats was straining the airline's manual system, resulting in poor inventory management, overbooking, and lost reservations. Manifests, arriving barely before passenger loading, were invariably in error — and the greater speed and seating capacity of jet aircraft, which C. R. Smith was committed to acquiring, would exacerbate these problems.

Smith's routine field visits had turned up Ammann's analysis of the airline's reservations systems' needs and, inclined toward an electronic solution, Smith had acted upon it. Advised by his maestro-to-be that the technology could not maintain an accurate, up-to-date, remotely accessible inventory of passenger seats, Smith, to forestall further degradation in customer service, had authorized Charles Ammann to pursue a partial solution.

Ammann subsequently interested the Teleregister Company in producing a prototype, and Smith's involvement legitimated the effort. Although Smith informed the airline's board of directors and kept his vice president of Finance apprised of financial needs, he effectively ran the project with Ammann and the reservations manager. He was able to maintain momentum with only modest oversight, relying on his knowledge of individuals and the force of the culture to create and fill positions. He was an orchestrator of movers and shakers.

PHASE 2. BUILDING IT COMPETENCE. Beise tracked his initial IT project closely, meeting weekly with the SRI team to review design decisions. He continually altered project objectives to suit the bank's purposes, authorizing additional funding as needed to carry the project forward. Recognizing the potential to outflank manufacturers in producing a bank-oriented design, Beise backed away from a full-blown banking system in favor of a more readily developed limited functionality pilot for check processing to prove the design quickly.

Beise had approved Zipf's request to explore additional opportunities for using computers. The CEO wished to gain perspective on the economics and personnel needs associated with computing and on the idea that the exercise might serve to season a manager for the system that was to emerge from the SRI project. But he also viewed the exploration as an opportunity to test his new maestro's ability. Beise met weekly with Zipf and frequently discussed alternatives with him on the telephone, a practice he continued throughout his tenure.

As former operations managers, Zipf and his team brought to their analysis of loan-processing applications firsthand knowledge of the managers and procedures. It was thus relatively straightforward for them to work with the responsible managers to redesign work flows. After performing time studies and developing new flow diagrams, the teams defined the procedures to be altered or eliminated and detailed system costs for auto loans and credit applications.

When it became apparent that Bank of America's first application would provide management information about the process it was to automate, a user team was assigned to assess the system's impact on overall management of activities as well as work flow. Zipf and the technical teams worked with the managers and work-flow analysts to sort out new jobs and functions in parallel with system development. When the system was ready for test, individuals trained by the Operations group as test agents were available to evaluate proposed job descriptions and functions. Their direct involvement led the credit managers to become as committed to the project as the system team and established a tradition of involving work-flow analysts and line managers early on to consider role shifts.

The loan systems were subsequently programmed and tested by the technical teams while Zipf continued to oversee SRI's development of the prototype check-processing system. Implementation audits of the loan systems projected a positive cash flow from savings in the fourth year and a net profit from labor savings in the fifth (the systems promised to eliminate 200 man-years of clerical work). Moreover, costs remained relatively fixed as volume increased and the programs could be expanded to include more functions, generating more labor savings. Finally, skills and knowledge derived from development of the loan systems were directly transferable to most consumer credit products. These kinds of results enabled Zipf to pose automation opportunities to management as positive cash-flow ventures and thereby establish IT as an acceptable form of business investment.

American Airlines' reservations problem, although tougher than the bank's check-processing bind, was more focused, and Ammann, a brilliant engineer, understood it and could work with electronics engineers. The systems he developed with Teleregister tested the economics of electronics and established the value and potential of accessible electronic memory as the core of the reservations system.

With the deployment of the electronic memory Reservisor system, American's planning focus shifted from hardware testing to implementation. In the absence of an overall integrated plan for exploiting IT, Smith worked with individual departments to develop new procedures for linking to the system.

Reservisor improved the accuracy of reservations data, thereby reducing the occasional flailing over status, and provided an additional inventory control check. The system did not appreciably change the organization beyond reducing the number of telephone calls agents were required to make and reducing somewhat the number of agents and clerical staff. It did add a few technologists and required some new skills by reservations operators. A compromise system designed to enable the airline to keep pace with the increased productivity of jet aircraft, Reservisor lacked the important capacity to accommodate passenger name data. Nevertheless, two versions of Reservisor afforded Smith an appreciation for the complexities and costs associated with electronics and perspective on the magnitude of the problem and potential for a solution.

PHASE 3. EXPANDING THE SCOPE OF IT. Beise, recognizing almost from the beginning that the technology would have a strong impact on Bank of America's organization, had begun early to alter organizational structure to take advantage of the potential of IT, and the bank had exhibited a willingness to experiment. Beise, who knew that ERMA provided a leap to all-electronic banking, sought to assure that the new product met the bank's needs, not the manufacturer's. His decision to go with General Electric (GE) reflected an economic and strategic persuasion; Beise knew that Zipf would ensure a fit with their needs and that GE would not fail in such a high-profile project. To provide an added base of experience, he expanded the scope of the IBM 702 across all credit products as well as trust services. In the process, Systems and Equipment Research (S&ER) grew to be the most influential force in bank operations.

Zipf managed to mold the design of ERMA to include proofing as well as automating bookkeeping, assuring the bank and the industry of eliminating manual inputs, which created the base for all-electronic banking. With that in mind, he expanded to the IBM 7070 and introduced services to small businesses, creating not only a new use of IT but also a large new market. The planning for the potential implementation of ERMA in parallel with the development of the system is a model of the deployment of innovative IT systems.

Organizational maturation was in evidence in Bank of America's ability to manage simultaneously two highly complex system expansions while experimenting and providing new services. The bank had mastered the art of detailed long-range planning for service-oriented computer systems. That the most serious glitches in the ERMA rollout were construction delays caused by weather is attributable largely to the bank's balanced focus that held human and systems planning to be equally important.

Planning at the bank never stopped. Management reviewed current and anticipated demand, expected alternatives at least quarterly, and involved staff in tracking outside developments; senior management continually reviewed customer needs for market opportunities; technology scanning was combined with an ongoing review of capacity and how bottlenecks might be alleviated by new technologies. When a need existed and a system to meet it did not, the technical teams confidently created one.

American Airlines had shifted from an incremental to a massive development program with the inauguration of the SABRE project. Bill Hogan was charged with managing costs and risks, Marion Sadler with integrating IT into operations, and Fred Plugge with leading the project. Because the airline lacked deep technical expertise, it engaged Arthur D. Little to evaluate the vendor's efforts. Regulated competition and service on assigned routes being key in the airline industry, Smith was not given to strategic discussions. Nor did he institute a formal planning process, the critical decisions being related to obtaining routes and aircraft and attracting customers. Smith held American's strategy in his head and discussed it with his management team; the latter expanded uses of IT within the context of improving service and inventory control and exploiting through marketing the availability of computerized reservations. The team understood the strategy, and Plugge delivered within this framework.

Early IT innovations at American had proved the value of information processing and the long-run economics but had not made an appreciable impact on the organization or on the management of its business. The technology was capable only of automating a portion of the task and for a relatively small segment of the market. Therefore, management had no experience with an all-electronic base. Implementation had consisted of automating clerical tasks at one or two reservations sites. The potential of SABRE was to centralize the organization's inventory status, leading to dramatically centralizing the airline's procedures. Sadler was responsible for reorganizing the effort and directing the marketing program. He focused on developing a training program and marketing the promise of reliable reservations to American's customers.

PHASE 4. IMPLEMENTING THE DESIGN. As he gained perspective in developing ERMA on the organizational impact and potential of his banking systems, Clark Beise began to envision how IT innovation might enable Bank of America to become more efficient and expand market share. To take advantage of newly available economies of scale and realize the fullest payback on its IT investments, he dramatically increased the number of branches.

His conviction that IT could serve Bank of America as a means to achieve competitive advantage led Beise to press for its assimilation into the broader processes and activities of the organization. Beise centralized check processing and decentralized marketing as the new system supported more rapid product growth. He had pursued decentralization more broadly by designating functional field staffs to oversee branch operations from regional centers. As automation transformed the branches, S&ER had become a dominant influence, seeking out the best-run branches and establishing a strong field network of "doers." To encourage them to function as business developers and emphasize customer service, branch managers had been given dual reporting responsibilities — to the president and regional credit managers and to Al Zipf and his area managers.

Zipf had further extended the domain of IT by strategically placing key members of his core teams. Mel Gienapp, who had managed the bank's highly reliable data operations function, lobbied in Corporate Personnel for staffing and salary levels and the delineation of career paths for S&ER; Hugh Dougherty, a key systems project leader, managed new developments that led eventually to the formation of the Business Services group; Russell Fenwick was a key planner of new projects, facilities, and systems. The base of Bank of America's IT competence was distributed throughout the organization. Most managers had been involved in planning and implementing IT systems, and as bank operations became more dependent on these systems, their planning and operation became topics of discussion at all levels of management. Beise had effectively made IT a normal part of bank operations and management.

Beise's longer-term goal was to make Bank of America the low-cost deliverer of, and market leader and innovator in, new electronic-based services. Beise shared with a handful of senior managers an emerging vision of how the organization might function around an improved electronic information-processing base. His discussions with Zipf about such strategic issues as the status of outside suppliers and the progress of the check-processing system and credit applications established a continuing dialogue on electronic banking that Beise subsequently formalized.

Attesting to the efficacy of the bank's strategy were growth in the customer base and number of services per customer and more rapid growth in profits than in market share, suggesting that economy of scale had been achieved. By 1960 the bank had a five-year plan for new products and was awaiting the arrival of a new-generation computer and installing a low-cost microwave communication system. Continuing to hustle for new markets for IT, Zipf, by then a member of the senior management committee, compiled a portfolio of useful projects. On finding an interested user, he would commit his technical team to work with the group to establish the scope of the project, develop a project proposal, and provide systems analysis support. He gradually institutionalized this process, thereby embedding in the overall management scheme the transition from pure entrepreneurial effort to managing an evolving strategy.

As it emerged a technological leader, Bank of America was besieged with proposals from innovative electronic companies throughout the country. The bank maintained close contacts with most innovators in electronics and provided funds, project management, and professional support for trials of emerging technologies. It was a test site for early commercial microwave, which met its needs for electronic communication among its many branches. Even joint ventures that failed in the literal sense, such as two early image-processing systems, lent the bank perspective on what might work.

Marion Sadler, subsequently charged with managing the deployment and encouraging use of the SABRE system, distributed terminals to airports and operations centers to provide timely information for flight preparation and crews. American Airlines' SABRE system had multiplied manyfold the airline's capacity for handling telephone calls, accommodating seat availability inquiries, booking reservations, and selling tickets. Moreover, the system provided a solid foundation of technology and skills to support further system development aimed at improving customer service, flight operations, and management control. Most important, it provided an accessible base of accurate information that could be used to improve operations, marketing, and planning.

The American team exploited throughout the airline information made available by the SABRE system. George Spater developed a marketing program that reduced double booking and guided the development of a flight operations system designed to tailor numbers of meals, fuel, and service requirements to expected numbers of passengers. Hogan developed a detailed flight profit analysis system that optimized the use of jet aircraft with respect to load factor. Plugge improved SABRE's reliability and strove to improve the airports' and marketing groups' management information. These aggregate efforts resulted in profits that exceeded the industry average within one year.

Smith and Sadler quickly moved to centralize reservations services and to exploit the potential of the accessible accurate data, which were to become the nerve center for the airline's strategy. They were quite effective in marketing their advantage in accurate reservations and grew in market share. With SABRE's elimination of manual clerical activities, the limiting factor became the load the computer system could support, whereupon the technical team's focus shifted to maintaining stable operations and dealing with technical problems. As the number of airports linked to the system increased, a new communications system emerged; it centralized previously local activities such as flight status and rendered the airline a more coordinated entity. Yet Smith did not alter formal organizational structure; except for a modest set of centralized activities, the airline remained geographically organized by airport.

PHASE 5. EVOLVING IT STRATEGY AND EMULATION OF DESIGN. The size of the banking market and existence of an American Bankers Association committee charged with developing a standard for check processing led a number of manufacturers to launch development projects aimed at influencing implementation of the standard. By the time General Electric delivered the ERMA check-processing system to Bank of America, IBM, NCR, and Burroughs, among other companies, were selling future deliveries of their systems. Market forces and a specified standard had created an operational base for design.

Clark Beise continued to innovate and to sustain an evolving information technology strategy by building on Bank of America's electronic base as a means to grow market share and broaden product line. Confident the electronic base could avoid earlier debacles, he initiated the credit card effort as a new form of financial services, and Zipf proved Beise's point. Beise later supported Zipf's entrance into Business Services, which established one of the first demonstrations of the value of an established electronic link. Over the next four years the bank expanded scope via this link and grew markets.

The critical resource in implementing a standard-conforming check-processing system was management competence to initiate and oversee development of innovative applications, electronics systems experience, and willingness to invest in hardware and staff. Manufacturers, though willing to train staff and provide services, were strapped for capable personnel, making it difficult to assemble and field competent teams. Bank of America's leadership in proprietary services and credit applications was solid, as imitation would require equivalent technical competence. Early entry into the market and economy of scale had enabled the bank to evolve an IT-based business strategy well in advance of its competitors. Moreover, its experience with credit applications afforded perspective on bringing up its check-processing system, a transition that, because of equipment failures, cost many other banks customers.

The shift in leadership could not have happened at a worse time, as Bank of America was facing its first true information technology crisis since the early days. Neither the bank nor IBM understood the true complexity and magnitude of the processing requirements. The continued failures and drop in earnings caused by interruptions resulted in a dramatic shift in power away from IT and to the unsympathetic and uninformed line managers' focusing on overseas markets. The rapid growth potential in California was gone and IT's overseas potential seemed modest. With no clear replacement for Zipf, the bank became maestroless and its competence atrophied over a twelve-year period.

As American Airlines was gaining momentum, Smith left for Washington, Sadler retired, and Spater took over. Spater, who lacked hands-on experience in the development of IT systems, left the project leaderless as he became enamored of external projects and allowed their momentum to slacken and then stop. The centralization of the organization of reservations, planning, and marketing ground to a halt. Fortunately, Plugge sustained the airline's technical and therefore IT competence, allowing Robert Crandall, on appraising the system, to quickly make IT a vital top management issue. He hired James O'Neill and encouraged Max Hopper to roll out terminals to regain organizational competence. Its ability to come from behind and pass the leaders is a testimony to management's IT and leadership skills.

The histories confirm the force of IT as a perpetual change agent in unlocking new opportunities for knowledgeable IT entrepreneurs. Thus, to stay in the lead, a firm must continually stay abreast of developments by exploring the use of emerging technology to better understand its potential impact on services and organizational roles. Crandall's evolving IT strategy has sustained American's lead and forced the airline's competitors to continuously match the leader's in order to stay abreast. The potential mergers of reservations centers may result eventually in four global multi-airline systems. Since the frequent-flier program, there have been no glamorous leapfrog innovations, but most airlines have continued to invest in improving their ability to manage yield, seat availability, and marketing efforts.[1]

Fast-Second Emulation

There were fast seconds in both industries. In banking, all the members of the American Bankers Association (ABA) technical subcommittees were experimenting with some form of information technology in the 1950s. They visited one another's sites and exchanged war stories. As Bank of America was receiving its ERMA, Mellon Bank, First National banks of Boston, Chicago, and New York, County Trust of White Plains, and Wachovia Bank had all brought up loan systems and were in the process of implementing MICR-type systems. Most were up and running within a year of ERMA. Industrywide standards provide a basis for all competitors that exchange information. The sooner all players adopt them, the more efficient all become by not having to deal with multiple systems. The ABA committee's purposeful educational program had made most large banks aware of the potential and need to change.

The airline problem was more complex than banking's, as it stretched the competence of existing technology in providing online access to a large inventory of seats by simultaneous users. Only Frank Heinzmann at Delta/Eastern had been staying abreast of the developments at American and IBM, and he quickly began to develop a system on IBM's emerging new model 360 to meet the needs of a large airline. IBM itself reengineered the product to a smaller hundred-plane system because it knew that it would find a ready market. Most small airlines quickly acquired the SABRE system.

United Airlines, which had been working with Univac, had automated maintenance and a few accounting activities. It was in the process of experimenting with a Univac system for reservations when SABRE was announced. Neither Univac nor United Air Lines managers had the firsthand experience of on-line storage processes and grossly underestimated the capacity requirements. TWA, which had been working with Burroughs on financial accounting applications and worldwide ticketing, also lacked the real-time perspective that IBM had gained with the development of the early-warning SAGE system. Both also underestimated the system requirements. For the medium sized airlines, the hundred-plane IBM system was a godsend, particularly as IBM trained their systems personnel and developed a programmed implementation process.

Within five years of the debut of American Airlines' SABRE system, most small airlines had respectable reservations systems. With all airlines possessing roughly equivalent capabilities, it became management's prerogative to use the systems merely to process reservations or as a means to compete. American chose the latter course, leading — and being followed — in cultivating the travel agency channel for ticket sales and introducing innovative programs such as its frequent-flyer plan.

In both industries an IT dominant design emerged which fundamentally changed the nature of competition and became necessary to complete. In banking the system provided enormous cost savings and true economies of scale in an industry that had been limited by manual check processing with modest potential in punched-card systems for automation. In the airlines the new system was a competitive force because an airline could guarantee a seat in a market where competition was based on service. All competitors quickly adopted it and have made marginal innovations since. As information technology continues to grow in power and dramatically drops in cost, merely making marginal improvements in processing may not be adequate, as shown by Bank of America and American Airlines. A new design emerged in both their industries within seven years after they had established the dominant design.

The airline hiccuped and lost its leadership position, but the IT management team maintained its technological base by swapping software and moving to the new system 360 to stay abreast technologically. When the Casey-Crandall team took over and reinstituted an evolving IT strategy, American could quickly regain momentum and take the lead in establishing the next move in the dominant design. Since that time it has sustained its leadership with the frequent-flyer plan, yield management of pricing, and customer-focused marketing.

The bank in shifting to new leadership also changed strategy to an overseas focus and did not perceive any competitive advantage in IT abroad. Shifting leaders uninformed on the nature of IT quickly eliminated the bank's managerial competence to guide an evolving IT strategy at a time when the technology was gaining momentum in banking. Moving to a cost focus and ignoring IT at the top lost the bank its leadership and technical competence and eventually created the need for an enormous investment over several years to regain its competence and catch up with the evolving design.

The technology today is changing at an accelerating rate, and new opportunities exist for management teams that understand its potential and have the competence to create and implement new designs. Our analysis documents the competencies of the pioneers. To substantiate its validity in the present era, new pioneers must develop and innovate architecture that exploits the potential of IT.

Generalizing the Model

It is often the case that models seem almost intuitive with hindsight. Thus, it might seem entirely reasonable that a firm which would execute technological innovations of strategic import would require a technological maestro who has the interest and support of the CEO and the commitment of an effective technical team. It might not be as readily intuited that industry-transforming innovations are precipitated by industry crises, but phases 3 and 4 of the cascade, expanding the scope of IT and using IT to drive strategy and enable structure, are subjects of one or more books, and phase 5, emulation, draws on work done on dominant design in manufacturing by William Abernathy and James Utterback.[2]

What the model does tell us is new and interesting is (1) that all these elements, the three roles and five phases, are essential to industry-transforming innovations, and (2) that it is highly idiosyncratic, being influenced by a host of factors, including the nature of the industry and crisis, the state of the technology, company culture, and the personalities, management styles, and skills of the individuals who fill the various roles. Bank of America and American Airlines, as we have seen, filled these roles and negotiated these phases in sometimes dramatically different ways. But both companies stalled when one of the roles went unfilled or one of the phases was neglected. The essence, even at United and TWA, was to learn how to use the technology competently and adapt the organization to exploit its potential.

But inasmuch as we have acknowledged that the bank and airline were pioneers, and that technology changes rapidly, the question that might be asked is, Does the model hold for companies attempting to innovate in the context of modern technology? In the following chapter, we examine three companies that have more recently transformed, or are in the process of transforming, the dominant design of information processing in their industries.

Notes

1. Espen Andersen, "American Airlines: The InterAAct Project (A) and (B)," Case Nos. 9-193-013 and 9-193-014 (Boston: Harvard Business School, 1993).

2. W. J. Abernathy and James M. Utterback, "Patterns of Innovation in Technology," *Technology Review* 80, no. 7 (1978).

Chapter 6

Industry-Transforming Information-Processing Designs and Modern Technology

American Airlines and Bank of America employed an infant information technology to create dominant designs for information processing in their industries. The challenges and opportunities associated with molding fledgling devices and techniques into effective state-of-the-art processing systems are substantively different from those associated with engineering such systems from mature technologies offered and supported by an experienced vendor base.

We identified in the bank and the airline the essential roles of CEO, maestro, and technical team and delineated the five phases of the cascade. To establish whether these roles and phases were peculiar to the act of pioneering or essential to the creation of a dominant design, we studied the players in, and paths taken by, three other companies that have established, or are in the process of establishing, the dominant design for information processing in their industries. We selected United Services Automobile Association, Frito-Lay, and American Hospital Supply on the basis of differences in their market strategies, innovative use of information technology (IT) systems, and management processes.

United Services Automobile Association and Frito-Lay initially had to catch up to an existing dominant design for information processing before creating innovative systems that changed it.

American Hospital Supply, on the other hand, had invented in a punched-card inventory system a forerunner of electronic data interchange; the company's task was to integrate this innovation into a standard logistics system. The CEOs guided their management teams through the grid from automating to a strategic use of IT by transforming their organizations. We introduce each company and its key players and trace its progress through the cascade of activities that yielded, or is in the process of yielding, a new dominant design for information processing in its industry.

American Hospital Supply

Founded in 1922 by Foster McGaw, American Hospital Supply Corporation (AHSC) grew beyond its original base near Chicago into a nationwide distributor through regional offices, its growth spurred by McGaw's policies of fair published prices and a tradition of timely service. After World War II, the company expanded into such patient-care products as prepared intravenous solutions and began to manufacture as well as distribute hospital supplies. It continued to grow rapidly with McGaw's emphasis on customer service — meaning low price and reliable delivery — fostered by encouraging all units to be measured on bottom-line results and to operate as individual profit centers. McGaw's style was to encourage innovations that helped the customer. Published price lists represented the lid; all salespeople had data on full costs and could set prices to achieve sales and profit objectives.[1] In 1956 McGaw authorized his chief financial officer to implement a punched-card system for inventory control and to automate accounts receivable.

In 1958 the company split into two divisions, the Scientific Product division, which included several independent companies that produced and shipped supplies and equipment, and the AHS division, which managed the regional warehouses that supplied hospitals. Warehouses, like divisions, were rewarded according to their bottom-line figures and operated independently of headquarters.

In 1963, the Stanford Medical Center and an enterprising AHSC West Coast regional warehouse manager initiated a crude electronic data interchange. This system, which provided the conceptual base that expanded throughout the company, enabled AHSC to grow faster than the rest of the health care industry during the early years of Medicare; AHSC reached $1 billion in sales in 1975 and $2 billion in 1979. By 1984 AHSC boasted approximately 150 distribution cen-

EXHIBIT 6-1 **Development of the AHS Dominant Design**

Year(s)	Event	Significance
1956	McGaw authorized punched cards for inventory control	Provides an organized set of procedures
1963	Regional manager creates automated order system	Provides electronic link to customer; improves sales
1964	McGaw backs broad use of Tel-American	Gains operational competence with links to customers
1965	McGaw approves computer study of inventory control	Initiates system design of inventory/order cycle
1966	Doerhoefer develops into maestro; builds system in house	Involves managers in appraising IT; develops IT competence
1967–1972	Convert TelAmerican to distributed systems and links	Improves link to customers with IT
1973–1975	Bays becomes CEO; focuses on link as means to grow	Provides proactive IT strategy — ASAP with programmatic objectives
1976–1985	Actively manage customers; tighten interdependence	Relies on customer information inventory; full product line
1985–present	Merge with Baxter; networks continue to evolve	Expands ASAP to broader market; sales expand dramatically worldwide
1986–present	Competitors finally create links and begin to contest	

ters worldwide; products created in its more than 4 million square feet of manufacturing space constituted 46 percent of sales and had a 42 percent share of the hospital supply market. In 1985 it was acquired by Baxter Travenol. Exhibit 6-1 summarizes the management actions in AHS/Baxter Travenol's course through the cascade.

The AHSC Innovation Team

Two American Hospital Supply Corporation CEOs, Foster McGaw and Karl Bays, led the company's development of an industry-transforming information-processing design. AHSC's assimilation of IT began in the late 1950s with McGaw's support for the implementation of a punched-card system designed to streamline order entry, inventory control, and invoicing. Exhibit 6-2 traces the events in the development of AHSC's IT strategy.

The 1963 electronic link allowed customers to telecommunicate order information recorded on punched cards. The link not only reduced costs and improved accuracy, but its convenience led to

EXHIBIT 6-2 **American Hospital Supply Cascade**

	CEO	**Maestro**	**Technical Team**
Phase 1 Information- processing crisis and search for an IT solution 1963–1964	Promotes TelAmerican punched-card inven- tory-control system; urges local managers to link to system	No maestro involved at this stage	Small team of accoun- tants payables and re- ceivables personnel design and installs inventory-order punched card
Phase 2 Building IT competence 1964–1968	Overcomes distrust after system halts cen- tral operations; ap- proves expansion; organizes IT as a profit center; hires Doerhoefer as maestro	Halts deployment; shifts development from accountants to managers; reviews IT plan and implements system	Technologists imple- ment minicomputer warehouse systems; extends TelAmeri- can's needs for new system
Phase 3 Expanding the scope of IT 1968–1972	Approves expanded functionality; 1965, De- Witt CEO; 1970, Bays becomes CEO; pro- motes links to custom- ers and establishes IT as basis of strategy	Oversees develop- ment of central sys- tem; maintains tight control of funds and gains support of us- ers; creates evolving IT system	Develops central system and transfers from minicomputers; adds functions and continues database to initiate ASAP support
Phase 4 Using IT to enable structure and drive strategy 1972–1985	Focuses on customer; contracts for volume and guaranteed cost; reinforces links within the organization and with customers	Analyzes management and customer needs and develops cus- tomer systems; estab- lishes strategic- product portfolio	Develops system to customer specifica- tions; expands func- tionality and provides seamless services; converts old systems to new ones
Phase 5 1985–1987	Baxter acquires AHS; continues evolving IT strategy Competitors finally build their own links to suppliers		

increased sales volume. McGaw quickly encouraged other regions to adopt the process, which was marketed as TelAmerican.[2] The electronic link captured the imagination of Chicago regional sales manager Karl Bays, who became a product champion for IT as a means to reduce hospital supply costs and grow market share.[3] Bob DiVall, CFO, proposed to McGaw, on the basis of their accountants' analysis, that they automate the punched-card system with a computer system. McGaw approved the project because it promised improved service and reduced costs. DiVall relied on the accounting firm to develop the system, with an AHS sales manager as coordinator.

Harry DeWitt, on becoming CEO in 1965, emphasized traditional sales efforts over IT, but Bays, when he succeeded DeWitt in 1970, restored IT as the cornerstone of AHSC's strategy. In 1971 Bays named John Crotty vice president of Planning and charged him with developing a plan with a longer-term focus. The resulting strategy, based on expanding the functionality of the managed electronic link between AHSC and its customers, set the stage for a massive new investment in IT that fueled double-digit growth and dominance of the hospital supply business (see Table 6-1).

AHSC's first maestro, Ed Doerhoefer, a division controller with prior IT experience, sustained the momentum of IT development through three CEOs. DiVall asked him to complete an inventory-control system that had been proposed and designed by AHSC's accounting firm and to push more general use of information technology. Doerhoefer first developed an implementation program designed to raise managers' understanding of their role in and the resources needed to complete the system design. He subsequently recruited a group of outstanding technicians, among them Lynn Brown, who was to become the technical architect and developer of AHSC's systems. Doerhoefer's annual challenge was to gain budget commitment from users; the CEO could lead, but the maestro had to provide the context.

Division managers developed their own budgets, and the Information Systems function charged for services with the objective of showing a zero balance at year end. Doerhoefer expended considerable effort gaining management's understanding of IT costs and benefits. Over the next fifteen years, his team was to create an evolving link that moved from order entry to managing inventories. Reluctant to convert to a new system because of timing issues, Doerhoefer moved on to a senior IT planning role, whereupon Mike Heschell became Bays's new maestro. Heschell initiated a massive conversion to a new IBM system; after a brief hiatus for system adoption, it improved reliability.

Lynn Brown, director of the R&D Systems Group, expanded the early TelAmerican system and added several major enhancements. The key technical architects of a series of innovations, he and his team subsequently sustained the system through two major computer conversions while continuing to support systems implemented as early as 1965. Carl Steiner, an early systems planner, became a metronome for the planning activity as AHSC rolled out multiple new services. An able and forward-looking integrator of the divisions and IT group, Steiner worked with users to define new applications, providing the impetus for Doerhoefer to create the electronic infrastructure.

TABLE 6-1   American Hospital Supply Corporation, Financial Comparison 1974–1984 ($ in millions)

Operating Statistics for Continuing Operations	1974	1975	1976	1977	1978	1979	1980[a]	1981	1982	1983	1984
Net Sales	$915.3	$1,065.3	$1,238.2	$1,364.4	$1,619.5	$1,928.1	$2,261.9	$2,260.0	$2,965.8	$3,310.5	$3,448.5
Earnings from Continuing Operations	$42.4	$50.2	$58.5	$70.1	$81.3	$100.0	$117.1	$133.5	$170.0	$211.9	$237.8
Increase over Previous Years:											
Net Sales	18.7%	16.4%	16.2%	10.2%	18.7%	19.1%	17.3%	17.6%	11.5%	11.6%	4.2%
Earnings	12.4%	18.5%	16.4%	19.9%	16.1%	22.9%	17.1%	14.0%	27.4%	24.6%	12.2%

Source: Adapted from "American Hospital Supply Corporation: The ASAP System (A)," Case 9-186-005 (Boston: Harvard Business School, 1986).
[a]In 1980, AHS changed to the last-in, first-out method of determining cost for substantially all U.S. inventories.

Genesis of an Information-Processing Design

Technological developments in science and electronics precipitated explosive proliferation in the health care industry. Electronic instrumentation, new surgical treatments, dramatic growth in disposable items ranging from bed linens to electronic solutions, and a move to cheap, disposable supplies expanded the industry's stable 30,000-item product base by hundreds of new items per year, necessitating increases in warehouse size and complicating inventory control.

PHASE 1. INFORMATION-PROCESSING CRISIS AND SEARCH FOR AN IT SOLUTION. In 1956 McGaw, with AHSC's accounting firm, initiated a study that led to punched-card automation of inventory control, order processing, and billing. The system that was subsequently developed improved accuracy and reduced clerical costs. However, the genesis of what would eventually become a dominant design for information processing in the health care industry was, as previously noted a rudimentary communications system developed by Frank Wolfe, a San Francisco sales manager, in 1963. He worked with Lamar Lee, director of the Stanford Medical facility, to improve delivery and service and reduce the institution's complex inventory requirements. Wolfe, relying on an IBM card reader, devised a means to transmit via telephone part numbers from the hospital to an AHSC keypunch. The easy-to-use system reduced errors, improved service, and increased sales, characteristics that led McGaw to encourage other regional sales managers to adopt the system. Packaged as TelAmerican, it eventually provided a vital link to more than 900 major customers. AHSC's systems group added a Telephone American component that enabled customers to call into a warehouse and order by numbers. A clerk selected inventory cards and inserted a customer's heading for order processing and billing. AHSC was an early user of IT for support and the first company to use electronic data interchange (EDI) with customers.

PHASE 2. BUILDING IT COMPETENCE. In 1964, concurrently with the introduction of the TelAmerican system, McGaw approved the recommendation of Bob DiVall, his vice president for Finance, to purchase a computer system to automate the ordering process. DiVall engaged AHSC's accounting firm, which conducted an analysis that promised solid cost savings from an order entry and accounts receivable system with input and printer systems located at each warehouse linked to a central system in Chicago. McGaw transferred a sales manager to ensure that the project preserved a customer focus.

When McGaw became chairman of the board, he was succeeded by Harry DeWitt, a seasoned producer of technically oriented products steeped in the decentralized philosophy of the Scientific Products division. DeWitt, uncomfortable with the centralization aspects of the new system, became a passive observer, delegating all IT responsibility to DiVall. Bays, the product champion for IT, was effective in maintaining momentum, while McGaw, as chairman, remained a presence.

After an eighteen-month conversion program led by the accountants' system group to install and roll out the system to thirty-two warehouses, the Chicago region tested it but was forced to shut it down because it generated inaccurate invoices and orders. DeWitt's hands-off attitude had so permeated the management group that no member had participated in the system's design or implementation.[4]

DiVall transferred Ed Doerhoefer from controller to IT manager to regain momentum. After studying the system and past project planning, Doerhoefer spent a month involving managers in an analysis of the system's potential and their role in guiding its design and implementation. With management agreement, he restarted the effort and secured DiVall's approval to shift quickly to internal development, the project representing a long-term investment that could be linked to the TelAmerican program.

The new system controlled inventories, billing, accounts receivable, and shipments to regional warehouses and customers. It provided a base to grow TelAmerican as an interactive link. Gary Nei, hired by Bays in 1969 to be product manager for systems marketing, began a study of new features that would allow TelAmerican to provide better services. His thrust was to help hospitals improve their inventory management systems to reduce their inventories as well as AHS's delivery cost.

The growth in sales pressed the distributed minicomputer system, and Doerhoefer, with Bays' support plus the strength of the systems market growth, shifted to a Burroughs mainframe system to centralize their effort. The new system proved a solid support and the base for further expansion of TelAmerican. On becoming CEO, Bays was immediately approached by Brown, who suggested a Touch-Tone telephone system complement to the TelAmerican system. Bays then authorized a development program as the first step in revitalizing TelAmerican.[5]

PHASE 3. EXPANDING THE SCOPE OF IT. Bays, DiVall, and Doerhoefer expanded the charter of IT from a cost focus to improving sales, and Bays promptly expanded the TelAmerican system to provide access to AHSC's entire product line. With his vision of becoming the prime vendor to hospitals, he inaugurated a program to help them reorganize their ordering procedures to reduce costs and improve service in the face of growing and expensive inventories. Bays named John Crotty strategic planner and worked with him and the management team to forge an IT-based strategic plan, the foundation of which was the use of TelAmerican as a means of providing service, reducing hospital costs, and expanding AHSC's share of each hospital's business.

Bays was unable to persuade three of the more successful Scientific Products Division's companies to join TelAmerican, as they enjoyed control and were very profitable. But when the CEOs of three of the largest and most prestigious hospitals complained about the added cost of dealing with these independents, Bays broke the tradition of independence, deftly coercing the divisions' CEOs to adopt TelAmerican as their channel of distribution. His objective was to provide a complete product line for AHSC's customers.

Crotty's plan called for establishing a prime supplier relationship with customers that would build on AHSC's broad product line and the strength of its electronic links. When discontinuation of support for the terminal component threatened disruption of the TelAmerican system, Brown, working with a Scientific Product division, developed a tailored TekPro terminal that provided customers a new level of functionality. Bays subsequently announced an improved link between hospitals and warehouses, dubbed Analytic Systems Automatic Purchasing, or ASAP, which placed renewed emphasis on expanding the functionality and sales capability of the TelAmerican system. Automating the link established a vital marketing system.

PHASE 4. USING IT TO ENABLE STRUCTURE AND DRIVE STRATEGY. In the mid-1970s, Doerhoefer was directed to develop full service connections for customer inventories. Crotty, in the context of the strategic-planning process, sketched out a series of increased functionality ASAP models to provide the links. Bays, with manager of Sole Sourcing Gary Nei, assembled a team with expertise in purchasing and inventory control to design a just-in-time type of materials management system to improve the hospital inventory management function, which tended to be staffed by low-paid, undermanaged employees saddled with inefficient processes. They organized a prime vendor program whose guaranteed lower inventory costs to hospitals encouraged them to contract with AHS to redesign their inventory systems and implement the latest version of ASAP. Doerhoefer and Brown formed an advanced systems team that developed a series of ASAP releases, each of which added functionality and strengthened the link to hospitals. They simultaneously expanded their product line to meet more than 80 percent of typical hospital needs. The program was an instant success, generating increased sales and eventually enlisting as subscribers 5,500 of the total census of 6,900 hospitals.

As the marketing effort gained momentum, the ASAP system was expanded. ASAP2, which permitted messages to be edited and substitute supplies to be recommended or back-ordered, was useful as a communication system between AHS and its customers. ASAP2 implemented two-way communication and made AHS's marketing program more service oriented, increased the company's market penetration, and supported field service teams. Innovations such as customer profiles that traced goods shipments enabled hospitals to establish economic order quantities, safety stocks, and reorder points that served to bring their inventory investment down.

AHS moved its systems strategy to a new level with the 1981 implementation of ASAP3, which supported inventory management by customers' using their own numbering systems and accepted bar-coded input. The terminal growth shown in Figure 6-1[6] resulted in the sales and profit growth shown in Table 6-1, providing clear evidence of the system's market impact. An adaptation to the mainframe computer system extended the capabilities of ASAP3 from receive and respond to full electronic exchange of information, effectively rendering AHS an integrated materials management function of the hospitals it served. At the same time, a reverse ASAP was created to support automatic ordering from outside suppliers.

With ASAP4, introduced two years later, AHS became an integrated service function for its more sophisticated customers, providing a seamless link that enabled customer systems to generate orders automatically using any part number from any published catalog. The system dramatically reduced AHS's operating costs by automating order processing, delivery, and customer confirmation. AHS sales teams included system analysts, materials management

FIGURE 6-1 **ASAP Installations 1979–1989**

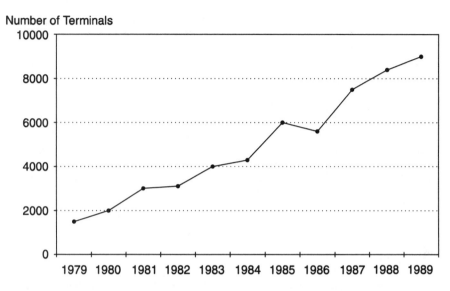

Number of Terminals

specialists, and trainers to help customers exploit the potential of ASAP4.

Even as the latest release of ASAP expanded AHSC's market share and profits, the company strove to maintain its links to hospitals, notably smaller ones, that continued to use previous genera-tions of the system. When ASAP5 was introduced in 1985, providing off-line entry via personal computers, 200 hospitals were still using the earlier teletype technology; AHS had successfully sustained service to its customer base over six generations of electronics.

PHASE 5. EMULATION. Until the mid-1970s, competitor responses to ASAP were nil. Johnson & Johnson established and then abandoned its own electronic hospital links, as most of its large divisions within its decentralized tradition continued to use ASAP. The industry was extraordinarily fragmented, with a few large national distributors, all of which used ASAP, and a preponderance of small regional distributors.

The industry situation changed in 1985 when Baxter Travenol

TABLE 6-2 **Market Positions after the Merger**

Product Line	AHSC Share	Baxter's Share	Combined Share	Market Position
Solutions	—	30.8%	30.8%	1
Parenteral supplies	—	18.8	18.8	2
Medical supplies	15.2%	—	15.2	1
Garments and textiles	31.0	—	31.0	1
Disposable kits and trays	24.9	3.0	27.9	1
Catheters and tubes	21.2	1.2	22.4	1
Respiratory therapy	20.0	7.0	27.0	1
Surgical packs	50.4	—	50.4	1
Urological packs	16.1	9.9	26.0	2
Gloves	—	28.5	28.5	1
Maternity products	40.8	—	40.8	1
Elastic bandages	11.5	—	11.5	3
Dietary supplies	30.2	—	30.2	N/A
Dialysis supplies	—	28.7	28.7	1
Identification supplies	14.7	4.2	18.9	2
Total Market	13.1	7.4	20.5	1

Source: Health Industry Today, February 1986, p. 25. Reprinted by permission.
Note: These are market shares for hospital sales only and do not include sales to non-hospital markets.

acquired AHS and merged the two firms into a giant producer-distributor with the significant market share shown in Table 6-2. Baxter absorbed AHS's information services group nearly intact and turned over to it management of its own IT services. Vern Loucks, CEO of Baxter, encouraged ASAP's continued evolution, leading to the 1986 announcement of ASAP8, which supported electronic invoicing and funds transfer and document interchange with requisite security measures and fail-safe procedures. ASAP8 cemented the merger and was a vital element in the megafirm's competitive strategy.

Although the merger went exceptionally smoothly for the partners, it represented a formidable market force and consequently generated tensions in the industry. Loucks responded with an industry platform called ASAP EXPRESS, which was to be operated as an independent hospital supply network on General Electric computer service systems under audit control of a Big 8 accounting firm. The move drew a mixed reception from competitors as several smaller suppliers agreed to participate in Baxter's initiative, but Johnson & Johnson refused, choosing instead to create a competing multivendor system, dubbed COACT, and Abbott Laboratories entered into a coalition with two other firms to establish an alternative network called Quik Link. With ASAP already in 80 percent of hospitals, however, Baxter continues to wield a decided advantage.

United Services Automobile Association

Based in San Antonio, Texas, United Services Automobile Association, commonly referred to as USAA, was founded in 1922 by twenty-five Army officers. It offered auto insurance to military officers, who often had difficulty obtaining reasonable rates because of their high mobility, overseas posting, and risky jobs. The company's mail and word-of-mouth approach to sales provided the base of experience that led to its mail and telephone customer services being ranked second in the industry in 1988 by *Consumer Reports*. Low rates and tailored services enabled USAA to capture a significant share of its target market — in 1992 it boasted more than 2 million policyholders. Expanding into financial services in 1983, within a decade the company owned thirty-two subsidiaries, among them mutual funds, real estate and discount brokerage operations, and a federal savings bank, and had accumulated $24 billion in assets.[7] Over this period the company had below-average loss ratios and its asset base grew at a faster rate than that of the industry, as shown in Figure 6-2.

A Military Demeanor

USAA's style and mode of operation reflect the military heritage of its top officials, mostly former high-ranking armed forces officers. Recruited by USAA in 1968 and named CEO early in 1969, General Robert F. McDermott, for example, embraced a management philosophy steeped in military tradition. Admirals don't tell captains how to run their ships; admirals develop policies and guidelines of acceptable actions, procedures, and objectives. So McDermott attends closely to selecting and supporting personnel and to maintaining traditions that value innovation and dedication to company objectives. He subscribes to the military philosophy that transferring individuals frequently helps to keep them innovative, and he stays in touch with managers whose projects he has nurtured.

Viewing the human resource function as an agent of change, McDermott leads annual companywide promotion reviews that emphasize managers' qualifications and organizational needs, a prac-

FIGURE 6-2 **Assets, USAA versus Industry Average (1974 = 100)**

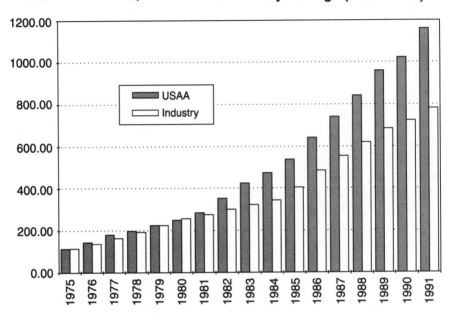

USAA Has Comparable Loss Ratios but Lower Expenses

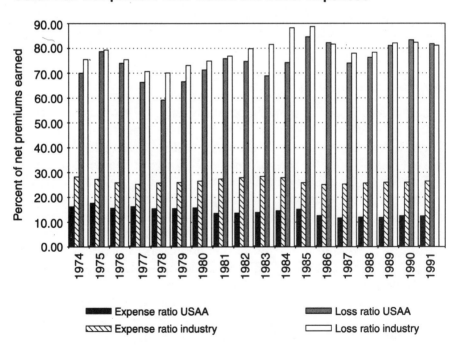

Source: Data from _Best's Insurance Reports,_ 1974–1991.

EXHIBIT 6-3   **Development of the USAA Dominant Design**

Year(s)	Event	Significance
1969	McDermott becomes CEO; goal "paperless office"; hires maestro	Focuses management on IT; starts to catch up
1970–1974	Implement standard industry system to automate	Gains competence in IT; reduces costs
1975–1978	Implement distributed system to users; expand product line	Shifts to new concept of IT use with new services
1979	Patterson becomes maestro	Involves managers in IT
1980–1982	Contract for IT architecture; initiate R&D effort	Appraises business IT; develops trial WORM system
1982–1984	Centralized IT services into IS division — customer oriented	Architecture provides quick access to all data
1984–1985	Lasher becomes maestro to create evolving IT strategy	Established user group to decide on IT portfolio
1986–present	Create customer-oriented IT portfolio; expand DSS	Use IT to empower customer service personnel

tice which leads to innovators' being frequently promoted out of their units to revitalize other units. He regularly schedules review meetings with direct reports and briefing sessions with managers to deal with problems, is open to informal routines, provided they are innovative and purposeful, and is willing to forgo the chain of command when that is useful and productive.

A highly visible leader, McDermott sees his role as "[articulating] a philosophy and an attitude that encourage employees to stretch to do the job better." He construes the search for better ways to do things as "a focus for change and continual improvement, not for acquiring more resources." McDermott sums up his vision for information technology in three objectives — create a paperless office, maximize convenience to customers, and make the work environment efficient for employees — all of which he takes very seriously.[8]

McDermott employed three maestros during the period we studied. Exhibit 6-3 traces the key events of his evolving strategy. Martin Fishel, an Air Force colonel with considerable computer systems management experience, was hired in the spring of 1969 to improve and bring up to industry standards the operating efficiency of USAA's information-processing systems. After installing a state-of-the-art system focused on reducing processing costs, Fishel was succeeded, in 1979, by James Patterson, a Property and Casualty executive with considerable experience in designing and implementing new organizational systems.

Although he had no direct systems experience, Patterson had been fulfilling a set of responsibilities that was directly relevant to what McDermott saw as the next step in USAA's information systems direction: involving users in the systems effort and establishing long-term direction. Then in 1984, with IT innovation taking form and gaining momentum, Patterson became involved in a project related to planning for the future and McDermott recruited as his maestro Donald Lasher, an Army major general who had managed information systems for more than twenty-five years and held an advanced degree in systems engineering. Lasher, building on earlier efforts, created an evolving IT strategy.

Among the technologists who participated in the development of USAA's modern architecture was Bob Woolridge, an early proponent of a client-server architecture with an accessible database, who served as overall systems architect. Woolridge shifted the company's emphasis from microfilm to image processing and recruited a brilliant technician, Charlie Plesums, to integrate such a system into USAA's overall design. Bob Wheeless, an innovator hired to move USAA toward a client-server architecture, later became project leader for the effort to shift to an accessible data base.

Campaign for a New Information-Processing Design

In 1969, USAA was an intensely clerical company plagued by annual employee turnover of 44 percent. Only payroll and accounting, which were in a pure accounting support mode, had been automated with computers. Policy applications and interaction with customers relied almost exclusively on mail and telephone. As the company grew, so did the volume of correspondence, rendering its paper-based information-processing systems cumbersome and ineffective. At any given time, 50 percent of customer files were unavailable because they were in use, in transit, or simply lost. A thirty-person contingent was specifically designated to work the night shift to look for missing files. The most intense processing bind was in the mail room, which received more than 10,000 customer service letters per day. Exhibit 6-4 documents USAA's progress through the cascade.

PHASE 1. INFORMATION-PROCESSING CRISIS AND SEARCH FOR AN IT SOLUTION. In his appraisal of USAA paper systems by walking around, McDermott found wasted time, space, and energy, leading

EXHIBIT 6-4 United Services Automobile Association Cascade

	CEO	Maestro	Technical Team
Phase 1 Information-processing crisis and search for an IT solution 1969–1970	Recognizes that company lags industry standard for information processing; recruits Fishel	Hires programmers; hires consultants	Works with consultants to design standard programs and replicate property and casualty system
Phase 2 Building IT competence 1970–1978	Pursues automation strategy of property and casualty (P&C)	Fishel develops standard insurance design for a mainframe-based information-processing system	Automatic data processing builds product file; focuses on efficiency
Phase 3 Expanding the scope of IT 1978–1984	Shifts focus to organization; hires Patterson to integrate IT into sales and decentralize its products	Patterson establishes links to most managers; involves users; initiates R&D program to explore WORM technology; engages consultant	Redesigns systems around customer (versus product); develops distributed systems; builds/tests pilot systems
Phase 4 Using IT to enable structure and drive strategy 1984–1990	Hires Lasher to create an evolving IT strategy; centralizes customer database; establishes senior management IT policy group; engages IBM in WORM R&D	Lasher establishes IT policy group and emphasizes IT architecture; develops customer-focused applications portfolio; guides IBM's WORM project	Consultant's activities migrate to technicians; organization expands to support emphasis on customer needs, universal product support
Phase 5 Evolving IT strategy 1990–present	Approves R&D funds to leading edge; emphasizes IT as basis of corporate strategy	Implements decision support; portfolio planning	Evaluates, builds, and tests R&D prototypes; maintains/enhances evolving dominant design
Competitors emulate	Several competitors were also moving to customer focus systems and adopted the WORM system		

him to announce, at the first management committee meeting he held as CEO, his vision of a "paperless" company arrived at through automation and computerization.[9] He subsequently hired Martin Fishel as MIS manager and charged him with automating clerical activities and creating an accessible electronic database of policy and customer information to support the company's agents. INSCO Automated Systems, the consulting arm of Continental Life Insurance of New York, was recruited to assist with the implementation of a systems base compatible with the insurance industry's existing, mainframe-based dominant design of information processing.

PHASE 2. BUILDING IT COMPETENCE. A newly formed Information Systems division was charged with establishing user requirements in accordance with an overall philosophy of a paperless system. The effort was guided by the consultants in close collaboration with an internal group of skilled technicians recruited by Fishel from other insurance firms and the Property and Casualty group. The team was to develop and implement, with the consultants' support, the standard IBM mainframe insurance industry computer system for Property and Casualty business. Special-purpose computer terminals were added to the design to provide on-line information support for agents who processed claims with customers over the telephone. This not only improved agent service to clients, it also involved salespersons with the system. His objective being to minimize computer cost by maximizing throughput, Fishel focused on reducing costs per account by improving overall system efficiency.[10] He automated the processing and moved to the factory stage of IT use.

PHASE 3. EXPANDING THE SCOPE OF IT. As USAA's systems were being automated, McDermott initiated a set of new services to broaden the company's financial product line. To provide specialized services, he organized a new IT unit to deal with them. USAA's early innovations soon fell short for a variety of reasons. A growing number of occasional references to isolated data that had been deemed uneconomic to store in the computer was impairing agent service to clients, and incoming mail was becoming a major bottleneck to improving customer services. Moreover, the evolution of USAA from a focused insurer of automobiles and homes to a broader casualty business had expanded its processing needs.

Systems analyst Robert Woolridge, recruited to analyze Property and Casualty's needs, concluded that the group would be best served by emerging personal computer products which would provide detailed customer information. The Information Systems division rejected the proposal, but Woolridge, with the implicit support of McDermott,[11] was encouraged to continue. A Data Point system was demonstrated to the head of Human Resources, Jim Patterson, Property and Casualty managers, and McDermott, all of whom heartily endorsed its rollout. Thus did USAA enter the distributed computing era. Fishel's transfer soon thereafter left Patterson in charge of IT.

Patterson had led a project that targeted each organizational unit every three or four years for an operational review and analysis of procedures, organizational responsibilities, and policies with an eye toward improving service and efficiency. Through these analyses, Patterson had become knowledgeable about the information-processing needs of USAA's various businesses and established strong working relationships with their managers. Unfreezing the organization's centrally controlled data-processing concept, he involved management in a participative process that considered organizational as well as technical aspects of systems portfolio development.

When McDermott had expanded USAA into a financial services organization in the late 1970s, all non–Property and Casualty businesses had been organized into a Financial Services group. Each entity acquired or spun off had its own identity and organization and operated its IT systems independently of Property and Casualty. Believing that the company needed an overall architecture that would support agents' on-line access to its complete line of financial services, McDermott and Patterson involved the senior managers in an IT management committee charged with setting policies and guiding overall IT development.[12]

USAA's IT management committee identified as critical a need to develop a long-range system plan to sustain company strategy. There was consensus that utilizing advanced technologies to deliver high-quality, low-cost products would enable the company to compete better. But the committee also agreed that USAA lacked the necessary know-how to move beyond the Information Systems division's budgeting process as the primary basis of planning. The committee subsequently issued requests for proposals for assistance with developing a long-term plan. Patterson and McDermott realized that engaging a consulting firm to develop an IT plan and design the critical systems would preclude the need to hire and then lay off a large number of people.

The management committee selected the Arthur Andersen firm to conduct the study and oversee the project, with Patterson as project coordinator. The committee also formalized Woolridge's efforts with Property and Casualty by creating a Research and Development department. Product management groups defined their requirements to Arthur Andersen, which analyzed the inputs to the study as to general and specifics to generate a systems architecture set of development projects.[13]

Incoming mail, which could exceed 100,000 letters daily and was growing, compounded by the large amounts of ancillary policy information that had to be maintained (e.g., descriptions of household

belongings and jewelry), constituted a certifiable crisis. An exploratory R&D project with microfilm was set aside in favor of image
processing based on write-once, read-many-times (WORM) technology, which was emerging from laboratories toward the end of
the 1970s. The system offered a solution to both the mail problem
and random access to particular background information. McDermott and Patterson concluded that there was great long-term potential for WORM technology. It was significantly cheaper than alternatives, and it supported rapid retrieval times. But collaborative
development of a pilot WORM technology-based optical system
demonstrated that existing technology was not sufficiently powerful
to support a production system. Patterson subsequently initiated
development of an experimental device with 3M Corporation that
furthered USAA's understanding of optical system requirements.
Then, in 1984, Patterson moved on to a corporate planning project,
ceding responsibility for information systems to Donald Lasher.

PHASE 4. USING IT TO ENABLE STRUCTURE AND DRIVE STRATEGY. A
million-dollar long-range IT strategic plan was two years in the making when Lasher assumed responsibility for the Information Systems division.[14] The core of the new architecture was an automated
insurance environment designed to enable agents to perform all
customer sales and service activities for all products on-line. McDermott suggested that to test the system, the design team define service needs, marketing opportunities, and information-processing
requirements for a series of critical customer events, such as the
birth of a child or retirement.

The plan had produced no tangible results and there was no
provision for keeping it current. The architecture was viewed as a
blueprint for the future. Arthur Andersen was developing the initial
design without USAA staff involvement, as the system was needed
as soon as possible. Lasher, who persuaded the committee that it
was essential to assume responsibility for IT development for economic and strategic reasons, launched a recruiting effort to expand
the Information Systems division's technical and system skills. To
ensure a smooth transition, he subsequently initiated a program for
transferring the consultant's competence to USAA systems personnel. McDermott expanded the role of the management committee
to a corporatewide information systems review board and formalized its procedures to support an ongoing planning process.

Eager to resolve USAA's paper-processing crisis, McDermott and
Lasher convinced IBM of the market potential of an image-process-

ing system. A project was then established to build a reliable compatible source of technology capable of supporting the company's integrated product strategy.[15] Lasher's team developed a fail-safe infrastructure capable of preserving the company's entire system — and economic future — through hurricanes, earthquakes, and loss of power. The team, working with users to develop decision support and other managerial marketing aids to facilitate new product development, has begun to experiment with linking customers' home computers for customer-initiated and controlled access to services. As a complement to this effort, an expert systems R&D team has created a software system that supports agents' selling activities. To afford the management team perspective and a map for the future in discussing project funding and architecture, Lasher has established a consolidated system schedule review that details all major systems efforts, past, present, and future.

The final innovation that established the dominant design of the future for the industry was to organize information with a customer rather than a product focus. USAA's expansion into auto and home, then health and life and other types of insurance and financial services, relied on product line files. Customer files, as was common among insurance companies, resided within the respective product lines. As a result, agents selling, for example, auto insurance would have no idea whether a given customer might be a prospect for homeowner's insurance. The McDermott/Patterson/Lasher effort had focused on the need for central customer files with access to all product information to promote opportunities for cross-selling to the entire customer base. Today, USAA agents can review a customer's entire range of coverage on-line while talking to the customer on the telephone. USAA has established an image-based design for information processing that is customer oriented. The industry is slowly and painfully straining to adapt such product-oriented IT systems with as much as eighty years of history. Many companies, such as Capital Holding and Northwest Mutual, were pursuing similar architectures independently and quickly built upon the availability of the WORM system. Again, IBM was an effective transfer agent.

Frito-Lay

When it was acquired by PepsiCo in 1965, the Dallas, Texas–based Frito-Lay Corporation, a consolidation of two snack-food companies founded in 1932, operated 46 U.S. plants and more than 150 domestic distribution centers and was listed on the New York Stock Exchange. Economies of scale and scope and national advertising enabled the company to realize double-digit profit and sales growth every year throughout the 1970s as it expanded geographically across the nation. By 1980, six of its products, with national retail sales in excess of $100 million, were among the fifty top-selling dry grocery brands. The fragmented snack-food market of the first half of the twentieth century, with its many small regional competitors, was by 1985 a $20 billion industry. After a slowdown in 1984, it regained momentum to grow sales over 10 percent in 1991 (see Table 6-3).[16] Of the top thirty market segments, Frito-Lay had 80 percent of one, 50 percent of another, and at least 30 percent of another four.[17] Exhibit 6-5 tracks the key events in the creation of Frito-Lay's evolving IT strategy.

Four Captains and Crew

Four Frito-Lay CEOs figure in the company's creation of an industry-transforming dominant design for information processing — Wayne Calloway, now CEO of PepsiCo, his successor, Michael Jordan, and William Korn and Roger Enrico (two others who served in transition roles had no impact on information technology).[18]

Calloway is a consummate executive who recruits managers with care and works to understand their approach and arrive at, then support, mutual objectives. He inherited in 1981 a finance-oriented IT organization focused on automating overhead. He promptly hired his IBM salesman, Charles Feld, and charged him to lead the organization with an eye toward achieving functional excellence and exploiting economies of scale. Calloway worked with this new maestro and then vice president of Operations Michael Jordan to establish the development program that would become a competitive force for Frito-Lay. Exhibit 6-6 is a summary of the management actions in Frito-Lay's course through the cascade.

Although promoted to corporate headquarters toward the end of the implementation, Calloway retained an abiding interest in Frito-Lay's competitiveness. That led him to continue to nurture the project and to help select Jordan, an engineer by schooling and a brilliant system designer with an engaging personal style, to succeed him. Calloway and Jordan subsequently played different but complementary roles in guiding the evolution of IT strategy at Frito-Lay. Jordan, an analytical genius, became involved directly with

TABLE 6-3 Frito-Lay Financial Comparison 1970–1991 ($ in millions)

Financial Summary	1970	1975	1980	1981	1982	1983	1984	1985	1986	1987	1988	1989	1990	1991
Revenues	$325.6	$806.7	$1,830.7	$2,177.9	$2,323.8	$2,430.0	$2,709.2	$2,847.0	$3,018.4	$3,202.0	$3,514.3	$4,215.0	$5,054.0	$5,565.8
Operating profit	$25.0	$89.5	$245.8	$298.5	$326.4	$347.7	$393.9	$401.0	$343.0	$548.0	$636.0	$821.0	$934.0	$787.6
Frito-Lay year-to-year revenue growth rate		25.1%	20.6%	19.0%	6.7%	4.6%	11.5%	5.1%	6.0%	6.1%	9.8%	19.9%	19.9%	10.1%

Frito-Lay, Inc.: market share (%)	1976	1978	1980[a,b]	1988[c]	1989	1990	1991
Potato chips	27.3%	30.9%	36.7%	34.0%	34.0%	34.0%	34.4%
Corn/tortilla chips	85.0%	70.3%	82.1%	76.9%	67.2%	66.7%	NA
Cheese curls/balls	51.6%	51.8%	57.8%	41.7%	41.5%	54.8%	50.0%

[a] Years 1976–1980 compiled from Melinda B. Conrad, Lynda M. Applegate, and Richard O. Mason, "Frito-Lay, Inc.: The Navigator Project (A)," 9-193-025 (Boston: Harvard Business School, 1993).
[b] Years 1982–1987 not available.
[c] Years 1988–1991 compiled from Snack Food Magazine, various issues, 1988–1991.

EXHIBIT 6-5 Development of the Dominant Design at Frito-Lay

Year(s)	Event	Significance
1981	Calloway hires Feld as maestro; gives full support	Initiates IT; appraises system
1982	Feld involves users in design and managers in IT group; test HHC; propose logistics	Users gain ownership accountability; IT respected; gains IT competence
1983–1984	Jordan CEO, roll out logistics; restart HHC; competition tough	Develops overall architecture; intense need for market data
1985–1986	Korn CEO, accelerates HHC rollout; decentralizes without control	Empowers field with new IT; timely information; no means to use
1986–1990	Jordan CEO, organizational design; decentralize P&L to field	Focuses on decision support for effective marketing decisions in a timely fashion
1990–1992	Create robust system; create 221 profit centers; delayer 1,800 staff; shift to a continuous annual planning horizon every four months	Provides analytic support for either a product line or a market manager

the technology, while Calloway, who had created the context for innovation and remained an interested and organizationally powerful observer, orchestrated its deployment as a strategic force. Jordan migrated to corporate headquarters in 1985, but returned to the helm of Frito-Lay two years later when his successor, William Korn, unable to meet profit goals, resigned. When Jordan left again in 1990 to head Frito-Lay's International division, he was replaced by Roger Enrico, an experienced sales manager who relished lively, one-on-one discussions with his managers but was indifferent to IT.

Charles Feld, a tough-minded systems analyst with a friendly style and a penchant for experimentation, provided continuity across these CEOs. As the company's former IBM salesman, intimately acquainted with Frito-Lay's information systems and their limitations and liabilities, he was eager to see them turned to competitive advantage. He won his spurs early with the development of a sound logistics system and went on to create, with a middle-management team, a highly sophisticated executive support system.[19]

Feld trained the existing team in new techniques and working with customers. Subsequently, Planning and Control manager Dori Reap instituted a system that enabled users to develop IT projects

EXHIBIT 6-6   Frito-Lay Cascade

	CEO	Maestro	Technical Team
Phase 1 Information-processing crisis and search for an IT solution (1981–1982) Calloway	Hires and makes Feld part of management team; funds logistics project; integrates IT plan into business	Involves users in effort to build state-of-the-art IT infrastructure; develops corporate IT plan	Expanded organization establishes links to, develops systems jointly with management; experiments with hand-held computer technology
Phase 2 Building IT competence (1983–1986) Jordan-Korn	Focuses on markets; revives/funds hand-held computer project; approves/funds database project; seeks funding from regional managers	Initiates hand-held computer project; builds on/enhances IT infrastructure	Tests planned rollout of hand-held computer technology
Phase 3 Expanding the scope of IT (1986–1988) Jordan	CEO restores emphasis on decentralized architecture; focuses on new product introduction/profitability	Initiates design of executive decision system; continues development of decision support system; establishes field test team and defines requirements	Develops pilot system for marketing; establishes links to areas; establishes field reporting conventions and data standards
Phase 4 Using IT to enable structure and drive strategy (1988–1993) Jordan-Enrico	Establishes evolving IT strategy; secures funding for systems development; distributes profit responsibility to areas; eliminates layer of staff	Develops decision support system architecture; contracts for system development; establishes headquarters/field team to decentralize decision making	Tailors and installs off-the-shelf on-line system; develops expertise in supporting/building screens for decision support system; develops remote support capability
Phase 5 Evolving IT strategy (1994–present) Calloway-Enrico	Emphasizes IT as basis of corporate strategy and encourages exploitation of IT infrastructure; monitors competitors' activities		
	Competitors emulate with focused market competition		

for budget proposals and track progress toward specific functions and economic objectives. Systems Development director Monte Jones orchestrated the implementation of the hand-held computer project described below so that users eventually managed the entire process. And director of Communications and End User Services Mary Cass involved users in the development of standards and definition of the functionality required to establish an integrated, reliable, and adaptable information system.

Navigating the Cascade

By the early 1980s, Frito-Lay had deployed some 10,000 salespeople who routinely placed the company's products in more than 300,000 retail outlets throughout the nation. To grow market share as it expanded to serve the entire U.S. market, the company had shifted from a geographic growth to a new-product strategy. Its product set already numbered 200 and was growing by two to five items per year.

The complexity of its new products was straining Frito-Lay's antiquated production planning system and creating a need for more timely sales information, both the firm's own and that of competitors. The existing system provided information only on 80 percent of gross national sales, and that two weeks after the fact. More critical was growth in products, which had confounded production scheduling and led to goods' being shipped late or too early. Using two-week-old, incomplete data to manage the nationwide flow of 2 billion bags of product with a thirty-two-day shelf life began to impair margins seriously. The forty-six plants relied on paper forms and a financially oriented mainframe system at the company's Dallas headquarters. There were no electronic links.

PHASE 1. INFORMATION PROCESSING CRISIS AND SEARCH FOR AN IT SOLUTION. Frito-Lay entered the 1980s looking for (1) a technology to relieve its route salespeople of excessive paperwork, and (2) a logistics system capable of accommodating an expanding product line with regional manufacturing sites to support nationwide distribution. Wayne Calloway, keenly aware of the information-processing crisis, recruited Charles Feld who in turn engaged a consultant to audit the company's existing systems. The audit suggested that the company's financially oriented systems required excessive hardware and incurred above-average costs due to poor design, employed obsolete procedures, and operated independently of the business.

Because the Information Systems function reported to Finance and systems managers chose new projects, users had no responsibility for, and were uncommitted to, development projects. Calloway subsequently authorized Feld to alter funding procedures to afford users greater accountability within an overall Information Systems–designed architecture. He also authorized William Korn, then vice president of Marketing, to undertake an R&D effort to design a hand-held computer for route salespeople and Michael

Jordan, then vice president of Operations, to develop an up-to-date logistics system.

PHASE 2. BUILDING IT COMPETENCE. His first priority being to develop a competent technical group, Feld initiated a team-building process to instill in the Information Systems organization his vision of the future. To this end, he invited Calloway, Jordan, and Korn to relate to the IT business and functional managers their views regarding how IT might provide a competitive edge. These discussions, coupled with the new funding approach, empowered users and encouraged their involvement in scoping out new projects. The discussions boosted IT morale and empowered the managers to work with users as a team. Feld subsequently recruited talented entry-level individuals to extend the organization's technical capabilities.

Jordan and Feld, both experienced in the development of such systems, jointly designed Frito-Lay's new logistics system. A variety of managers and professionals involved in the system's design became the implementation team. Users themselves, they were in a position to lead an effort to reorganize the functions around the architecture they helped develop: a programmatic, integrated product flow from suppliers to distribution centers based on sales forecasts. Korn, in parallel with this effort, initiated the development of a hand-held computer designed to eliminate salespersons' paper forms. Early trials of the technology proved it too unstable, and the project was tabled. As the logistics system was being rolled out, Calloway departed for headquarters to assume the helm of PepsiCo and Jordan became CEO of Frito-Lay.

PHASE 3. EXPANDING THE SCOPE OF IT. To counter aggressive regional competitors whose frequent product introductions and weekly price changes were nibbling at its market share, Frito-Lay needed a replacement for its existing sales update system. Running weekly, it left headquarters' knowledge of store sales ten days in arrears. Jordan and Feld envisioned the core of the solution as a data warehouse containing timely product sales information by store for every delivery and market as well as competitor data for purposes of evaluating and interpreting market results. Given the system vision of wholly electronic order preparation on the basis of expected sales and daily delivery updates, the hand-held computer system instantly became a strategic necessity and a new design was tested with a manufacturer.

To capture and render accessible daily information on product sales per store, per route would require an entirely new information architecture. The data warehouse was to be linked to terminals to support decentralized, market-oriented decision making. Feld's efforts to explain the overall architecture and project its impact on markets and corporate profits was cumulative: he first established the design in IT architectural terms such as files, processing activities, and communication functions, then used these terms to describe new functions such as automatic store orders. A standard package of definitions, levels of architecture, and organizational impact emerged from Feld's efforts to guide management understanding of company needs and functions. Figure 6-3 reproduces a slide Feld used to articulate the elements of the architecture.[20]

In 1985, with the architecture and hand-held computer system still in development, Jordan followed Calloway to corporate headquarters, and Korn took the wheel. Under pressure from the parent company to achieve double-digit profit growth, and believing that he could not wait for the information and management systems to be in place before implementing the decentralized business strategy, Korn delegated price and marketing strategy to regional brand managers under local competitive pressure. Without an effective means to focus on profit, these field managers emphasized sales, driving margins down, at times even selling below cost. Sales grew by 6 percent, but profit by only 2 percent, well below target.[21] Korn subsequently resigned, whereupon Jordan returned as CEO of a merged domestic and international snack-food business. Expected growth in overseas markets afforded Jordan a funding base for continued investment in IT.

A field test of Frito-Lay's hand-held computer system evidenced service, but not sufficiently dramatic economic, improvements. The system conserved drivers' time, eliminated paperwork, reduced errors, and enabled salespeople to build accounts and perform their jobs in a more professional manner, but incurred added costs in system support. Feld documented the cost savings needed to meet the hurdle rate and Jordan, recognizing that the benefits would not be realized unless the field sales force was committed to implementing changes in the way it did business, required each local field sales organization to commit to a one percent reduction in cost of sales. It was left to the individual organizations to determine how to meet the new productivity target (e.g., by decreasing "stales," increasing sales volume, or rationalizing routes). Jordan's intent, to encourage the field sales organizations to identify ways to use the technology to change the way they did business and ensure that

FIGURE 6-3 Information Technology Architecture

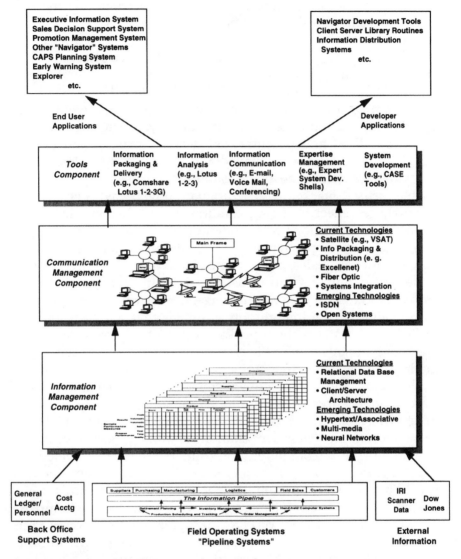

Source: Lynda M. Applegate and Nicole A. Wishart, "Frito-Lay, Inc.: A Strategic Transition (C)," Case 9-190-071 (Boston: Harvard Business School, 1989).

they achieved the anticipated benefits, was fulfilled — all field sales managers reduced cost of sales by at least 2 percent, and the sales force experienced a significant boost in morale.[22]

PHASE 4. USING IT TO ENABLE STRUCTURE AND DRIVE STRATEGY. Soon after introduction of the hand-held computer system had begun, Jordan, Feld, and the management team developed a five-year plan for migrating to a hybrid organizational structure that would leverage the information collected by the new system to the benefit of both centralized and decentralized decision making and control. An IT infrastructure was detailed and an architecture designed to support decentralization of decisions with embedded controls to enable focused marketing. The annual budget was to be updated quarterly to reflect changing conditions and identical time increments. Data definitions were standardized, as were metrics for all functional planning activities to facilitate integration. R&D, Logistics, Production, Sales, and Finance were all to use precisely the same unit definitions and measures. Relevant information was to be made accessible to senior managers, who were to be provided with analytical decision support terminals that would respond to "What if?" questions about price cuts, advertising ploys, and other marketing initiatives with likely scenarios derived from sales information and data on demographics and competitors' past responses.

The architecture was to grow incrementally as system developers learned how to organize the information more effectively and determined what constituted useful decision guides for managers. Development of an intelligent workstation was undertaken with IBM as system integrator, communication firm, and software developer to create a tailored system that met the firm's needs. The development was to be led by Feld's team while it pursued an in-depth study of the information needs of managers at all levels of the company. The study revealed that Frito-Lay managers preferred access to the numerical details of graphics displays, specifically tabular information, on which they could perform their own analyses. Access to such detail, they believed, would enable them to learn how to interpret the data and identify which relationships among different information items might be meaningful. This became the guiding premise of the architecture.

Jordan's goal for Frito-Lay's evolving information system was to support management at each step in the business process rather than simply report final outcomes. Continuous analysis of the impact of marketing decisions on individual product sales profitability,

Jordan believed, improved understanding of the business and challenged many old rules of thumb. The information made available by the system suggested new opportunities for enhancing growth and managing costs and fostered more prospective and predictive thinking on the part of managers. But the real value of the information, according to Jordan, would be realized when decision making was pushed down to the people in the field.[23]

Jordan and Feld were among the first to receive the executive and functional manager workstations that the Applications Development team began to roll out in June 1989. Jordan estimated that it would take about eighteen months to learn how to use the system information to manage the business and create a shared understanding of the direction the company needed to take. He found the internal information on regional and channel profitability and external information on competitor market share and pricing most helpful. The internal information cast the dynamics of the business in a new, thought-provoking light and revealed how company strategies influenced profitability; the external information served as an early warning signal of industry changes.

The creation in 1990 of four area business teams with profit responsibility was the first step to decentralize decision making to more than 200 focused profit center marketing areas. The technical infrastructure to support the teams was robust, but the requisite organizational procedures and tools to support on-line decision making were in a state of rapid change while their developers were learning by using in a process tightly controlled by Jordan.

Field managers' understanding of the system was evolving with system use and the organization was learning how to decentralize strategic decisions without adversely affecting the bottom line when Jordan left to head Frito-Lay's newly formed international division. Feld, with Jordan's support, persuaded Roger Enrico, his successor, to conduct a field trial. His interest piqued when the region trying the system exceeded its profit objectives while other regions were having difficulty meeting theirs, Enrico began to ply Feld with questions about how the system worked and at the annual profit planning meeting introduced a new version of the terminal support system, which Enrico praised to his managers.

A subsequent organizational analysis of roles and responsibilities led to the creation of four area divisions and the further decentralization of market responsibilities to twenty-two market area teams with bottom-line responsibility. The ensuing reorganization eliminated 1,800 managerial/professional personnel, 800 from headquarters and 1,000 from the field. Frito-Lay had become a broader, flatter organization, its market force distributed among twenty-two locations instead of four, all linked by its evolving information system. The system continues to be expanded in scope and capabilities, its efficacy confirmed as much by competitors' shifts to decentralized IT-supported decision making as by the quantifiable benefits it has brought Frito-Lay — stable or increasing market share and solid growth in profits.

Comparisons with Pioneers

These modern sagas document both the vitality of and variations in the cascade model. For recent innovators, the breadth and speed of change in information technology is greater, all paradigms of information processing are changing, particularly the management role, and there exist many more external sources of IT competence. Yet CEO involvement, the dynamic role of the maestro, and the salient role of the technicians, as well as the nature of the genesis of change, remain consistent with the experiences of the pioneers. Bank of America and American Airlines set out to solve operational problems and discovered marketing opportunities. The same is true for the firms described in this chapter; AHSC addressed an ordering problem, USAA a lag in state-of-the-art claims processing, and Frito-Lay a logistics problem. The difference is that these innovators had access to off-the-shelf systems and in most cases were able to copy existing designs. Yet, again like the pioneers, they assimilated IT gradually and, as they came to recognize their systems as a competitive market force, actively managed the evolution of their IT strategies.

Variations in the way key players executed their roles reflect considerations of available useful technology, the nature of the problem, and the cultures and strengths of the organizations. In part the divergences are due to each market's idiosyncratic differences in information-processing needs and capabilities of available IT. Figure 6-4 traces the growth of the companies as they gained competence and developed an evolving IT strategy in the strategic grid. All started with similar moves, then diverged as each developed an evolving IT strategy.

American Hospital Supply was in the mainstream of data processing in automating its order entry in the mid-fifties to reduce inventory and improve control with punched cards. Inventing a means to transfer order information with the customer created a

FIGURE 6-4 **Strategic Growth**

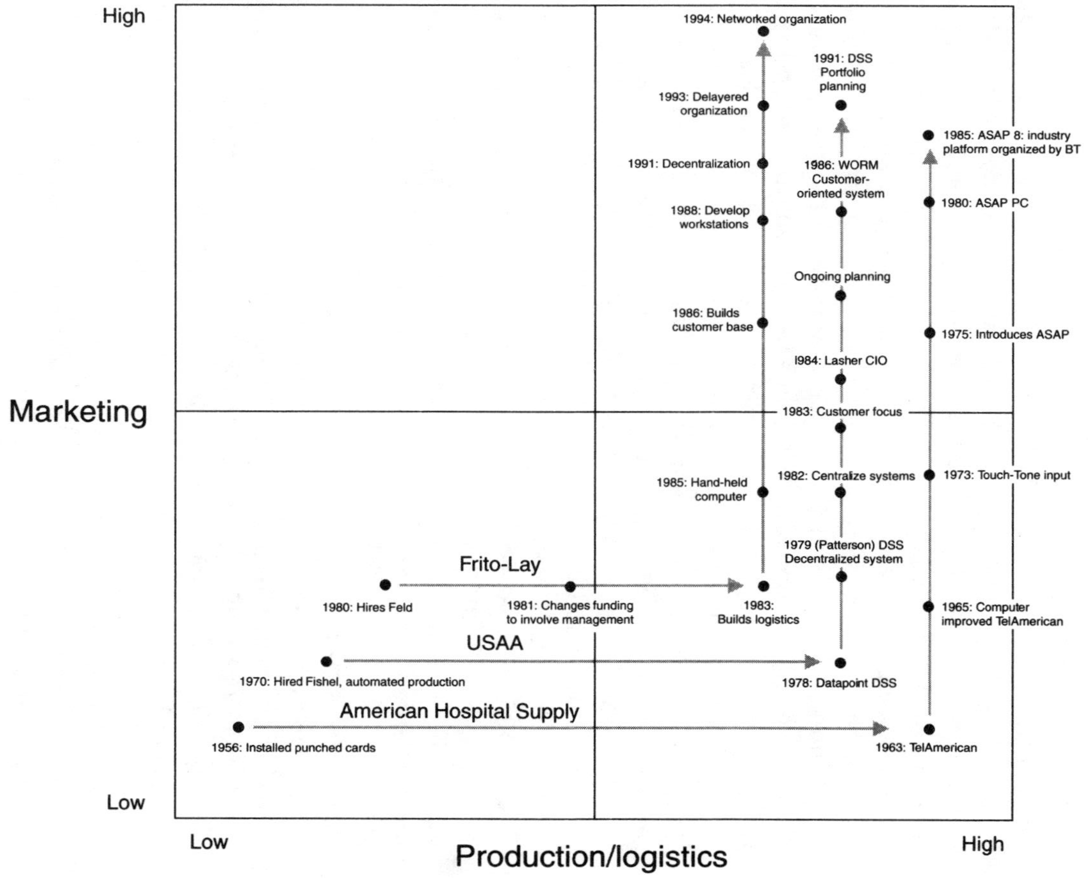

communication link that AHS grew to an elegant system, proving processing concepts can work. However, its first IT automation was typical of the sixties — using IT for accounts receivable and inventory control, essentially automating the punched-card logistic system. As Karl Bays began to see the potential of the link American Hospital Supply's strategic move was to improve the functionality of the link to allow computer input and provide an all-electronic connection. AHS refined this process to control the movement of goods with the customer. The link enabled its eventual second strategic move of managing its customers' inventory in a seamless system tied to the customers' use of supplies. AHS was rewarded for its vision and ability to exploit IT as a first mover. It continued to manage the evolution of this link over a thirty-year period and still benefit from its connection to the hospitals.

AHS gained significant market share on the basis of a relatively modest, but highly innovative technological base. Enabled by Ed Doerhoefer's groundwork, it championed the novel concept of partnering with customers through an electronic link; Bays, on becoming CEO, moved quickly to develop an IT strategy. The new marketing concept of prime vendor that he and Gary Nei pursued through several generations of ASAP established market share and a defensible entry barrier. The wonder is that no competitor responded. AHS's market position, consolidated with the Baxter merger, is probably as secure as American Airlines' travel agent base.

The two recent movers could copy existing systems with the help of consultants and IBM as they lagged their industries in IT use. The benefits were obvious and the means well defined. Once up to speed, both became innovators in serving their markets. This is largely a factor of the unique nature of their markets and the maturity of IT for their production systems. For Frito-Lay there was an effective dominant design for production processes as well as logistics, and the gating factor was developing better forecasting methods. The company started by automating logistics and production because that had payoffs and provided experience with IT systems. The strategic trick was to capture sales data efficiently in a timely manner, and the team launched an R&D project that invented the hand-held computer to accomplish the function. This eventually led to an all-electronic system that provided on-line access to up-to-date shelf sales figures nationwide.

The financial services industry was just beginning a gradual transformation from narrowly defined functionally oriented companies such as casualty and savings and loan institutions to broader financial service organizations when Robert McDermott, like most managers in the industry, undertook to automate claims processing and billing by relying on known designs. McDermott ceased to follow the industry when he turned his attention to the needs of USAA's unique customer base. Because they understood the basic information-processing needs of their customers and the capabilities they required to meet those needs, McDermott and James Patterson were able to redesign the company's information architecture from the customer service point of view and focus research efforts on eliminating the processing bottlenecks. The architecture allowed modular development of functional programs capable of accessing the necessary data to both support agent terminals and provide management exception reports. This system has evolved to a networked on-line agent-management decision support system that links agents to product specialists.

USAA also had a model insurance information-processing system that was easily appropriated through a consultant. To better serve its customers it first had to automate claims processing to improve accuracy and reduce costs. This provided an organizational competence in the way to develop existing technology into an efficient IT processing system. Then the company could focus on how to serve a customer for a broad range of services. This required timely access to specific details from a comprehensive set of descriptive information. Its crisis drove USAA to an extended R&D process that resulted in a useful technology and a reliable supplier. Both firms' procedures were similar to the pioneers' in working with suppliers, and particularly IBM, to develop an appropriate technology to meet their needs. The WORM technology fit the need and management worked diligently to achieve a solid source of supply.

For USAA the challenge was to support a customer-focused marketing effort that would make it a preferred source for a broad product line of financial services. The critical factors were (1) to reorganize its system to focus on customer needs versus the product, (2) to train its service personnel to use the information to provide prompt courteous service, and (3) to grow the system as it expanded its services. This required reorienting all the product divisions from their systems to a common database as well as developing a system that could prompt on-line users to find relevant information from a broad variety of accessible data. USAA recentralized IT and created a single, customer-focused database with intelligent terminals able to support all products and services.

Frito-Lay was characterized by a strong bottom-line focus and a tradition of moving successful executives to deal with new opportunities. Charles Feld provided much-needed continuity in this context, effectively sustaining momentum through a succession of CEOs by marshaling resources to reduce costs as he implemented a new infrastructure. By dramatically increasing the productivity of information processing, Feld opened the door to rethinking the entire approach to marketing management. His way of planning effectively involved the entire management team, which was accustomed to planning only for the following year, in a staged process with a more useful horizon and incorporated a common set of concepts for considering IT investments in infrastructure in terms of market impact. The enormous change in systems and organizational structure completely transformed the gestalt of the company. A shift from one profit manager, the CEO, to 221 field-based profit managers is a learning experience, to say the least.

Given a solid system that met Frito-Lay's production and logistic control needs, Feld and team focused on expanding their company's markets by improving customer service, then on learning what customers wanted. They led the industry in developing programmed product introductions and tailoring their offerings to meet the needs of local markets. The necessary decentralization required a new form of IT — a market intelligence aide that provides decision support to plan and monitor a sales effort by tracking competitors, sales, and market trends to continue to grow the market. The organizational imperative was to develop simultaneously individuals with expertise in local market needs and product managers abreast of market trends in snack foods. Creating a system that provides informed individuals with common data and tools affords an operational base for understanding and decision making.

Frito-Lay's employment of distributed services has decentralized management control of markets through an IT system. The design of the system is evolving with use, but its core is a graphic display system linked to an organized set of data to provide monitoring information, user-friendly analytic tools, and decision support for such recurring decisions as product price or quantity. The design of the system is organizational specific to provide a set of framing schemas to support individual decisions, be they helping to determine prices and mix of products or market-testing a new item. The system accumulates history to enable the designers to improve it over time. Frito-Lay has used the system to increase competitive pressure in the market, forcing rivals to match its systems. The IT innovative process is continuing as marketers struggle for shelf space and profits. The organizational shift was massive and contin-ues as companies work to assimilate the new strategy based on timely marketing analysis.

The commonality between the recent innovators and the pioneers is the elapsed time necessary to develop a truly innovative system. In all cases, as documented in the cascade exhibits, they required at least seven years from the start of actively managing IT as a competitive resource to achieving a dominant role. As noted, the gating factor is the elapsed time required to train individuals and adapt roles to exploit the potential of IT. It required eight months to develop the hand-held computer at Frito-Lay and thirty months to implement it to its entire sales force. At USAA the development of the first terminal system took less than a year, but training agents in and converting all product files to the new system required more than two years. During this period, as new products were being added, USAA developed its own systems while Property and Casu-alty was busy converting. The first conversion at AHS to the mini-computers took two years; once it was automating paperwork, it still required training of personnel and testing. The second move to the centralized Burroughs system took almost two years, as AHS had to convert each warehouse to the systems sequentially to pro-vide continuous service. Shifting the basic processing infrastructure of an organization is nitty-gritty work that requires a thorough plan and meticulous implementation because business does not stop and servicing real customers has to proceed in parallel with both old and new systems for some length of time.

All these firms recognized the need and undertook to recruit ca-pable technicians, experiment with new technologies in partnership with manufacturers, and focus significant energies on the manage-ment of organizational change. A perhaps more remarkable consis-tency is that even in an era in which the technology is stable and professional talent readily available, it has still taken five to seven years to arrive at an innovative design. The gating factor that has not changed is human behavior. Maestros today are more likely to devote additional time to involving users and crafting presentations to managers to promote understanding and commitment. For USAA, linking entrepreneurial businesses with mature insurance organizations required focused effort and time for the technology to mature, but it also relied on the ability of McDermott and Pat-terson to articulate a vision of an architecture. Frito-Lay possessed the architecture necessary to support the rollout of its new technol-ogy, but needed time to build a database, train 10,000 route salespeople, and implement a new logistics system while maintaining operations. Finally, Bays and Nei understood the potential of managing customers' inventory, but developing the expertise and staff needed to convert customers and utilize customer inventory data required experience and an entirely new set of skills and management procedures.

Perhaps the most dramatic shift for modern managers is the move to direct involvement with technology as a managerial aide. Front-line managers in USAA, Frito-Lay, and AHSC use terminals to monitor progress and rely on electronic mail as a means of communication. Most are now tightly coupled into the IT system and have access to an automated plan versus actual reports on unexpected variances at a detailed level.

Frito-Lay's shift to decentralized marketing represents a complete overhaul of the company's skills in appraising market shifts, skills embedded in the marketing and senior executives' experience; most knew what to do, but not how they made decisions. Theirs was and is a craft occupation. To create a data-driven market alternative into a useful IT system involved working with marketers to scope relevant variables and design formats that made sense to relatively inexperienced market managers. The designers had to learn how to organize the information to enable a manager to search efficiently for useful alternatives as competitors moved or introduced new promotional gimmicks.

The technology was not as much a gating factor as the intellectual issues and organizational traditions, specifically, the notion of managers as keepers of intelligence. Distributing salient information in a timely fashion throughout an organization is far more sublime and involved than automating inventory control or the sales cycle. Linking organizational units and providing timely and relevant information requires a conceptual shift within the entire organization. Managers exploring the automation of strategic decisions rather than of someone else's job are, for the first time in the history of business, deciding how to automate and informate themselves.

A second divergence from the pioneering era is the generic nature, yet unique market focus, of architectures. We are witnessing a move from managing by exception to managing in anticipation. This switch, as we have documented, increases the pace of activities and the need for more and immediate information, both external and internal. The domain of IT thus continues to expand, to customers and suppliers as well as to competitors. At one level of analysis, all five organizations we have described have fairly similar IT systems. Each has a set of mainframe-based systems that drive operations and planning and activity data. The systems are organized accessibly to provide a range of individuals access to information they need via intelligent terminals that retrieve, organize, and analyze the data into informational displays. But each company also has a set of unique functions within these systems — AHS's link to hospitals, Frito-Lay's hand-held computer, American Airlines' link to travel agents, Bank of America's worldwide money-transfer system, USAA's enormous on-line image storage system — that reflect specific market needs.

The total elapsed time from development to implementation of a concept has decreased, since the days of the pioneers and AHS, with the availability of competent personnel, the accessibility of experts, and the reliability of software. Thus, Feld could bring up a logistics system in two years and an on-line database in less time than earlier efforts required. More time is spent on managerial tasks and less on details of systems as the basic IT infrastructure is well defined; clearly setting forth system standards and IT development processes are of primary concern. However, the Frito-Lay gating factor was the elapsed time required to tailor management tools to the business and to gain the acceptance and understanding of the organizational team.

The Role of IT in Developing Infrastructure

The role of an IT strategy is to stimulate exploration into how IT might improve information-processing activities and what organizational structures are best suited to particular applications. The stories related here identify the ingredients of a strategic program. CEO involvement is mandated by the lengthy incubation period of useful systems, often more than seven years, and the persistence of organizational change throughout this period. Perspective on required organizational adaptation and the development of necessary competencies is as important as the development of new skills and innovative systems. In all the companies we studied, organizational issues required longer lead times than system-development efforts. One might argue that the real reason for American Airlines' brief demise was failure to ensure that the future organization would be as firmly entrenched as the operation of SABRE; the company could easily have installed terminals two years ahead of its competitors.

The nature of technology has changed since the pioneers set out to exploit it. The question is no longer, Will a technology work? but, How much greater is its capacity, and what precisely is the nature of its functionality? Technology adaptation is in a more predictable developmental phase, with automation efforts such as electronic data interchange and automated analysis well defined. The challenge of the future is how best to employ information technology to assist the management of global organizations.

Organizational shifts were more complex at AHS, USAA, and Frito-Lay, since all three had to reorganize levels and functions into an integrated market focus; they devoted as much as or more time than Bank of America or American Airlines to furthering understanding and acceptance of organizational change during the implementation process. All have emphasized support for decision makers, whether agents or marketers. Subsequent changes are more likely to influence management procedures and decision processes, which is inevitable at the cusp of institutional and analytical procedures. Although the future promises more predictable and powerful IT, and organizational potential is great, developing and implementing useful systems has been made more ambiguous by the larger human factor.

Notes

1. James L. McKenney interview with C. Steiner and E. Doerhoefer, May 20, 1993.

2. "American Hospital Supply Corporation: The ASAP System (A)," Case No. 9-186-005 (Boston: Harvard Business School, 1986).

3. James L. McKenney interview with E. Doerhoefer, April 12, 1993.

4. Thomas J. Main and James E. Short, "Managing the Merger: Building Partnership Through IT Planning at the New Baxter," MIS Quarterly 13, no. 4 (December 1989): 469.

5. James L. McKenney interview with C. Steiner, April 12, 1993.

6. N. Venkatraman and James E. Short, "Strategies for Electronic Integration: From Order-Entry to Value-Added Partnerships at Baxter," CISR Working Paper No. 210, June 1990 (revised February 1991), 12.

7. John J. Sviokla and Joyce J. Elam, "Image Processing Project at USAA," Case No. 9-190-155 (Boston: Harvard Business School, 1990), 6-2.

8. McKenney interview with R. F. McDermott, October 17, 1993.

9. J. Elam and J. E. P. Morrison, "United Services Automobile Association (USAA)," Case No. 9-188-102 (Boston: Harvard Business School, 1988).

10. McKenney interview with J. Patterson, D. Lasher, and R. F. McDermott, October 17, 1993.

11. McKenney interview with J. Patterson, D. Lasher, R. F. McDermott, R. Woolridge, and R. Wheeless, April 23, 1993.

12. J. Elam and J. E. P. Morrison, "United Services Automobile Association (USAA)."

13. McKenney interview with Patterson, Lasher, and McDermott.

14. McKenney interview with D. Lasher, October 17, 1993.

15. Donald R. Lasher, Blake Ives, and Sirkka L. Jarvenpaa, "USAA-IBM Partnerships on Information Technology: Managing the Image Project," MIS Quarterly 15, no. 4 (December 1991): 551.

16. M. B. Conrad and Lynda M. Applegate, "Frito-Lay, Inc.: The Navigator Project (A)," Case No. 9-193-025 (Boston: Harvard Business School, 1993).

17. Lynda M. Applegate, M. B. Conrad, and Charles S. Osborn, "Frito-Lay, Inc.: A Strategic Transition (D)," Case No. 9-193-004 (Boston: Harvard Business School, 1993).

18. L. M. Applegate, "Frito-Lay, Inc.: The Early Years (A)," Case No. 9-193-154 (Boston: Harvard Business School, 1993); N. C. Wishart and L. M. Applegate, "Frito-Lay, Inc.: A Strategic Transition (B)," Case No. 9-187-123 (Boston: Harvard Business School, 1987); L. M. Applegate and N. A. Wishart, "Frito-Lay, Inc.: A Strategic Transition (C)," Case No. 9-190-071 (Boston: Harvard Business School, 1990); Applegate, Conrad, and Osborn, "Frito-Lay Inc.: A Strategic Transition (D)."

19. McKenney interview with C. Feld and M. Jordan, October 28, 1992.

20. Applegate and "Frito-Lay, Inc.: A Strategic Transition (C)."

21. Wishart and Applegate, "Frito-Lay, Inc.: A Strategic Transition (B)."

22. McKenney interview with M. Jordan, October 28, 1992.

23. Ibid.

Chapter 7

Sustaining an Evolving IT Strategy

The timing of this narrative could be considered ten years overdue. But though it might seem that all the first-mover advantages are gone and the world economy is in a grueling slugfest of the powerful, we are now facing two, if not three, of the most exciting opportunities in the history of information technology (IT). The first is the truly easy and natural intelligent linking of individuals to a broad range of useful information. The second is the impending shift from a million gate chip and eight-channel optical fiber to 64 million gate chips and 512 simultaneous channels, which will reduce the marginal cost of graphic/voice information to zero. A third opportunity is the ability to store information in a form retrievable by voice and the hoped-for, but perhaps improbable, means to translate human voice into any language automatically.

Organizations such as Frito-Lay and Wal-Mart have transformed their organizations — one decentralizing strategy to the field, the other centralizing the largest retail business in the world. The breadth of management options on strategy, structure, and scope, given a comprehensive IT-based infrastructure, are bounded by the creative instincts of the management. As the technology has become more user friendly, useful, and accessible, its mystique and power have eroded, and the mainframe has become an anonymous influence. This further accelerated the pace, forever eliminating the "check is in the mail" delay gambit. One can now consult a terminal to determine the status of accounts receivable.

The next infrastructure shift will be precipitated by pervasive networking and expansion of the media, from alphanumeric to audio and graphics. The coming era promises interesting storage and retrieval opportunities, for example, automated storage of television clips and verbal comments on their meaning among disparate users. The actualization of popular science fiction movies, in which the protagonist interacts with machines and enjoys easy connections to a wide range of services, is on the horizon. It will be challenging to manage the evolution from the present to a future in which one can link to anyone anywhere — in living color. If the past is any indicator, and depending on IT competence, present infrastructure, and managerial vision, this accomplishment will require significant organizational learning over a three- to seven-year period of experimentation. The overriding issue will clearly be how to deploy the system in an orderly fashion that builds on present competencies and expands the productivity of an organization as an entity.

The impact of changes of information-processing capability and capacity on the infrastructure is to allow more prompt and convenient sharing, computing, routinizing, and linking, which enables a broad range of ill-defined functions formerly done by humans or other machines or media, or not at all. Development of an effective infrastructure is still dominated by instinct and desire more than by systemic analysis. All the rationale in the world may not convince a forty-year-old manager to rely on a terminal — individuals must want to share their intellectual activities with a machine. Future IT will be even easier to work with and potentially more useful. But how successful its use will be continues to depend on managerial leadership and technical competence.

The Influence of IT on Dominant Design

The histories recounted earlier also document the influence of the state of the technology on the relevance and utility of IT as a solution to a processing problem. Until fairly recently, IT's capacity to meet an industry's processing needs was highly dependent on storage capacity and fast access to stored data. If there was one unrealized aspect of business processing that was not well understood, it was the enormous requirement for particularized data.

The early 1960s saw the development of a fad labeled "total information systems," inferring that computers could make all relevant information available on demand. These were partly based on large manufacturing systems and innovative designs in the oil industry to manage logistics and refining. Both systems required massive investments and indeed produced impressive results.[1] However, few had the uniformity or capital of both those situations. Some companies in attempting to define their total information needs discovered an impossible objective because the systems evolved with use, their needs changed, and the system design had to be revised. Managing the implementation of computers became an important task.[2]

McKenney made a similar discovery while helping to design a system to automate catalogue sales for a national retailer. The design completely underestimated the volume of items in a mail-order business. Seven months into the project, when it was discovered that there were 288,000 different men's socks, as they had to be inventoried by a combination of style, pattern, color, length, and size, an alternative design was suggested. Present mass storage devices and the ever-expanding communication links have the potential to provide access to specific information throughout the organization. In many retailing organizations, the store manager and the supplier simultaneously receive exception reports on the rate of sale of particular items directly from point-of-sale checkout systems. Today, systems can assimilate unlimited data in accessible form, given an appropriate design.

Technology has been and will continue to be a binding constraint for certain applications. Pioneering technologists eagerly sought new memories and more productive software, whose development was relatively slow. American Airlines' need for on-line access to an accurate seat inventory from a variety of locations, for example, far outstripped the capacity of 1950s computers. Bank of America, on the other hand, found automating loan computations to be a productive use of existing technology. It built on that experience to realize economies of scale from what, from today's perspective, would be viewed as an inept technology. The bank also learned quickly, how to derive more timely control information, which enabled it to support more complex products.

The art of the possible is best understood by experimenting on a small scale to appreciate the promise and learn to perceive the business relevance of potential systems. Experience with the Stanford Research Institute electronic recording machine systems gave rise in the bank to an all-electronic vision of the future, which would not emerge until the mid-1960s when computer systems became more powerful. Over the years, hardware has diminished as a force; for most businesses the cost and functionality of software and access to data are the technical constraining factors. However, the most critical constraints are the perception of a management team on alternative designs of a process and competent technologists to deliver a reliable and productive working system. With today's color screen intelligent terminals, the art of the possible had a broad set of solutions.

The future of IT still depends on chip size and clock speed, both of which are growing at an ever-increasing pace. IT will soon outstrip existing software, which may become the gating factor. In the mid-1970s, the rate of chip growth was in the thousands, from 2,000 to 64,000 circuits; in the 1980s, it jumped from 64,000 to 128,000, then in steps of 100,000. Today we are moving in steps of millions; there is strong evidence that a 16 million-gate chip is possible. The joint effort of Toshiba, IBM, and Siemens is directed to building a 256 million-bit memory chip. The rate of change is increasing and will continue to accelerate. The window for response will narrow and competence will be key not only to perceiving useful systems but also to adapting the structure and modifying the strategy to exploit them.

With IT, the challenge is to keep up with its increasing functionality, which from the solid state period has had a predictable growth in capacity as the chip expands in increments of the power of two. American Airlines' original constraint, memory access, was not resolved until two generations after the introduction of IBM's model 360. But American's IT managers were aware of the necessary technological developments to facilitate a broadly distributed terminal system, albeit with less than the desired functionality. When he initiated the design of the cooperative travel agent system, Max Hopper understood that if he waited, the technology would be more effective for the application and more cost effective for the airline. The cost and functionality of computers were not economically feasible at the start of the Joint Industry Computer Reservations study.

Most industries today have an accepted dominant design for information processing that may shift as IT changes. Industries in which markets and production systems are stable and more timely or precise information is not critical may adopt a dominant design that appears to meet all needs and may not change dramatically. Computer-based process control systems in paper mills linked to sales-driven scheduling systems have integrated the value chain, resulting in most firms' making money in good times and inefficient firms' closing down in depressed periods. It is strategic to have the best of these systems, but radical redesign may not occur. Rather, companies must stay abreast of innovations in existing design to remain competitive. Such industries may be in the midst of a transition to utility-type IT services much the way that, in the 1920s, electricity shifted from in-house to utilities as significant economies of scale in electricity generation dramatically reduced costs. This eventually may be forestalled to the extent that the chip allows smaller computers with specialized software to provide more bang for the buck.

For a significant segment of industries, the continuous shift in power of the electronic chip and communication channels will provide a basis for a new design that could supply a competitive advantage. We are presently in the midst of a dramatic shift in retailing to just-in-time deliveries as firms learn to exploit the information from point-of-sale devices directly to the production line. This provides actual sales rates throughout the logistic chain and allows significant cost reduction possibilities. It was not possible until the early 1990s because the mass of information flowing from the checkout counter was too great for the average store processor. Now the systems can handle the flow easily. Wal-Mart and Procter & Gamble are leaders in this evolution to create the new dominant design.

An example of a futuristic organization's use of IT is a popular clothing chain's approach to developing new styles. Agents with video cameras visit fashion shows worldwide. If they find an item they feel would fit their niche, they transmit the views on the model electronically to company headquarters. Merchandising groups review the tapes biweekly to select promising designs. The chosen designs are detailed and created in electronic format and forwarded, with material and color specifications, to producers in Hong Kong, Korea, Singapore, and Taiwan. These suppliers, in turn, airfreight a set of samples for the line within 48 hours. If the merchandisers decide to move, they place an order to the manufacturers electronically. They then develop a new store layout to accommodate the new product, typically eliminating one or more lines, and create merchandising material, advertising copy, sales training brochures, and an update to the in-store computer system. The company can have a new model in a store in eight or fewer days.[3]

Developing a New Dominant Design

The histories of the firms we have traced have common threads in that all were led proactively by a management team driven to change its processes through the means of information technology. Early on all created a vision of the outcome, be it electronic check processing, electronic reservations, or providing better customer service. Yet each was persistent in framing its issues within existing technology, which whetted its appetite for deepening the use of IT. Early results demonstrated economic returns and promised greater potential as those involved could perceive other uses. In most of the sagas, the CEO soon created a vision, whether Clark Beise's electronic banking, C. R. Smith's on-line reservations, or Robert McDermott's paperless office. They pursued these visions in practical steps that changed their procedures and gained perspective on potential uses of IT.

In today's terms, the CEOs defined a goal and with their maestros persisted in gaining adequate insight to develop an architecture of their processing systems and how they could support their customers. This became a basis for determining how to transform their organizations and provide the required training. In many of their innovative moves the organizational shifts, not the technology, were the gating factors. This will be particularly true for most future innovations as the technology has a direct impact on how to link the value chain for improved control and how to manage new product development and inventive services. Exhibit 7-1 documents the shift in the firms' "architecture" as they gained experience with IT and the technology grew in processing capacity. The range of designs and paths documents the commonality of use of the technology and differences related to the unique needs of their businesses. However, all their infrastructures have evolved to a customer focus with centralized policymaking and some centralized marketing.

A macroanalysis discerns that all the firms began to automate a gating factor in processing critical information and learned to master the technology. Most second moves were to link to the customer or to make detailed information on the customer accessible to a responsible agent. Again, this was a learning-by-using activity in which all gained competence in linking geographically disjointed organizations electronically. Such linkage opened new opportunities, which tended to create large central databases of customer-related information. In time all created means for managers and professionals to access this information; in the process they decen-

EXHIBIT 7-1 Comparison of Management Actions in Cascade

Different Stresses and Management Responses

	Bank of America	American Airlines	American Hospital Supply	United Services Auomobile Assoc.	Frito-Lay
Crisis	Growth of check usage	Impending jets; travel growth	Prodcut proliferation	Growth in number of customers	Product proliferation
System input/storage	Signature/check	Paper/blackboard	Paper record	Forms	Forms
File system	Customer name	City origin	Product name	Customer ID	Product name
System focus	Automate check	Automate reservations	Automate order entry	Automate account processing	Automate logistics
Complementary actions	Automate credit-added products	On-line inventory to travel agents	Link to hospitals; grow functions	Decision support; grow product line	Hand-held calculator; integrated marketing
Expanded vision	Electronic banking	Computer-based analysis/marketing	Provide service; help control costs	System access to all products/customers	Link between shelf and factory
Emerging strategy	Expand product line to customers	Focused marketing; create links to sales	Maximize sales; share savings	Broaden product; focused selling	Micromarketing; comprehensive DB
Organization; customer plus	Branch focus	Travel agent focus	Hospital focus	Family focus	Store focus

Similar Responses

After automating, all extended the system to more focus on the customer
Decentralized sales efforts while maintaining centralizing marketing policies and system design
Developed centralized databases and retained control over product development

tralized certain responsibilities and eliminated others, reducing the number of staff/customers in the process. In large measure, the sagas depict a gradual empowerment of customer-oriented professionals with adequate information-processing services to meet their customers needs promptly. One could surmise that a large number of firms currently engaged in downsizing have not evolved as quickly.

Our evidence documents that insightful IT managers with senior management support are the architects of IT dominant designs. This is true because innovative IT systems must be market- and product-service specific and usually require significant organization adaptation for effective implementation. Managerial insight and market awareness are essential to leading an organization to a new plane of operation. However, the stories demonstrate the competitive value of a working system designed to solve a critical problem as a model for others to imitate or acquire quickly as the system becomes a technology necessary to competition. IBM exploited SABRE by building PARS (Programmed Airlines Reservation System) and selling it to most of the smaller airlines. The banking design took a year or so for all the other manufacturers to catch up with GE. IBM, Burroughs, and NCR had been working on competing designs, so they quickly developed the magnetic ink character recognition system and within a year were selling banking systems for future delivery. As described, MICR check processing was just one element of banking and most of the competitor banks required three to four years to reach the efficiency levels in check processing that the Bank of America had achieved by 1958. Being first provides a significant advantage. One piece of evidence of the existence of a dominant IT design is the number of fast second followers of the design that emerges.

The advantage of a general-purpose computer is that a design can be functionally copied, since the programs have only to replicate the necessary activities, and new technology typically allows improvements on an old design. The hurdle is organizing the development of a new design, deploying the systems in an orderly fashion, and gaining competence in exploiting the potential of the result. In the airlines industry American created a working design of a reservations system for which the technology became adequate to support on-line access. IBM saw an opportunity and developed a system for medium-size airlines which realized that they could not afford to build their own. One of the few IBM industry systems that proved to be a standard, it made that company quite capable of helping airlines convert. Further, it met an obvious need because it was primarily automating clerical operations. IBM, with a 60-plus percent market share in the mainframe era, was customer focused and proved to be an effective technology transfer agent. It was instrumental in four of the innovative companies described. In the present era the issue is more toward terminal software standards and database architecture as communication standards are gradually evolving for most industries.

American Airlines, an early user of the information for planning, has continued to lead the industry. With time this allowed the airlines with varying competencies to move gradually to an integrated planning and marketing system and be co-hosted with other airlines whose systems were identical. In banking; however, the short-term challenge was greater, as the MICR system opened a path to an all-electronic production system, not the automation of inventory. Firms that were experimenting, like Mellon and First Chicago, quickly adopted MICR because it blended into their program of automation of paper processing. Quite a few banks automated check processing to meet clearinghouse requirements. But because they did not revise many other systems, their costs increased, which often led to their eventual merger with a successful IT innovator.

Although technology transfer of a dominant design can be difficult, it is usually feasible, depending on the experience of the IT team and how closely the new functionality relates to the old. USAA and Frito-Lay, with the help of consultants and IBM, were quickly able to bring up the existing dominant design. Their new IT functionality automated processes and eliminated clerical operations, which were not massive organizational moves. With a purchased system and competent leadership of organizational change, emphasis can be on implementation and adapting the organization.

New Opportunities

The downsizing of large firms is due primarily to the accessibility of rich stores of information that humans can analyze through the power of new chips and user-friendly software. On-line databases of trillions of data files on a formatted screen are usable in a few seconds. Powerful terminals, connected by visual menus that noticeably characterize important events and allow the user to browse intelligently through the facts, are replacing analytical staffs and some middle-manager roles. Frito-Lay eliminated two levels of management as it rolled out its new system and downsized the corporate marketing staff.[4] Even American Airlines is in the midst of an organizational shift, linking all middle managers and analysts with powerful workstations supported by a broad range of analytical tools connected through a client server network to their enormous set of databases. Each department agreed to reduce head count to bring in the system.[5]

The 1960s experiments conducted at SRI, MIT, Xerox Park, IBM's Advanced System Laboratory, and other experimental groups studying man-machine collaboration finally have the computer power to support the human ergonomics they developed to make them an intellectual aide. Our best information receptor is the eye, which can discriminate three angstroms of color, record objects of one millimeter or less, and absorb millions of bits of information in a large picture. The ear, which processes a wonderful array of information in real time faster than any computer, is, however, limited to narrow sources of coherent information, has difficulty operating in parallel, and has an appreciable error rate. The trick in human communication is semantics. For example, an analytic system still cannot discriminate the salient difference between the phrases "the black bear" and "the bare bottom"; we instinctively understand the meaning. Developing visual schemas that organize events in an informative structure allows individuals to quickly grasp both the big picture and easy access to useful details. That is, a clever screen provides the semantics of the information and allows a rich set of interpretive activities by a knowledeable operator. The ingredients of the present Apple Macintosh, first demonstrated at the 1963 Fall Joint Computer Conference, included linking two terminals through a computer with an on-line picture of the other partner, and each one able to manage a "mouse" on both screens.[6] The newly available chips will allow that to happen with emerging software on generally available systems.

The telecommunication systems are also exploding with available capacity as they develop switching systems that can manage multiple messages on an optical light pipe. The old copper wire went from two simultaneous messages in 1894 to 64,000 in 1990. Now the optical pipe transmission capacity can ship 8,000 simultaneous signals and will soon provide 64,000 channels at speeds of 10^{19} versus copper wires of 10^{12}. Furthermore, the technology allows easy linking through switches that are elegant special-purpose computers. Global banking, relying on an error-free flow of billions of dollars, continues twenty-four hours a day.

The critical differences for the future are learning to develop relevant filters and framing schemas that provide easy access to useful information in a timely manner. Many organizations, such as Frito-Lay, have experience with color screen systems, which provide an effective tool for analysis and exploration by competent individuals. Frito-Lay has an elegantly engineered system that is growing through use of a comprehensive set of decision tools. Firms that are not experimenting with on-line decision support systems may be at a disadvantage. In the restaurant supply market, salesmen are carrying laptops that show a restaurant manager how a plate of their products looks, the cost per serving, and the profit at a range of prices. The illustration can be modified to change size, product, and prices. Once the customer makes a selection, he or she receives a set of diagrams, menus, recipes, and the order and delivery schedule. The laptops have proved to be an effective sales tool. The gating factor has been training mature sales personnel to learn the system and become comfortable with the tool as a sales aid.

Keeping Abreast of IT

An important technology transfer process in most industries is the ongoing dialogue between knowledgeable IT managers on innovative systems. In the petroleum and chemical industries, the two mainstreams of IT innovation are the process engineering groups and management scientists. These groups have strong professional societies in which the state of the art in information technology is a subject of continual discussion and joint experimentation. In banking, two organized consortiums of noncompeting banks swap technology, for example, Bank of America providing the credit card system to Mellon. They became a useful force in gaining perspective on the impact of new IT and its potential. In the airlines, which were regulated and at the leading edge of IT use, maestros met quarterly to exchange views. When the operating software failed to meet their needs, they jointly developed a multihost network on America's system with programmers and managers from the other major airlines. These exchanges continue.

There is also strong evidence that successful firms with IT have the option of being a leader or following a fast-second policy. Both require an IT program to maintain competence and continuous scanning of alternatives to discern the probable designs of the future. The leaders continually experiment and test for new designs, while

the fast seconds stay technologically abreast and track the innovators. Both integrate IT planning as a normal aspect of their management process, one by experimenting for implementation, the other
by testing new systems with innovative groups. Absence of investment in up-to-date IT creates a lack of competence to understand
the nature of potential changes and their impact on the industry
competitive situation. Equally important, firms without IT knowledge have no management skill in understanding the impact and
may lack the perspective of how to lead necessary organizational
adaptation. That skill, which is hard to purchase from consulting
firms, is expensive when needed.

The reason for constant surveillance and occasional testing is that
an emergent design goes through an evolution that depends on the
needs of an industry, its history, and the innovativeness of firms'
exploitation of emerging technology. Future designs are not well
understood at the beginning of the development cycle and evolve
with experience into a reasonably well-understood vision that continues to shift with experience and changing technological opportunities. For instance, early point-of-sale efforts, directed toward capturing information at a store and making it available to the store
managers, proved interesting but not very useful. The managers
could obtain the same information by walking the aisles with a
clipboard, which was cheaper. Now an in-store processor can capture and display actual sales versus planned sales, shelf status, and
replenishment orders in graphic form that serves as a vital aid to
the manager. Those stores which experimented with EDI links to
their suppliers and using store information or replenishment have
a two-year lead on their competitors. That delay will be costly.

The real problem in most firms is not the technology but the
ability to adapt the organization to take advantage of the technology. This requires an understanding of how the organization might
function as well as a readiness for change. Changing purely for the
introduction of new IT is often akin to automating and difficult. If
introduced into a context of improving the firm's ability to compete
and make money in a believable manner, a system will realize its
potential. A modest investment in an ongoing experimentation with
systems allows the organization to learn how to test new technologies and appreciate their limitations and potential. It also creates a
context for learning how to use IT.

The term "evolution" has been used to characterize a process in
which technology is shaped on the basis of experience rather than
design, as the ultimate design is initially obscure. Competent man-

agers and technicians shape a design as their understanding of the true potential emerges. While they shape the design they are also shifting the organization to take advantage of incremental changes, creating an environment where adaptation to take advantage of better information becomes a norm. Typically, as at American and Frito-Lay, this has been proved to expand the community of experimenters broadly across the organization. Such breadth tends to toughen and deepen the capability of the proposed system as well as prepare the organization for change. The Bank of America story clearly documents the growth in the rate and breadth of change as the bank gained momentum; that is, once the system is up to speed, the issue is one of managing the rate of innovation, not worrying about initiating a change. Progress toward new industry designs is not driven by the technology, which is an enabling force, but like all general-purpose technologies must be shaped by market need. In the case of IT, innovation has been the domain of knowledgeable users from the start.

Future Challenges

The challenges of the 1990s, though similar to those of the past, are increasingly more pervasive and accessible. The basic driver of the technology, the chip, is expanding in leaps of millions versus thousands of transistors, and communication costs are dropping at a faster pace. Cost is not as important an issue as functionality and standards. A networked organization is the norm, and there exists a broad range of disparate information-processing systems that can function as aides to professionals and managers. The documented similarities are an active management focus on training, reorganization, and the implementation of IT as a means of improving the overall process, not just automation. Companies in industries dependent on it must continuously invest in information technology to improve or maintain their position. Nevertheless, the few that are not vitally dependent on future IT investment have strong IT dependencies in operations and financial matters. For example, oil companies have massive on-line infrastructures that capture data throughout key variables in the value chain from the wellhead to the gas pump. They have evolved a system that tracks degree days for heating oil and samples passenger miles for gas consumption, which drives an elegant logistic marketing system. However, one of their most sophisticated sets of systems scans newspapers, links to experts, and has knowledgeable interpreters of the political situation in the Mideast — anticipating swings in the price of crude oil is a critical success factor.

With fewer short-term technological risks, an active IT planning process, and a core of competent technologists, an up-to-date organization can decide whether it wants to lead or become a fast second. As noted, none of our innovators decided to invent a dominant design, but one emerged as an integral aspect of each firm's evolving strategy. In today's fast-shifting world, with intense competing demands on resources and management attention, a CEO and management team may decide to shift to a surveillance mode of new technologies and continue to invest to stay with the leaders. Such an alternative might not include investment in R&D that could lead to new processing systems but could support investment in promising technologies to stay abreast of changes. Key to this process is maintaining IT as an active focus in planning and organizational development as the technology becomes more embedded in the infrastructure. Few firms can afford to manage IT as a passive, inconsequential technology.

A vital element of both tactics is to maintain a competent group of technologists and to stay abreast of software innovations. Falling behind a generation or two of technology atrophies and technical skills, loses key employees, and most of all entrenches existing systems as the answer to everything — individuals learn to make do and lose resiliency. The gating factor today is a combination of outmoded technologists and addicted users that are experts with their existing systems in spite of its cumbersomeness. The Luddites are alive and well among us, as outdated Lotus spreadsheet users can demonstrate. Personal computer users who are locked into the idiosyncrasies of their systems become quite creative in inventing elaborate systems that grow obsolete. The modern challenge is keeping groups of users, rather than the technologists, adaptable. The best tactic is to have a user committee experimenting with the latest word in systems.

The driving force of either an innovative or follower IT program is a planning process that reviews the IT portfolio, state of competitor moves, likely impacts on the organization, and market strategies. As demonstrated at Frito-Lay, the CEO does not have to be the product champion, but there should be at least one other enthusiastic senior manager besides the maestro. An innovative manager provides a foil and a sounding board for means to visualize how best to adapt the organization and the technology to the needs of the market.

Sustaining an IT Strategy

The critical time for sustaining an IT strategy is when the CEO moves on. At Frito-Lay, Wayne Calloway served to sustain the continuum. It is a challenge for incoming CEOs, who usually face a new set of problems. If an IT crisis has been resolved, the CEO will not take the time or be inclined to pay attention to what appears to be a technological situation that is working fine. Bank of America did not lose its competence by an overt decision but by default. The leadership of the bank lost its competence to manage IT as it moved its focus overseas and implicitly shifted to a cost minimization focus when there was no effective maestro. The brief review of the bank's saga to regain competence speaks to the complex set of issues and the comprehensiveness of the need for a dialogue at the senior level to attain an understanding of IT's potential. The bank's senior management ignored the issue at a time of some of the more dramatic changes in banking. It took a heroic effort at a significant cost — to climb back into the competition.

American Airlines was in a different context when it lost momentum. Its industry was suffering from overcapacity and learning to cope with jet planes. American's new management cut costs and diversified — a painful period for the company. The crisis at the airline was ameliorated by Fred Plugge's adroit action in exchanging software with Eastern's Frank Heinzmann to allow American to stay abreast of technology. In some sense, it was a matter of competitive timing and the technical situation. The airline was in deep trouble, as was most of the industry with the arrival of jets, and in three years nothing dramatic had happened with the technology. Further, the next management understood the nature of the problem and quickly reversed the direction of the airline. The SABRE system is still at the heart of its strategy.

Frito-Lay demonstrates the latest model: create a planning process that covers multiple years and involves all management levels. Furthermore, it should be a cumulative process and within the business context focus on IT as a means to compete. It should also outline organizational issues, costs, and cash-flow objectives in realistic terms. In the act of creation, a vision gains momentum and gathers from past investments the funds necessary to building the infrastructure. For USAA and Frito-Lay, coming from behind was an advantage. Each knew what to do and that its new system would reduce costs and improve service as it replaced those which were obsolete. This base established a track record and gained them credibility.

USAA and Frito-Lay moved when the technology was increasing the pace of change to the leaps in chip capacity and the availability of nationwide broad-band communication. They were able to build high-capacity links and gain experience ahead of the pack. Firms in consumer-product industries that did not stay abreast are in the midst of "reengineering or transforming" their organizations to attempt to struggle back into a competitive position. Interim results of a longitudinal study of twelve firms which started three or more years ago substantiate that it still takes at least relatively incremental careful planning and competent managers. Consultants that parachute in to start a process and then depart can create more turmoil than they resolve.[7]

However, the organizational shifts in the recent innovators became more complex, because they had to spend as much or more time on implementation than the pioneers did to gain understanding and acceptance of change. Both sponsored support for active decision makers, whether they were agents on a phone or marketers deciding on a price. These changes, which affected management and decision methods, were inevitably a combination of judgment and individual empowerment. They seem typical of what is likely to happen in the near term as we provide more comprehensive information to professional workers and managers. While the future brings more predictable and powerful IT with great organizational potential, developing and implementing useful systems becomes increasingly uncertain.

The real issue is that system evolution requires a program establishing how an organization will function in the future. The likely new processing activities should be broadly shared and continually shifted as the new technology and resultant organizational design become better understood. The concept should provide an overarching view of the future organization and probable management actions to move toward a new design. Without such a view organizational shifts may become subject to unique, purely evolutionary incremental changes in response to IT innovations. The result often resembles a woodpecker's sculpture in reflecting the location of immediate opportunity.

In all cases, it seems that the outcomes were determined by a mixture of luck, timing, intuition, and knowing the real issues. The dominant theme in developing an IT-based strategy appears to be persistence. This probably depends on both the maestro and the CEO's willingness to try and their ability to learn by using, given competent people to make things work. The design evolves with experience into a competitive force. The strategy is clarified in a few artifacts and maintained in the shared concepts of the active participants: their vision. Its tangible form is the portfolio of projects under way and the proposals being studied. In today's environment, the objectives are often determining ways to distribute individual support systems or reapportion tasks as roles shift.

The interpretation of a vision and its impact, hidden like an iceberg, is 90 percent within the intellectual fabric of the organization.[8] The token plans, budgets, and hardware are akin to a musical score that requires an effective conductor to elicit the coherent sound of an excellent orchestra. The experience to make insightful judgments as to when to invest, when to experiment, how to trust one group to do advanced work and allow another only to automate, is not quantifiable. The CEOs of our companies knew how to recruit and test their maestros and to build momentum. Once it was attained, the leaders had the capacity and understanding of technological entrepreneurs to disseminate the results in myriad directions because of their perception of emerging functionality and the new economics of IT. On the other hand, all our innovators had a formal agenda that articulated future plans, experiments, and proposed new products or services. These normal rituals of business are essential to integrate the IT function into the overall fabric of a business. However, they are not sufficient if new management is uninterested or incompetent in leading an IT effort.

As USAA and Frito-Lay demonstrate, all their learning did not come from using. They gained a significant amount of insight from observing and discussing the experiences of other companies and managers in their own or other industries. They acquired intelligence by hiring experienced computer specialists to provide training in new technologies. The predictability of the technology processing capacity is well defined; the greatest uncertainty is determining which software will become the de facto standard. The political issue today, to gain commitment to a potentially useful internal standard, is as complex as any of the issues the pioneers addressed.

The essence of the leadership of the CEOs in these stories is their adapting the culture to accept and exploit the computer and developing systems that supported the culture while changing the organization and the culture. One could argue that Bank of America's mainframe development changed the operational culture and improved the bank's ability to process more information quickly and accurately. However, that did not change the relation of the bank to the customer or consolidate its personal style. Thus, it was ill prepared to extend the technology to linking customers with ATMs, which threatened its tradition of branch banking. Keep in mind that these changes are not obvious at the start; the nature of the changes emerge only as the stories develop. When Clark Beise started to automate check processing, he had no vision of centralizing operations or installing on-line banking. However, he and his team, by pursuing the use of the technology to its best advantage, were able to capitalize on their appreciation of the potential and exploitation. Their understanding came from their management of the technology through carefully defining their objectives and potential rewards and measuring the results. This process provided the bank measured experience with the technology and its impact.

The trick we are trying to describe is the art of pursuing an emerging vision as it becomes reality. The art is marshaling the activities of individuals so that they become competent at better understanding the potential of the technology and how their particular organization can exploit the opportunity. As their confidence grows and they gain commitment, they gradually develop a process of organizational change to assimilate the technology and continue to search for new means. It is related to the scientific management era of the early 1900s, when thoughtful, systematic study of activities that had evolved with experience proved valuable in gaining significant improvements in productivity. The similarity is in analyzing processing systems for potential innovations with IT and conjecturing possible changes and savings or added value. However, information technology is dramatically different in that the new process changes not only the production and distribution of a service or goods but also the management of the entire process. For the first time since the beginning of the Industrial Revolution, the designers of IT, like the craftsmen who invented machines, may make themselves obsolete.

Though all the designs appear to have similar infrastructures and focus because all have an on-line customer database and are accessible from thousands of intelligent terminal systems, each implementation is unique. Although the Bank of America's and USAA's files are active records of customer transactions, each has a unique market focus: the bank has a broad range of corporate and individual services whereas USAA's basic data are a consistent set of potential data files for all customers.

American Airlines' data files, which focus on individual customers by city and frequency of flying, operate independently of the data sets that are the nervous system of the operation, whereas Baxter Travenol's system is both part history and the driving force for replacement and delivery of its products. Frito-Lay employs the most articulated decentralization of decision making through its organized support systems. The airline was the first to go to a nonorganizational distribution system as the decision maker; American Hospital Supply started with such a shift and gradually transferred the responsibility to the actual customer. The bank was an early leader in turning over to their customers the decision making for corporate funds management. USAA is in the process of allowing its customers to manage their own accounts.

The architecture of the future will reach from the customer as far back into the value chain as practical. It will be able to provide up-to-date information to well-defined useful schemas. Providing a fire hydrant flow of data is nonproductive. The range of alternative tactics will grow. It is clearly possible to conduct on-line R&D efforts with systems that involve customers who agree to purchase an imaginary product or service. The real trick is to design the process to sustain managerial control and anticipate exceptions and the art of the possible. Extra information is useful, but insight can be more reliable. In our experiments with managerial cognitive style, Peter Keen and (McKenney) found several of our executive subjects never defined the problem but instinctively searched for similar situations in their experience and conjectured solutions to choose alternatives.[9] They scored significantly better on our tests and were the leaders in their companies. Effective information amplifies the talents of capable people.

Notes

1. M. K. Evans and L. R. Hague, "Master Plan for Information Systems," *Harvard Business Review*, January–February 1962.

2. J. W. Taylor and N. J. Dean, "Managing to Manage the Computer," *Harvard Business Review*, September–October 1966.

3. Jiro Kokuryo, "The Impact of the Retailing Industry's EDI-Based Quick Response Systems on Vendor Logistics Operations," Harvard Business School, 1992.

4. Lynda M. Applegate and Melinda B. Conrad, "Frito-Lay, Inc: The Navigator Project (A)," Case No. 9-193-025 (Boston: Harvard Business School, 1994).

5. Espen Andersen and J. L. McKenney, "American Airlines: The InterAAct Project (A)," Case No. 9-193-013 (Boston: Harvard Business School, 1992).

6. "ACM Conference on the History of Personal Workstations: The Augmented Knowledge Workshop," film, Association for Computing Machinery, New York, December 1989.

7. T. H. Davenport and D. B. Stoddard, "Reengineering: Business Change of Mythic Proportions?" Harvard Business School, March 1994.

8. Richard E. Walton, *Up and Running* (Boston: Harvard Business School Press, 1989), 68.

9. J. L. McKenney and P. W. G. Keen, "How Managers' Minds Work," *Harvard Business Review*, May–June 1974.

Index